Distinctive Design

Distinctive Design

A Practical Guide to a Useful, Beautiful Web

Alexander Dawson

A John Wiley and Sons, Ltd, Publication

Distinctive Design

This edition first published 2011

© 2011 John Wiley & Sons, Ltd

Registered office

John Wiley & Sons Ltd, The Atrium, Southern Gate, Chichester, West Sussex, PO19 8SQ, United Kingdom

For details of our global editorial offices, for customer services and for information about how to apply for permission to reuse the copyright material in this book, please see our Web site at www.wiley.com.

The right of the author to be identified as the author of this work has been asserted in accordance with the Copyright, Designs and Patents Act 1988.

978-1-119-99298-1

A catalogue record for this book is available from the British Library.

Set in 10 point Benton Sans by Melanee Habig, Jennifer Mayberry, and Andrea Hornberger

Printed in the U.S. by CJK

About the Author

ALEXANDER DAWSON (@AlexDawsonUK) is an award winning, self-taught, freelance web professional, writer, published author, and recreational software developer from Brighton (UK). With more than 10 years of industry experience he spends his days running his consultancy firm HiTechy (`www.hitechy.com`), writing professionally about web design and giving his free time to assist others in the field.

In recent years, Alexander has become an established web writer providing articles for some of the industry's most respected sites including *Smashing Magazine*, *Six Revisions* and *SitePoint* (where he regularly assists others through their popular forums). In addition, as a member of the Guild of Accessible Web Designers he actively promotes and advocates the benefits of a good user-experience and web standards. When Alexander isn't coding or writing about design and development, he enjoys a game of tennis (or chess) and watching movies.

Credits

Some of the people who helped bring this book to market include the following:

VP Consumer and Technology Publishing Director
Michelle Leete

Associate Director- Book Content Management
Martin Tribe

Associate Publisher
Chris Webb

Publishing Assistant
Ellie Scott

Development Editor
Beth Taylor

Technical Editor
Michael Tuck

Copy Editors
Debbye Butler
Melba Hopper

Editorial Manager
Jodi Jensen

Senior Project Editor
Sara Shlaer

Editorial Assistant
Leslie Saxman

Senior Marketing Manager
Louise Breinholt

Marketing Executive
Kate Parrett

Senior Project Coordinator
Kristie Rees

Graphics and Production Specialists
Melanee Habig
Andrea Hornberger
Jennifer Mayberry

Quality Control Technicians
Melissa Cossell
Susan Hobbs

Indexer
Ty Koontz

*For the long suffering professionals who work tirelessly
to make the web a better place, and those individuals who continue to strive for
a more accessible, standards compliant Internet.*

Acknowledgments

There are a number of wonderful individuals who have helped and inspired me throughout the journey of writing this book. My thanks firstly have to go out to the entire team at Wiley who have shown me continued support and helpful advice over many a Skype or e-mail conversation. Just a few of these people include Chris Webb (who's recognition of an article and enthusiasm lead to this title), Ellie Scott (whose patience with my questions seemed never ending), Beth Taylor (my long suffering editor who has helped transform my brain's contents into what you're reading), and Michael Tuck (my friend and technical editor who ensured that what I wrote made sense).

I must also give recognition and some well deserved appreciation to the amazing people who have given me opportunities to write for their wonderful sites. Without their support and friendship, this title certainly may have never been written. Thanks must go out to Jacob Gube (*Six Revisions*), Vitaly Friedman (*Smashing Magazine*), Aidan Huang (*OneXtra Pixel*), Amanda Hackwith (*FreelanceSwitch*), Kristina Bjoran (*UX Booth*), Walter Apai (*Web Designer Depot*) and both Jonathan Anderson and Tiffany A. Hampton (*UX Magazine*). If you don't read these awesome resources, you should do!

Next, I'll give thanks to my friends over on *SitePoint's* forums, Learnable, Skype, Windows Live Messenger, Google Talk, IRC, and real life, who've kept me going with interesting, lively discussions throughout the entire writing process. This Includes: Andrew Cooper, Christian Ankerstjerne, Troy Mott, and Ursula Comeau. Finally, my thanks go out to you, the reader who has chosen to support my hard work (and hopefully gain some useful content in the process). Without you, the book certainly wouldn't have been worth it, and if my musings and Web design knowledge can help a single person become a better professional, it will have been worth the effort made.

Contents

Part II: The Art of Distinctive Documentation   61

CHAPTER 3

Principles of Information Design 63

CHAPTER 4

Design Concepts and Theories 99

Part IV: User-Centered Considerations   217

Part V: Designing for Ubiquitous Users   273

Setting the Stage

Some details for the journey ahead

WHEN THE WEB was new, the role of a web designer was fairly limited. Designers used HTML and liked it, CSS was lacking widespread, graceful support (some things never change), and the concept of designing good interfaces for the visitor was just being explored. With things gradually improving we've lived through two browser wars, the first via desktop browsers and the second (still ongoing) via handheld devices, both with plenty of casualties!

As the web continues to evolve with new standards, so must the methods for dealing with the demands placed upon its infrastructure. With the number of Internet users rising toward two billion, more browsers and devices than you can count, and with networks like Facebook gaining an enviable user base, the need to customize experiences and provide a non-intrusive way of showcasing content is critical.

As I move through the book, I shall not only focus on the key technologies that now influence how content is designed, structured, and visualized (HTML, CSS, and JavaScript.) I also give you plenty of diagrams (because this is a design book and the visuals are what much of our work comes down to). As such, design can and should be considered (whether distinctive or otherwise) both an art and science (with some philosophy thrown in).

Introducing distinctive design

Hopefully, as you examine distinctive design, you'll get as much enjoyment from reading about the material as I've had from writing it. Luckily, I'm a fan of simplicity and straight forward ideas so you don't need to be a rocket scientist or a brain surgeon to take part. Whether you're getting started in design (but know enough code to implement the changes) or have a background in it, you'll still find some useful nuggets of goodness to help you improve your design work.

I've also been of the opinion that designers want to do what's in their visitors' best interests. I've no worries if you've made some designs that have caused other experts to begin crying. My primary focus and goal is to let you know about the wonderful options that exist and allow you to make informed choices for yourself (in what's appropriate) – because one size simply doesn't fit all when it comes to your identity!

One of the benefits of this approach is that I'm firmly in support of trial, error, and continuing your education. So as you examine the theories, patterns, knowledge and perspectives laid out in this title, feel free to experiment (at your own pace) and take opportunities to learn more about the subject either using the links I'll provide, or through your own user research. Self-motivation is important to any designer (it's almost as important as having creativity).

Motives and Motivation

When I was first approached to write this book, the principles of distinctive design were firmly at the forefront of my attention. My passion for accessibility (at an almost religious level), my enthusiasm for writing, and my empathic need to help future generation of designers (and developers) has shaped how I not only build websites, but has also challenged and enhanced the knowledge I currently hold.

Although giving up the knowledge I've spent years learning may seem crazy to onlookers, design problems are so widespread, and the topic of good design both technical and theoretical that while you may benefit from what I'm providing (by opening your eyes to new ideas and methods to boost your designs visibility), it's almost certain that good practices will take some time to gain traction.

It's also worth stating that I love my job and find it deeply rewarding. The web has become such a dynamic environment that you'll never run out of things to learn (and those who say they know all they need to should be approached with caution). While the diverse nature of the web has driven a few of us crazy (literally), I jumped at this opportunity to showcase a subject within the scope of design that many aren't aware of (which is quite unfortunate).

The web is an amazing medium with scope for an almost infinite array of unique designs and potential improvements. Although much of what you'll read is common sense or practical advice, it should apply in equal measure to whatever you create. With this in mind, I hope to challenge the way you view your designs and spark that creative "self-improving" spirit.

The need for a book that highlights the importance of distinctive design was born of this enthusiasm. Putting things simply, while designers are able to make something pretty and usable, few really examine the intricacies of the page (and its content) whilst taking time to consider, control, and hone the focus and attention to which visitors can gain benefits from.

A Primer on Distinction

The principle behind distinctive design can seem quite daunting once you look through the table of contents of this book. We'll examine subjects like psychology and information design, findability and interaction design! There will be plenty of cool abbreviation usage (which won't help your scrabble score) and some things you may not initially think of as web orientated.

Without going into a lecture about why this is important, I'll let you in on a secret . . . distinctive design is simply about making things stand out and controlling the attention parts of a page receive! Department stores literally spend millions in researching how to lay out their shop floors to attract customers. Movie directors spend just as much trying to emphasize what's on the screen to try and engage the viewer's emotions.

The world influences how our attention is caught on a daily basis. Examples include the signposts we read, the ways in which our senses are "hooked" via television or radio, and even the spam that get's shoved through the mail (as much as you wish the marketing men would leave you alone).

As the web is equally perceptive to similar techniques (just with different implementations to print, visual, or physical design), it seems only natural to want to explore how such methods can be leveraged to give your designs and layouts that distinctive sparkle of attention. You wouldn't want to build a car unless you understood your tools, the same goes for the web.

Although you may be aware of core concepts like usability, accessibility, and their functions in a design's success, the ability to maximize the way in which people recognize and respond to the interface is almost as important as ensuring that it can be seen and used (at the most primitive level). This book is therefore aiming to go beyond what you would find in your average design or usability title and highlight such inherent benefits.

At this point it's worth establishing that I'm not saying you should all start dumbing down our layouts and stylistic creativity so that the aesthetics or content suffers as a result. The whole process of wielding these ever more fanciful and useful technologies should engage your need to experiment and get your visitors involved in seeking (rather than just being served) attention-worthy content. Getting it shiny and noticeable is pretty much the ultimate goal.

Much of design is an illustration showcasing our ability to reflect our audience's needs in a consumable format. Doing this with accuracy (rather than guesswork) will not only make your awesome content and services more usable (and probably more awesome by the fact that people will see it, perhaps with feedback!), but it will help you target your sites visitors in ways that could give you an edge over the competition . . . like the idea?

Great Expectations

So now that you've heard the sales pitch and gained a brief insight into the concept of distinctive design, it's time to learn exactly what you should expect from this package. Because this title is based around design rather than development, there will be a few expectations of your skill set. Remember that even a novice can learn as they progress.

To keep this book at a readable length, attempts have been made to keep it from becoming a technical manual. While this title does cover a wide scope of subjects, keeping it in a format that's digestible is as important in print as it is on the web (and what kind of web designer would I be if I turned this title into something as huge as your telephone directory).

Secondly, because this is quite technical (relating to design) you'll need some basic skills to keep up. It doesn't matter if you're not artistic; it doesn't even matter if you're still learning to code. What is important is that you are passionate and are willing to learn the applicable skills (code or otherwise) to implement the techniques you'll uncover throughout the chapters.

Hopefully at this stage, things are looking peachy. If you do find that you do come up against a brick wall in a particular subject, it doesn't mean that the book is entirely useless. I've planned this title so you can apply the principles in any order, either as a supplement to your existing skills, or you can simply implement the techniques as you learn to develop. As with many things in life, it's the awareness of issues that matter, not the background you possess.

Beyond this, I think common sense and logic must prevail! This title certainly isn't feature complete (on every possible angle as you'd need hundreds of volumes) and to quote the phrase "here be dragons," there's elements that still require a lot of research and discovery. With this in mind, as developments occur in the future you'll want to be under no illusions that designing is a constant effort, so keep reading blogs, sites, journals, magazines, and books.

Frequently Asked Questions

I'm sure at this stage you have plenty of questions, such as what exactly are we going to talk about! Without giving away too many secrets at this early stage I decided that it would be in everyone's best interests if a few immediate concerns were resolved. As such, the following list of frequently asked questions aren't frequent (in the sense that my inbox is getting swamped) but they're incredibly valid at this stage and are usually asked within computer or design books.

Q: Do I need to know everything, and can I learn it all?

A: *Because of the web's evolutionary pace, it's impossible to know everything about designing for the medium. While you can become quite proficient with a good range of knowledge, you won't have the time to learn it all (so focus on what you need to know)!*

Q: What is the right way to design or build a website?

A: *Everyone has different needs, expectations, and ideas of what a good design is. While aesthetics are only part of the job, a good experience is made up of more than just eye candy! So there's no right or wrong way, just potentially helpful and unhelpful practices.*

Q: Does this information work for every type of site?

A: *Of course! Different websites will have different requirements and require a varying range of information to be displayed in the browser, however that doesn't detract from the nature of showcasing and giving distinction to a page (so that focus can be drawn).*

Q: Can I use these principles outside of the web?

A: *Absolutely! Although print (like magazines), visual (like video), and physical design (like architecture) have their own unique sets of challenges and requirements, it's perfectly possible to cross over many of the concepts in this book to other visualized formats.*

Q: Will this teach me how to create my first website?

A: *Sorry, although this book has plenty of newbie-friendly material and would make a great companion to a development book (or something that teaches you how to build your very first site), this will cover some advanced ground and focuses on improving experiences.*

Q: Should I pay a professional or do it myself?

A: *If you have the money to splash out on a guru, it may be worth the money as their years of experience will obviously cover a wider range of skills than this title can provide in a single volume. If not, self-testing is a better alternative to having no testing at all!*

Q: Is there really such a thing as bad design?

A: *Although this is a subjective answer, it's quite probably yes. Some sites can be really badly implemented, some can be impossible to use (for able-bodied and disabled individuals alike), and some are just plain ugly or annoying (or bad to the point of scary)!*

Q: I just want to have a simple site. Should I know this stuff?

A: *Although many individuals these days rely on content management systems like the mighty Wordpress or a template that was provided either for free or at cost, there are still improvements you can make. Why settle for average when you can be distinctive!*

Book Conventions

Like most books, this one follows a series of conventions. Regarding the personality of the content, an emphasis on being concise but useful is maintained. The last thing you want is to hear me waffle on about some *amazing* aspect of design to the sacrifice of something else of equal importance. In addition, it's always fun to see more than reels of text, so lists, tables, images, diagrams, and other cool "widgets" will be used in addition to visualize the principles.

Some of the things you'll find:

> **Screenshots and Diagrams**: To see a real-world implementation.

> **Wireframes**: Mockup interfaces to visualize specific concepts.

> **Tables, Charts, and Graphs**: Flow, bar, pie, and other useful data.

Alongside these elements, you'll find a series of special calls to action that will give you some extra nuggets of useful information. They'll be quite distinct in appearance and have icons to let you know what type of details you shall receive. As for what they represent, I've included a complete list as follows (so that you will know what to look out for). Remember that in the case of website links, occasionally they may disappear (so check the book's errata for corrections).

Call to action conventions used:

> **Note**: A technical term or abbreviation that requires an explanation.

> **Reference**: A useful site, book, or something else to continue learning from.

> **Tip**: A best practice or personal recommendation relating to a subject.

> **Important**: A warning or reminder that may affect what's being attempted.

E-Book Bonus Chapters

Distinctive design is comprised of many components. Although this book covers a wide range of these valuable theories and practices, many more exist for you to explore. The supplementary e-book covers three additional subjects that can help you improve your sites visibility and ease-of-use. You can find the e-book at `www.wiley.com/go/distinctivedesign`.

The Bonus Chapters are

> Bonus Chapter 1: Understanding Information Architecture

> Bonus Chapter 2: The Influence of Sociology

> Bonus Chapter 3: Accessibility: Removing Disability

Down The Rabbit Hole We Go!

Congratulations, you have completed this stage of the journey. Now that all the disclaimers and overview segments are complete, we can get down to business and this is where our distinctively unique quest for a better design shall begin. Just like in Alice, we shall go down the rabbit hole and tumble into Wonderland where nothing is as it seems (hopefully there won't be any animated GIFs of the Cheshire cat going on your site anytime soon)!

From this stage forward, the focus of this book shall not be aimed at either me (as the author) or you (as the designer or developer). Our focus is simply and quite literally aimed at the visitor (that fabled creature that often seems like a mythical beast). After all, we build sites and experiences for our visitors to enjoy, consume, and (in some cases) pay for. The greatest ace in the designer's handbook is to design for your users, not force users around your ideas.

Part I

Designing for the Web

The Distinction of Web Design

Principles and variables of a visually appealing layout

CREATING THE IDEAL, aesthetically pleasing, distinctive design seems like an impossible task to many. While most web industry fields have their own methodology to improve and yield results in the layout and the structure of the content, a few basic defining concepts underpin the whole process of forging beautiful designs. Essentially, the goal is to achieve maximum impact on users.

Within this first chapter, I highlight the justifications for creating a distinctive design, the variables affecting the end users, and the importance of visibility. In addition, I provide a solid introduction to critical basic design concepts, including neutrality or balance. I also explain how to emphasize the right content, how to prioritize and analyze content in order to clean up an interface (using tools like minimalism), and how to avoid conflict and inconsistencies with websites.

Taking You Back to Basics

Within the realm of user experience, complexity has become the enemy of the people. Often at the most basic level, the need to create more intrinsically dynamic and functional designs causes website visitation (and the users who browse those sites) to suffer. Although the concept of "designing with purpose" is nothing new, how people read and recognize objects, and how much attention people give to some components within a layout compared to others, can be summed up in the four words shown in Figure 1-1.

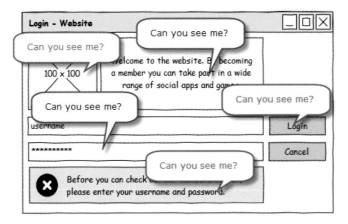

FIGURE 1-1: Each and every element asks, "Can you see me?"

Treating the elements of your website like a living, breathing entity may seem rather silly at first, but the visualization it produces accurately reflects the situation. Just picture each part of your site as someone within a crowd. The loudest individuals are shouting above everyone else. This clashing certainly results in quieter voices going unnoticed, even if that voice is important within the project's context.

Gauging every object's importance against the level of noise and distraction elsewhere on the page is central to assigning a level of purposeful distinction to your pages. Your users have a limited attention span, and by ensuring that the objects on the page have a well-balanced proportion of importance versus voice, you create a distinctive—and visible— design that people can enjoy and browse without constraint.

Tip

To learn more about the average Internet user's attention span (or lack thereof), check out this article by usability specialist Jakob Nielsen: `www.useit.com/alertbox/timeframes.html`

If something is visibly useful to a page, assign more attention to it (see Figure 1-2). Less important items on a page require less attention. You have little time to impress visitors before they hit the Back button or look elsewhere. The exact amount of time is up for debate, ranging from zero points of a second, as people subconsciously pre-judge what they see, to five or ten seconds. Web professionals often forget that selective emphasis holds importance!

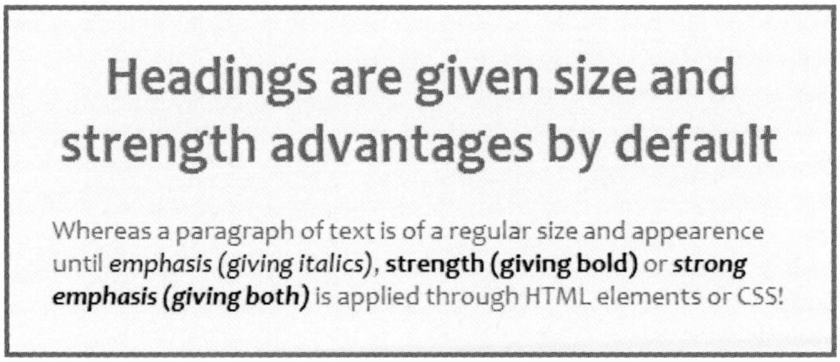

Headings are given size and strength advantages by default

Whereas a paragraph of text is of a regular size and appearence until *emphasis (giving italics)*, **strength (giving bold)** or ***strong emphasis (giving both)*** is applied through HTML elements or CSS!

FIGURE 1-2: A stylistic flourish within a page often depicts emphasis and strength.

The balancing act can be quite tricky. You should analyze and self-critique your methods as well as ask others to give feedback. Even negative feedback is helpful; actually, in many cases, it's more helpful than positive feedback. The justification for many design choices rests upon those four essential words (refer to Figure 1-1); by wielding such control over a page, you ensure users find what they want (or need) at the point they require it.

Remember that feedback is quite subjective (and should be taken with a grain of salt). Don't implement changes that users request on a whim without a good reason. Some things can actually make a design worse, and the last thing you want to do is destroy all your hard work!

Time, space, and relativity

Understanding the needs of your content is central to the concept of distinctive design, but the user experience demands more than simple information visibility. Although an inanimate object, your content has a few primary needs that must be accounted for in the overall layout, such as visibility and accessibility. Many variables can affect the duration and extent of a visitor's experience, and while some of these are more imposing than others, such as pesky browser bugs and page availability, some can be tied into human perceptions and the amount of resources or self-sacrifice web professionals choose to assign to a service.

Time, space, relativity, and other variables speak volumes to the finite resources humans often temporarily assign to a site for the duration of their stay. Each variable ties deeply into the other because they are often measured upon the perception of whether the effort exerted by visitors matches the importance level of other events going on around them.

Check out this list of finite resources:

> **Time:** There's only 24 hours in a day, and users rarely spend all of those browsing a single site. How much of this precious resource a visitor uses on your site depends on the value of the content.

> **Space:** The freedom to browse a site without inhibition is important to the overall user experience. If users feel restricted or forced into jumping through unnecessary hoops, they may exit!

> **Relativity:** The relationship between content and sites is important to the web. If a site's content connects to a concept or subject introduced by another site, it may gain added attention.

> **Money:** Services with defined costs have to work even harder than free or ad-supported sites for attention. Since the content is provided behind a "paywall", money is needed to gain visibility.

> **Patience:** The average visitor feels a great variety of emotions when browsing a site (some of which you can manipulate). If barriers to entry are high, the willingness to continue may be lost.

> **Attention:** Objects on a page are always vying for a user's focus, and in polar opposition, users are themselves trying to get the attention they require from objects. This must be accounted for.

> **Loyalty:** By providing good experiences and reducing the levels of background noise, users are more likely to return to our sites.

> **Trust:** Use of a site is based on the value of its content and how reliable users deem its source. If your content is full of lies or inaccuracies, the content's value is lowered.

> **Energy:** Users are expected to undertake so many activities within a page. Clicking, typing, and perhaps even more! Tiredness can work as an inhibitor when browsing the web. Don't make users exert themselves.

These end-user functions (rather than controls of an interface) are subjective to every individual, but this doesn't mean that they can't be accounted for or measured. Don't assume, for example, that visitors can (or want) to spend hours looking over a 5,000-page site filled with content. (Admit it: You'd lose *your* sanity if you had to scroll through them, so why would you torture someone else with such a process?) The balance between distinction and the variables mentioned earlier is important to get right; the two relate quite heavily to each other.

Tip

Making a website fun and engaging is among the best methods of distorting the time field of an end-user. People regularly waste endless hours playing games on the web, and if you are a creative individual, you can provide that sort of experience (and functionality) on your own site!

Albert Einstein once said, "Put your hand on a hot stove for a minute, and it seems like an hour. Sit with a pretty girl for an hour, and it seems like a minute. THAT'S relativity". Einstein's quote is a perfect reminder that a user's experience should not be painful or unendurable to the point of feeling abandoned. A visitor shouldn't feel useless in her quest for information. More importantly, it also shows that you can manipulate the variables that people use to measure your work's value (such as time and trust) and affect the impact upon a user (see Figure 1-3 for an example).

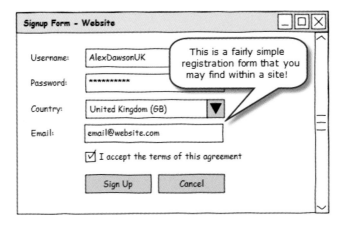

FIGURE 1-3: Straightforward forms are much less time-intensive than complex documents.

Distinctive design influences the time it takes to locate important details within a page. It also sets the tone for how tedious or enjoyable finding that information is (and by association causes relativity to take effect). Understanding the connection between the actual amount of time visitors devote to your site and the perception of time they devote to your site provides you a rare opportunity to stand out, which, in turn, gives visitors the desire to return.

Consider the amount of time you spend playing a game in comparison to undertaking a job you don't find particularly enjoyable. As you spend time doing something you enjoy, the focus you place on time spent is reduced, much like the famous saying "time flies when you're having fun." The "time flies" ideology (known as "Tempus Fugit") is a classic example of how variables can be manipulated to encourage continued use.

Information must be visible within the confinements of the page it's held in, or else the distinctive focus that may be drawn simply cannot exist. If you create a page that includes content or features with low visibility, (like creating elements that inadvertently minimize other elements' importance or you intentionally apply a negative emphasis to certain content or features), the content lacking visibility inherently diminishes in importance in the end-user's experience and could result in users missing the message.

Defining the ideal perspective

Of the variables and principles that impact your capability to serve visitors effectively, the most common failures occur as a result of either obtrusive subjectivity (doing what you think is best for the end-user rather than what actually may be the case) or a lack of attention to detail. Appealing to the widest possible audience is critical to underpinning a distinctive design. The concept of a best-case scenario puts forth the idea that if you aim to design in ways that will generally apply to all users, you reduce the chance of confusion. Distinction isn't about just standing out. It's also about aesthetics and providing a visual appeal to match the visitor's plentiful expectations!

Note Many people (excluding seasoned web professionals) confuse professionalism with the visuals or aesthetic a website provides. The public associates quality products with quality layouts! Unfortunately, spammers and scammers regularly exploit this assumption by creating slick designs.

A beautiful website engages more visitors, and an unattractive website gives off the impression of unprofessionalism, making users turn away as a result. Distinctive design showcases and attempts to reflect the need for a balance between beauty, usability, and awareness within the pages' unique layout. The immediate beauty of a page (just like human attraction) is great for the short term, but substance over style and the attributes that make your site great and unique are critical to a long and happy visitor relationship.

This may seem worrisome to some people, who may feel that trying to make something beautiful, unique, distinctive, and usable—all in one package—is close to impossible. It's actually *easier* to make a beautiful website once you know how (Figure 1-4 gives us a quick three-step process). If you build a website that is usable, the content's identity will be visible to those who read your copy. If your content portrays your site with depth and richness, viewers can identify with these characteristics. And if your site is distinctive, the uniqueness and aesthetic identity can be formed around it. Like with most things in life, it's a case of everything in moderation!

Granted, this is a best-case scenario, and there may be times when you may think that no perfect solution exists (perhaps one good solution has not yet been innovated), but you can compromise those ideals to a certain extent, as long as the final effect nets you the intended response. Perfection isn't possible in design (several factors cause a lack of control over the rendering canvas), but that doesn't mean you can't keep improving things to reflect the experience as optimally as possible (even though the web isn't print).

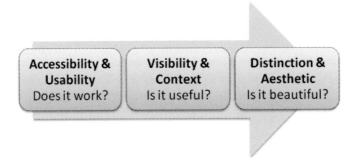

FIGURE 1-4: Building a distinctive and beautiful website is simpler than it may appear.

Designing with Neutrality

Beyond the variables I have previously mentioned relating to distinctive design and the idealistic intentions they naturally seem to evoke in giving your visitors everything (with as few consequences as possible!), the principles of how distinction is formed relate to a range of certain design concepts that exist not only within the context of the web, but also within the scope of print design. Of course, digital media and traditional print are quite different in their capabilities and limitations, but some useful lessons can be drawn from the study of concepts that branch both disciplines.

One of the biggest variables that influence distinctive design (and the print world alike) is the concept of neutrality (and the Zen-like state it produces). As you're still balancing within the realms of theory rather than practice, it may seem surprising that neutralizing visible elements of the page (and making them less visible or attention-seeking) plays a part in achieving distinction. But if you think about it, without balance, chaos reigns supreme!

Thinking of your website in a Zen-like format helps you understand that to ensure a clear and enlightened perception (both in giving accurate knowledge and being easy to follow) you need to self-reflect upon the issue at hand. As a designer, you need to analyze the choices you make for the benefit of your visitors, and you also need to provide a clear method of showcasing wisdom through careful planning and resourcefulness.

The principles of a Zen-like design are:

> Keep the components of your site's visibility in balance.

> Consider your options wisely before you apply them.

> Keep your visitors enlightened (offer them knowledge).

> Maintain clarity and reduce noise pollution.

Implementing the Zen concept within distinctive design and following the ideals of a neutral interface is relatively straightforward. Designs composed of well-balanced content (in which the required distinctive features take precedence over less useful information) allow you to draw focus to the parts of a page that require attention. Reducing noise pollution on a page and giving that balance where it's required keeps distinctive content—well—distinctive and lets the rest be calm, silent material that remains on the page but is noticed only as further page inspections occur.

Beautiful balance

Taking the concept of Zen neutrality beyond what was previously mentioned, a design that is clear in its separation of distinctive design elements from additional flourishes or extended attributes, gives your design added stability. The elements of your website are weighted (much like those in Figure 1-5) with distinctive elements holding more natural weight and value on one side and the other content balanced on the other. If the level of distinction either equals or extends beyond the neutral (less unique) content, the power of its influence lessens.

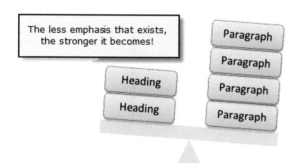

FIGURE 1-5: Although the balance may be offset, the need to complement such elements remains critical.

When looking at existing layouts, an unnatural balance must exist between a design and the emphasis (unique components) within a page. And just like Earth, if something is thrown seriously out of whack, it seems to naturally correct itself by reducing the strength of emphasis in which attention-seeking content retains. On a page with paragraphs of text and a single heading, that heading's distinctive nature stands away from the page (yet, if the page includes several headings, none stands out). This is due to how humans are naturally attracted to uncommon sights. Gaining a user's eye requires a clever mix of eye candy and offsetting the layouts equilibrium.

If all of your content has little to no emphasis (such as just paragraphs of text), the readability of that content is diluted to a neutral level. Yet, if you have too much emphasis (such as stuffing everything into headings like in Figure 1-6), the strength you intend to attain dilutes itself! Only when the critical mass is reached will emphasis and strength sustain itself.

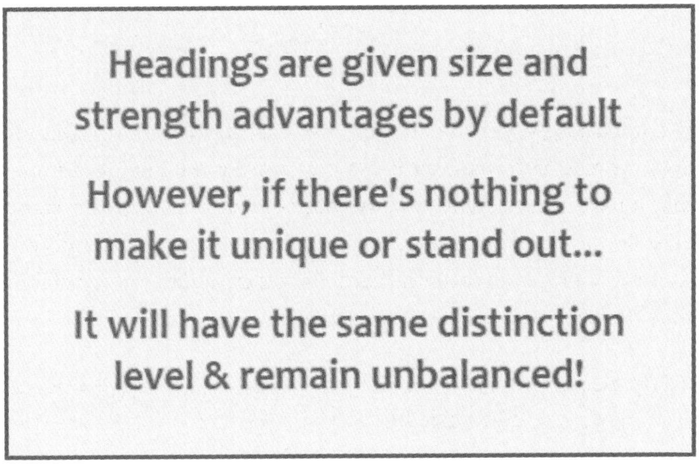

Headings are given size and strength advantages by default

However, if there's nothing to make it unique or stand out...

It will have the same distinction level & remain unbalanced!

FIGURE 1-6: If you place emphasis everywhere, nothing stands out.

Before leaving the concept of balance (for the moment), it's important to highlight the value of eliminating or repositioning balance whenever possible. The key to gaining a visitor's attention is to provide distinctive content, but neutrality is the direct opposite of this. The trick to good design is to provide as much distinction as you can, without pushing it too far (and diluting the effect).

You can apply distinction in many ways, including use of color, whitespace, and more! What this means is that if you're smart enough to apply emphasis equally through various means, rather than on one aesthetic point, you make your content distinctive without risking the issue of over-dilution. Generally, dilution only occurs visually with a lack of context within its implementation, not just as a result of an abundance of balanced objects.

Emphasizing the essentials

If you've been coding with HTML for a while or have any experience with producing websites, you should already know that certain HTML elements provided within the W3C specifications, such as strong and em, provide visual emphasis not just on the screen within the browser window (with default styles that can be overwritten) but in context within the content itself.

Tip

For those without coding experience, HTML stands for Hypertext Markup Language. It is the primary language web designers use to structure content within a page. Think of it as the candy wrapper that holds the goodness in pretty, identifiable containers (if they are labeled correctly)!

Taking the principle of emphasis beyond the context and restraints of the HTML language, providing a flourish or distinctive marker helps users recognize a point of importance. You can emphasize a particular element in a number of ways, as long as it stands out from its surroundings. Because emphasis remains at its strongest when it stands with fewer competitors for attention, give only essential content this critical boost in visibility. Used sparingly and appropriately, emphasis can draw attention quite quickly.

Some methods of providing distinction are quite direct and in-your-face; other methods can be quite subtle. While subtle methods take longer to be recognized, it's quite likely that they are more reliable. The proliferation of advertising that fights for people's attention illustrates this theory, because people tend to develop a level of "immunity" to patterns they recognize as negative (users automatically mentally block out blatant advertisements). See Figure 1-7.

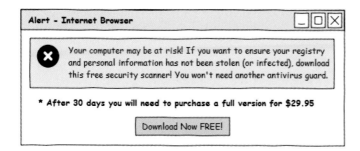

FIGURE 1-7: An advertisement like this won't hold your attention if you know it's trying to sell something.

One of the principles maintained through this book is that content must be emphasized tastefully, with serious consideration about how your visitors may be affected by the increased level of awareness to one item (against the lessened awareness of other content). Remember that balance affects your content and the value it inherits. Your goal is to ensure that viewers regard the obvious material on a page as useful, not as a blatant spam attempt.

Important   Opinions may vary on the extent you can emphasize content, but it's recommended that unless you know what you're doing, avoid forced actions such as pop-up windows, protection scripts (like anti-right-clickers), and the ever-annoying automatic music-playing jukeboxes.

Negotiating neutrality

When you remove emphasis from a page, what remains will increase in strength. Using neutrality effectively is an inspired concept, isn't it? In many ways it's like a talent contest. When fewer people enter, it's much easier to identify the most talented individuals, but as the numbers increase designers rely more on comparison and elimination (perhaps unjustly) to give ourselves the best chance of finding the stars amongst the masses.

Focusing on what's on the page and what already has emphasis is easy (because attention grabbing is what it intends to do). But the capability to disinherit and demote enhancements and flourishes (while involving some difficult choices) can both reduce the level of noise that exists within an interface and bring some stability to the page (Figure 1-8 highlights how attention is spread). The more neutrality you assign, the more direct the effects are upon content that retains its status and levels of importance.

If you already have a website, strip away all of the excess, both graphically and contextually (from existing emphasis). Once your content sits on an unstyled and visibly similar page, it becomes easier to see when you have an excess of information, thereby making your distinctive content harder for the reader to identify. This action could encourage you to apply emphasis more intelligently or with greater constraint. By doing this you deconstruct the aesthetic using *reductionism* (a principle examined later in this chapter).

Important   Whenever you change your source code (or critical files like images), make a backup or use a version control system just in case you need to return to the older edition later! It's common sense to safeguard your work, especially if you're making potentially dramatic changes to it.

Distribution of Attention

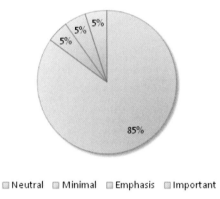

FIGURE 1-8: Balancing a page using less-emphasized content (of various types) redirects attention.

So far, you have seen the benefits of becoming Zen-like in your design approach by redrawing the balance when you feel it can improve the way information is conveyed, and by balancing neutrality and emphasis, which reflects the opposing sides of attention-focusing. In the next section, I go over the more straightforward principle of simplicity. It is one of the most primal methodological forces for improving the distinction of what remains visible on-screen (and without it, things would get very cluttered indeed).

The Sum of All Parts

Holding your visitor's attention with plenty of active elements on a page can be difficult. Because distractions on a page can reduce the visibility of key information, it's important to preserve the integrity of the emphasized content that already exists. If adding emphasis to such content seems like the only answer to your problems, never fear; there is a less popular but equally powerful way to give a cluster of content emphasis. That method is to take away any unnecessary clutter from the website's foreground and background (think of it as spring cleaning for your visitor's benefit).

Note

For every element, property, and function, keep asking if what's sitting within your pages is really necessary. If you can't justify it, remove it entirely! Or if you need to include it on the page, you can progressively disclose it as required (making it visible only when it's needed onscreen).

With increasing techniques to provide content on demand, the capability to perform such a function has become more widespread and popular. A website is essentially the composition of its many parts joining together in harmony. Distinctive designers need to reduce information overload and simplify the overall experience. Luckily for us, the web is evolving rapidly in ways that are helping you to achieve the design goals you set ourselves.

Perhaps because of its implications in search engine optimization or the assumption that more is better, removing emphasis (thereby stating some content is less important) or objects from the page can be quite a scary prospect. Simplifying the interface and maximizing the use of the space is critical to reduce unnecessary content removal. Instead of purging the material entirely, you can hide the content until necessary.

Methods that give content on demand a fresh appeal include:

> CSS3 selectors (like target or checked)

> JavaScript and JS libraries (like jQuery)

> AJAX (which has wide browser support)

An interface with fewer components inherently has fewer elements fighting for space and visual recognition. Such an interface also encourages visitors to read the full page rather than scan it. Don't be afraid to use some of the effective tools in the modern designer's toolkit—simplifying the interface, reducing content (or emphasizing the content's value in more efficient ways), clearing out any unhelpful or boring content, and heuristically assigning value (thereby temporarily hiding less valuable assets).

Tip

For those without coding experience, CSS stands for Cascading Style Sheets and represents the visual style. JavaScript is used to control behavior-based events, and AJAX is a method of processing data between a user and the host's machine. All three can help you avoid page refreshes and provide a seamless, content-packed experience!

Beautiful emptiness

Picture an empty website void of content, graphics, color, and every other asset of emphasis and distinction you can include. This emptiness may seem boring, but it actually showcases one of the most primal and fundamental aspects of design. Emptiness and space can be beautiful (see Figure 1-9 for a lovely example of how an empty space could appear). Such a visual representation is the epiphany of balance and a Zen state of being. If anything were to be added to it, the distinction would be at its strongest.

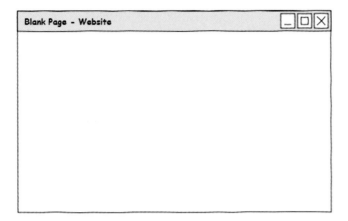

FIGURE 1-9: This is one of the cleanest environments known to man . . . a blank website.

Obviously, as a web designer, you are required to include content or items of interest for the visitor, and this coincidently means the addition of material to your once derelict yet simplified blank page. Clean can be very beautiful, but context and richness have more value! One beautiful example of simplicity in effect is the www.madebysofa.com site, which shows that combining quality content with a basic layout can still be rich in distinction.

Individuals building a website from the ground up, in which nothing is set in stone, should take time to examine not only what options are available to provide emphasis where it's needed, but also to refrain from applying stylistic, graphical, structural, or behavioral emphasis and distinction within the web page unless absolutely sure. If you can get away with simpler, it may work to your users' benefit.

Individuals adapting an existing site to make it more distinctive (and perhaps more valuable to the visitor) should consider reformatting all of the content back to a neutral state like plain text. Otherwise, you can simply examine the various individual components of your site and decide on individual changes as needed.

How you choose to transform the emptiness or existing construction into an elegant and optimized environment is up to you. (Figure 1-10 shows a basic example of how a more technical interface can be simplified.) What is great about distinctive design is that you can implement it progressively over a period of time, or you can use it as a basis for a design built from the ground up. The result of your work will be an interface that benefits more users.

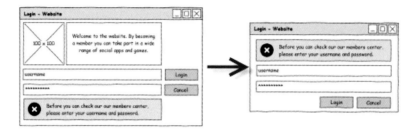

FIGURE 1-10: Progressively enhancing or gracefully degrading, both are great design philosophies.

Sanitizing the interface

Four primary methods accurately depict how to remove content that is otherwise deemed unnecessary from an interface in order to better portray the content that already exists. Although each tends to come with a varying set of definitions (as everyone seems to have a different interpretation of its meaning), they all play an essential role in design. Figure 1-11 identifies the bond each has to the design process.

FIGURE 1-11: The four cornerstones of distinctive cleaning. If it isn't needed, it should disappear!

Simplicity

Simplicity is one of the most fundamental aspects of a clean and efficient user experience. The acronyms KISS ("Keep it simple, stupid!") and YAGNI ("You ain't gonna need it") explain this principle in a highly direct method. Making things overly complex irritates users, and unless you genuinely need a function or a visual representation in the interface, don't add it. If there is a way to achieve something on the page with fewer objects, elements or visual points of interest, it's worth doing, as the likelihood for distraction will be minimized.

Minimalism

Minimalism is a method that encourages simplicity by preventing the enhancement of elements until it is required. It is about taking something of existing complexity (like an existing site) and stripping away every element that doesn't need to be complex. This concept aims to deconstruct and improve the site with fewer or an equal number of features of the same complexity level. With simplicity, you aim to strip existing objects down into their core components. In minimalism, you start with only what's necessary and build upon that (when improvement is demanded).

Reductionism

Reductionism follows a more scientific process than the previous two; it is the idea that if something complex is taken and reduced to its most fundamental parts, you can better understand its nature. Within the scope of distinctive design, you find that if you investigate how particular parts of a site function, you can determine where emphasis may occur. From there, you learn to improve the object. As an example, take the search engine results page. Consider where your eyes are naturally drawn. Decide if that's where you would like your visitor to look or if it should be changed.

Holism

Finally, it's worth noting the *holistic* approach, which acts in opposition to reductionist theories (within design). Aristotle said that "the whole is more than the sum of its parts," and within the concept of design, this often holds true. Although you can reduce a site down to a basic level to understand how things function, you need to visualize those parts in context of the whole page. Never just assume that making a site simpler or smarter will resolve every problem, because some issues result from outside influences that are difficult to measure. This effect is magnified on the web.

Tip

When assigning a level of importance to the components of your website, separate text from images and other forms of media (providing their distinction levels) because the level of emphasis a video and other input mediums (like audio) endure are far greater than what text provides.

Being Consistent is Critical

Consistency is an important aspect of a web interface. With regard to your visitors and audience, learning new things can be a particularly scary idea if they are forced to use trial and error to find what they are looking for. One of the main reasons why most websites don't have a totally different look for every page is that visitors need to effectively navigate around a page without getting lost (imagine the learning curve if every page is visually different).

Visitors often scan a page to proactively seek what they are interested in (rather than reading a page in full, as shown in Figure 1-12). They are more likely to use a mixture of guesswork and quick responsive selections to find the closest match to their needs. If they don't find what they're looking for, they'll return to the original starting page to try again. They are even more inclined to guesswork in an attempt to speed up the results. Although this erratic style of behavior may seem impossible to assist, clearly defined, well-labeled, distinctive layouts work wonders.

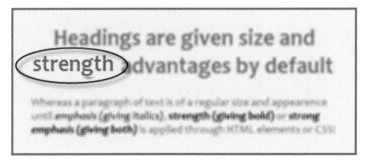

FIGURE 1-12: As your visitors scan for specific keywords, their focus ignores what doesn't associate.

If your visitors are fairly inexperienced with technology (as many Internet users are), they probably depend on conventions or trends (recognizable objects on the page like navigation menus and clickable logos) to help them navigate around a site. Major changes between designs or pages can therefore lead to widespread confusion. To quote Homer Simpson, "In times of trouble you've got to go with what you know." That's precisely what users do. If they feel something is too hard or inconsistent (and you have competition), they leave to find an easier source of information!

Important

Although it does not apply to everyone, the numbers of users who scan information for relevance first and read second are in the vast majority. This may be related to the reduced amount of free time people generally have (though research with exact figures is limited).

Part of the justification for emphasis within a website is to lead your visitors by the hand and guide them to the content that matters most to them. Titles within page sections aim to give visitors an idea of where certain data is located; images and navigation menus help visitors get to a resource they require; and even conventions like the underlined link (as shown in Figure 1-13) helps visitors establish whether they need to click or continue reading!

Hyperlinks are like portals to another **world**. They're powered by an underline, cursor, and color convention by default.

FIGURE 1-13: The default underlined link is often depicted by a selection of browser-induced trends.

Distinctively barrier-free

The problem of inconsistent design forces website visitors to re-evaluate everything they know about an interface, which isn't helpful because you want to keep the process as smooth and streamlined as possible, but punishing your users by accident can also be a problem that many designers fail to account for. Overcomplicated visuals, dense or heavy content, and invasive or abusive functionality disrupt the flow and distinction.

One clear example of this problem in action is the issue of repetition. As users examine the distinctive regions of your site in order to associate that location and content with a specific function (such as a navigation menu), confusion occurs if repetition exists in another format. For example, many advertisers use these techniques to fool visitors into thinking that their computers' security may suddenly be at risk.

Arguably, using existing distinctive elements may yield results from individuals who progress throughout a site without thinking, but the need for ethical practices in promoting distinction takes precedence. If you produce a distinctive page element that misguides the visitor, that user's trust in your brand (and any other distinctive elements within the site) may be permanently damaged, thereby turning the distinction into a negative.

Important

On rare occasions, a distinctive design can suffer a negative impact. This is only caused when the visitor's finite resources suffer and run dry (such as a lack of trust or loyalty to a particular brand). Avoiding such events will be straightforward if you follow any prescribed guidelines.

No visitor wants to endure the frustration of trying to adapt their skill set to match your site's requirements. Allowing a visitor to drift among the elements of your site undisturbed requires the capability to navigate around a site "brainlessly" (without thinking twice). A user's satisfaction increases if they have few obstacles to work through, and the barrier to entry is as unobtrusive (or intrusive) as possible, so it's worth the effort. In Figure 1-14 you can see how simple page numbering provides some sense of the site's depth to help users make basic, yet informed, choices.

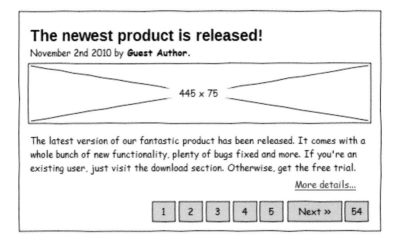

FIGURE 1-14: Page numbering within a blog helps visitors know how long an article might be.

When a site provides barriers to entry or an inconsistent, non-transitional interface, the visitor is likely to become reliant on interpreting (usually on a whim) the exact nature or depth of the content being explored. This coping mechanism of trying to stumble on what he or she is looking for usually comes at the cost of reducing the user's patience, making him or her feel inferior, and increasing the risk of a fast exit. Consider a popular site like Amazon. The sheer number of products acts as a barrier to entry as browsing without a product in mind could lead you into spending days stumbling around one category listing.

Consequences of distinction

The benefits of a user-centered experience are justified within distinctive design because you ensure those who use the information on your site have access to it. With visitors often finding themselves unable to locate information that should be visible within a site, it's important to guide users without limiting their interaction capabilities.

Reference A number of aids that can assist users exist, but increasing usage scenarios make the web developer's job harder. These range from the browsers or devices people use to the way their brains function and the tools that exist to help with certain disadvantages (like screen readers for the disabled). It's your job to ensure that these tools work for our users.

The consequences of emphasis and distinction will be felt wherever they are placed. By boosting the visibility of important content, neutralizing (or eliminating) less relevant details, and accounting for the principles that dominate your page's appearance, you increase the readability and visitor awareness of the content you want to showcase. Although it won't suddenly turn a poor-quality site into something amazing, it certainly goes a long way to improving it in a way that benefits your readers.

Summary

The beginning of this chapter examines the slogan that depicts the need for elements to have attention so that users recognize them. "Can you see me?" speaks to them on behalf of your site, so if the answer is no (and it's the data your visitors are looking for), something is amok and needs immediate attention! These principles are fundamental to a site's capability to showcase distinction and empathy toward the visitor's needs.

Visitors devote a finite amount of resources (such as time and trust) to you on a temporary basis during their stay. A distinctive design should not only look and feel better, it should feel effortless, obvious, and self-explanatory. Plus, because there's little additional work involved, there is no valid excuse against making your visitors happier and more comfortable with your user interface.

Designing for Different Devices

The hardware and software that demand your attention

THE MANNER BY which designers create designs for the web has evolved through changes in how humans use the Internet. Standards have evolved; new methods of attaching functionality are being explored (such as frameworks); and new browsers, devices, and hardware reach the public at ever increasing rates. In addition, presenting information in both digital and analog formats (for the web and otherwise) have made our attempts to stand out challenging.

In this chapter, I explore the rapidly changing market to see how distinction differs between virtual and tactile environments. I also examine how extensible tools, such as Flash and PDFs, impact your work as well as the importance of applications — both browser based and independently coded. To round out the chapter nicely, I conclude with some important information about the influence of print on distinctive design and why print still matters.

Designing for More than Desktops

Designing for the web presents a unique mixture of opportunities and problems that you need to address in order to maintain a useful interface. Because sites aren't tangible objects and are rendered on the fly rather than fixed upon a piece of paper, you are limited in the amount of control you might wish to hold over visitors and how they experience your site. How you approach distinctive design must therefore resolve pitfalls by using a design methodology that is both flexible and (for the sake of older versions of Microsoft Internet Explorer) quite durable.

Basically, you don't have any control over the following:

> Hardware or physical web connections

> Software that could interact with a page

> Browsers, extensions, or accessibility aids

> Scripting or plug-ins that are turned off

Unfortunately, you're stuck with the user's personal choices!

With so many devices, browsers, and users to cater to (all with their own requirements of the technologies you choose to implement), compatibility ranks high on the distinctive design agenda. Your layout can be as beautiful and as exquisitely crafted as you like, but if certain basic usage requirements cannot be met, or technologies are disabled, an entire site can be reduced to nothingness. There's no distinctive quality in being invisible!

Figure 2-1 shows the ultimate sacrifice a site makes if it demands that certain plug-ins or capabilities be enabled.

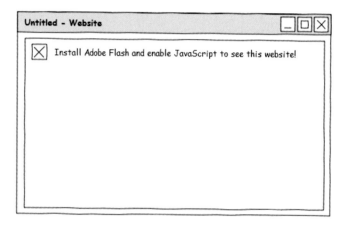

FIGURE 2-1: A site made entirely by using Flash is useless if the user disables Flash or does not have it.

The mechanics behind a distinctive interface take into account much more than the visual illumination that a design provides. The design inherently has to account for the method in which your site will be consumed as well as the tools at the visitor's disposal that affect the appearance. If that isn't enough, limitations can result from specific requirements. As a simple example shown in Figure 2-1, a Flash-based site may look distinctive on the desktop, but it fails entirely on an iOS device.

With more and more individuals browsing the web on a range of different devices, the web is quickly evolving into a medium unlike any other. While authoring tools become increasingly more agile in recognizing and dealing with such ranges and can even help those in restricted situations get an adequate browsing experience, it's important that as a designer you understand how impossible the "one size fits all" model actually is.

Distinction exists in many forms, and different variables account for the on-screen result your visitors see. Although having no real control over your interface's final look seems frustrating, it motivates you to maintain a flexible attitude, and an open mind, toward how things may render. The benefits of such an attitude are profound, as the evolving web environment requires you to avoid designing for the present alone. Applying such a methodology to your workload can also serve in your best interests when dealing with new, unique circumstances.

Note Have you ever wanted to see the most primitive way your site can be viewed? Download the browser Lynx (`http://csant.info/lynx`). It renders no graphics or pixels; instead, it's a simple text-only browser that displays a site's content structure (which is as basic as you're going to get).

Distinction within hardware

Among the initial considerations about how distinctive a design can be, the subject of hardware is never far from the developer's mind. Many electronic devices provide Internet experiences (even if restricted), and the limitations of such technologies can, by association, impact your capability to provide your visitors with the best experience possible. You must consider not only the device itself (such as a PC or phone), but also the hardware and software inside it.

Always remember that hardware comes with limitations. Understanding this concept is important because it impacts your capability to build distinctive and appealing visual experiences for your users. These imposed and unique situations affect the people you want to target, and if you don't address issues, your design may fail. For example, in the scope of a project, this may require seeing the benefits in a smaller screen and learning how to turn that display into something attractive and appealing. It's quite a challenge!

Several types of hardware provide access to the Internet:

> Computers, netbooks, and laptops

> Tablets, phones, eReaders, and PDAs

> Televisions and game consoles

> Even vehicles and household appliances

Note At this point you are probably wondering what household appliances access the web. Well surprisingly, devices like refrigerators, microwaves, ovens, dishwashers, and even toilets are gaining access. Currently, they are in limited circulation (so that plunger script you coded isn't needed just yet), but a web-enabled house isn't out of the question, so be prepared!

Many aspects of hardware within devices impact the end-user experience. A device's limitations and how visitors interact with that medium influence how interactivity occurs.

For example, a device with a small screen (or monitor, as shown in Figure 2-2) has less visual space to catch people's attention, and speakers could potentially provide additional levels of engagement through the medium of sound—if the visitor has them.

Some devices are naturally more or less capable than others, and these core "environmental" issues (influences outside of the device) can literally change how your users benefit from a service. If you're browsing the web on a handheld device, you may be less willing to visit a bandwidth-hungry site because of data caps or roaming charges. Or a slow connection speed may affect your visitor's attention span or patience level, causing adverse effects. Data, speed, and connectivity aren't affected directly from a limitation of a device; often it's the fault of the carrier or location of the device itself.

FIGURE 2-2: Small screens aren't necessarily bad. Just make the most of what space you have.

Your visitors' hardware acts as a middleman and a portal to access the content you provide through your site. You need to customize the experience for a wide range of input, (allowing interaction with your site) and output devices (allowing people to receive your message in various formats). Consider these objectives mission-critical. Web browsers provide only one level of distinctive influence, and it's one of the few things you can control.

In essence, hardware plays a critical role in providing visitors with a useful, distinctive experience. Without a monitor or display, eye candy is invisible. Lack of a mouse or keyboard limits site interaction. Without speakers, the impact of audio is limited. When you build a site, consider that some of your visitors have limited hardware at their disposal, and you need to assist their input and output functionality by providing alternative usage methods.

The following instruments can help a user interact with a website:

> **Input device:** Mouse, keyboard, tablet, touch screen, tracker pad, remote control, joystick, digital pen or stylus, gesture readers, scanner, webcam, microphone, camera, camcorder, GPS tools, motion sensors and certain USB and FireWire devices

> **Output device:** Screen, monitor, television, projector, speakers, headphones, LED lights, E Ink, 3D glasses, and printers

The number of Internet-enabled devices is staggering. No longer are you simply limited to technology of the 1990s, which offered either a limited-functionality gadget or a regular desktop computer for browsing. Today, you need to adopt interfaces for cellphones, tablet devices, and even televisions. It's yet another opportunity for web designers to be distinctive and creative, and if you can entice more visitors to your site, and if you can beat your competition, you could become the sole competitor on that device.

Important

You must avoid over-thinking your methodology. Know that you can't design for every possible scenario, so you should only justify adapting a design to be distinctive for a certain interface if there's a chance your visitors will use it (not every site will need to account for all of the above). Check any analytics software and ask your users for some basic insights.

Browser-based ubiquity

Although hardware comes with its own set of challenges and problems (for example, a designer can't rely on a single screen size or input method being available), one of the most common considerations for a web designer is the web browser. Recommendations and standards for browsers can be problematic to follow effectively (see Figure 2-3 for an example).

Most people consider web browsers as a graphical method of displaying information, but there's more to browsers than meets the eye. A number of text-based browsers remain in use from the days of old (though mostly by designers testing their work's readability), and a wave of 3D browsers still provide that '80s virtual reality interface style. When you check to ensure that everything works fine, think outside the box about how you can give your brand unique distinction that others haven't considered!

Tip Although 3D browsers exist (namely 3B and SphereSite), their market penetration is rather slim. It seems that for now, people still enjoy browsing the web through conventional graphical browsers. This is great news for you, because it reduces your testing workload considerably!

If you think the differences in browser types are scary, consider the prospect of the end-user's operating system. While the browser takes care of much of what appears on the visitor's screen, components of the OS such as drivers for hardware, technologies like ClearType (font smoothing and anti-aliasing), hardware acceleration, and even the built-in browser can play a part. For example, Safari for Mac can render differently than Safari for Windows.

FIGURE 2-3: Safari and Chrome are built upon the same rendering engine (webKit), yet have their differences.

Each browser may have its own unique set of features to aid your visitor's experience of your site (such as the capability to zoom in on a page, which helps those with poor eyesight). However, the trend of some websites to have bugs, unfinished standards, and inconsistency in rendering pages means that you must give extra attention to the testing process. Sites should be compatible with the tools your visitors use as well as the browser itself. It's that simple.

Note Several browser bugs affect how your code appears to your visitors. To learn about some of the quirks and how to handle them (these are good, solid, real-world examples), visit `http://gtalbot.org/BrowserBugsSection/` and `http://positioniseverything.net/explorer.html`.

With regards to good practices and distinctive design in equal measure, it's worth giving users a consistent cross-browser experience just for the sake of knowing that they will find what they expect, where they expect it. Validating your code is a good option (by using the W3C free validator tools), but in regards to what browsers your site needs to be tested on, see Figure 2-4 for the top five. You should also look at your statistics and see what browsers your visitors are using.

Of the many web browsers, the most popular ones require the most attention. Within the scope of a good, stable interface, this means testing the top five browsers as a bare minimum (to ensure you cover the top 95 percent). Beyond that, testing on a wide range of mobile devices is also an important practice because these devices (in most cases) use their own specifically built browsers, and so pages may render differently.

Firefox

Safari

Internet Explorer

Opera

Chrome

FIGURE 2-4: Begin your compatibility testing with the five most popular browsers.

Since the days of the browser wars in which Microsoft Internet Explorer and Netscape dueled to see which had the better browser, standards have been quite rocky as older browsers still roam the top of in-use lists. Although much of the terrain has settled (though bugs and quirks exist even in newer browsers), the capability to provide a consistent yet distinctive experience, even with the ulterior motives of each browser, has become an important area of HCI (human-computer interaction).

Note Because a number of browsers, renderers, and versions exist, knowing which technologies each supports is important. Plenty of sites can help you with this task by giving tables of data (though none are complete). Useful places to visit include `http://webdevout.net` and `http://fmbip.com/`.

Distinctive design works best when the experience works for as many users as possible (not just the number of browsers you can patch in harmony). To aid your code development, Microsoft created a way (for their own quirky browser) to address browser or version-specific inconsistencies in browser rendering. Conditional comments (which works on everything) and code compilation (for Jscript, which isn't the same as JavaScript) both help avoid the need for hacks. So you could physically alter the visuals for browsers, such as Internet Explorer 6, thereby giving your site and its layout a different but appropriate level of distinction. The result doesn't have to be pixel-perfect.

While targeting individual browsers may seem like a great way to separate the distinctive impact assigned to devices of different calibers (such as providing a mobile-optimized experience that differs from a basic desktop experience), it's worth thinking about whether a change in the expected experience will give people a better or more reliable way of interacting with your site. Change can be great, but it's only appropriate and useful if it's implemented with a purpose. If you find an unfixable quirk in Internet Explorer, apply conditional comments to your code as needed and style it as needed, and remember to test each applicable rendering engine (as shown in Figure 2-5).

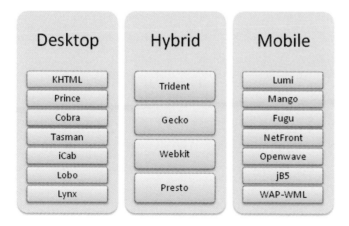

FIGURE 2-5: Plenty of rendering engines exist, but the top five browsers use ones in the hybrid category.

To keep the peace and ensure a consistent experience, spend time (how long is another question) testing on a range of desktops, handheld mobile-specific devices, and any independent browsers your visitors may use, considering the effects to nontraditional users. Testing on such a wide range of devices is time-consuming (unfortunately), but luckily, emulators can help reduce the cost of testing (if you don't have the actual handsets at your disposal).

Important Even though emulators (which simulate a device's capabilities and rendering) can help you get an idea of how a website will look on a mobile device, it's quite useful to test on the actual hardware, if possible. While emulators provide fairly consistent results, you may find slight differences in how an actual browser (or hardware or OS) renders.

Within browser-based environments, consistency and compatibility are worthy of a distinctive designer's attention. Although you cannot control the browsers or devices visitors use, your capability to cater an experience and keep the ride as smooth as possible reinforces the message and emphasis you portray online. Always emit professionalism on a site to gain user trust. If your site works beautifully, your user's focus will be where it matters!

Expandability with Extensions

Since the web's inception, the need for evolution and growth has been hampered by a slow procession of recommendations and standards by organizations such as the World Wide Web Consortium (W3C). While the work of these groups has lead to fantastic layers of distinction and careful craftsmanship such as HTML and CSS, their slow pace increased the need to forge alternatives in an attempt to give Internet users a richer experience without the wait for specifications to be recommended.

The work of the W3C should not be ignored because the recommendations they have produced make up the majority of what can be considered reliable code. It became reliable code because browsers embedded the technology (though it's not always a guarantee of support) at the rendering level. But with current limitations in how information can be showcased onscreen (you can use just HTML, CSS and JavaScript) and a historical lack of functionality, plug-in technologies like Flash appeared on the scene, attempting to fill the gap.

Tip Following standards is a good thing because it generally increases the chances of people being able to use what you produce. Using some strange language in a browser that doesn't know how to read it will ultimately leave you with a broken experience (and unhappy users).

As with most aspects of life, there's usually a catch. The limitation on these kinds of additions, which can be latched onto a browser, in this case, is compatibility. And, like with all proprietary technologies, it's up to end-users to ensure that they have the right plug-in, the right version, and the thing turned on before they can use it (as noted in Figure 2-6). If features aren't available by default, unavailability can become a prominent issue.

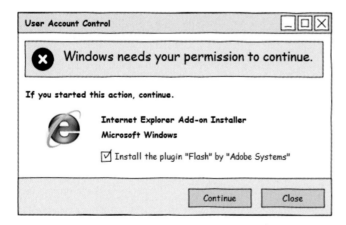

FIGURE 2-6: Usually, there is either a plug-in requesting to be installed or an extension at work.

These tools, created with the purpose of providing additional functionality during an online experience, while seemingly used everywhere, ultimately never received the same level of support that HTML and CSS have. When making use of such features within your design, you must offer alternatives in case these extras are unavailable. In today's online culture, you can't just expect people to download what you ask. They will likely be offended at the control you try to exert and rebel, clicking the Back button in order to find an alternative that isn't so demanding.

Tip

Some browsers come pre-equipped with commonly used plug-ins, which is great if you want to increase the chances that end-users have the extension you require. A potential problem is, of course, whether the version they were given is up-to-date (and if an update or installation is required to continue accessing the content).

As the web evolves, perhaps the need for such technologies will disappear (replaced by the latest standards of markup and scripting languages). But for the moment, it's worth taking the time to understand how such game changing (and radically different) tools affect the way you can create a distinctive design, how you can emphasize content using such mechanisms, and the benefits these tools can potentially bring to your upcoming distinctive design. After all, for all of their shortcomings they do still provide a unique opportunity to enrich a visually designed experience.

Plug-and-play design

The distinction of a site and how your experience will be portrayed depends upon several factors. Sometimes the hardware or operating system affects the rendering; other times, it's the browser trying to make the most out of the viewport (the visible window or canvas where the website usually appears). In the case of the plug-in (which embeds itself within the document), these rules generally do not apply because these extensions are self-contained and aren't browser formatted.

The concept of a plug-and-play device is easiest to describe when you examine something such as a USB or FireWire device. After you attach it to the computer, the device magically comes to life and performs a specific function. Such is the concept on the web, where if you produce a Flash sequence (see Figure 2–7) made up of animation, video, or other wondrous things, it will independently render the object and thereby be excused from the limitations or functionality that exists within a browser or the plug-in technology.

FIGURE 2-7: After you embed a Flash package in the page, it becomes active when downloaded.

Include cross-platform capability in your plans for a guaranteed, accurate rendering every time. Plug-ins have less constraints over how objects can be arranged and what those objects can do, which allows you to apply distinction to an interface that is only limited by your imagination or your willingness to experiment.

Important

Because plug-ins such as Flash render their own elements, browsers only need to ensure that the package (object) loads correctly. Therefore, you could technically class every major plug-in for web browsers as an independent rendering engine, capable of different, unique feats!

Deciding to use independent plug-in components can be tricky. Flash and other related technologies can be turned off, uninstalled, or rendered unusable. It's therefore going to be an either/or situation in which either the experience you provide will load, function (exactly as you visualized), and be fantastic, or it will impact the user, become unavailable, and result in the experience simply not existing for the session — quite a risk to take!

Because the concept of providing added functionality to a browser is quite appealing, a number of providers such as Adobe and Microsoft have created their own vendor extensions that give unique interactivity to a page. As with all plug-ins like this, you must realize that although many sites use these helpful technologies in imaginative ways, there's no real guarantee that they'll continue to be supported in the future, as standards evolve rapidly.

The plug-in technologies most widely used within sites include:

> **Adobe:** Flash and Shockwave

> **Microsoft:** ActiveX and Silverlight

> **Oracle:** Java

One reason why people use technologies like Flash is because in the days of old, designers were forced to embed media players from one of several independent providers to get various file formats to work (with no existing standard). The advent of Flash offered a useful method of embedding media within a page without end-users needing a specific media player installed; they just needed the right plug-in. That has satisfied many a user!

Tip HTML5 is making great strides toward employing video and audio directly into the browser. For now, you still need to supplement your approach with plug-ins so that most of your visitors get all of the distinctive extras, even if they don't support HTML5!

One of the main problems with such technologies occurs as a result of how they are both understood by people using them and the way certain websites implement the functionality. Although compatibility has shown itself to be a problem, it's been well established that search engines also suffer problems trying to read and index plug-in code, and accessibility aids can suffer quirks, too. Always consider the downsides before implementing!

Important Other elements of a website can also be turned off or disabled, and therefore can cause problems for your display. Visitors can literally flip the switch on HTML images, frames, and proprietary tags in addition to all CSS stylistic code and JavaScript.

Although standards are evolving to slowly eliminate the need for plug-ins and other proprietary technologies, there's no doubt that you can use such extensions to give your design some added flavor. As with the principles of distinctive design, the key is restraint. If you can offer a more widely supported method, use it. Otherwise, employ the technology with a good fallback. Many designers follow a concept called progressive enhancement that simply states if you ensure the basics work (think minimalism) and layer on the useful extras, if something goes wrong there will always be something that works for the end user (even if it's not what you hoped for or intended).

Within the scope of distinctive design, the additional levels of interactivity and functionality provided by Flash, Silverlight, and others provide a fitting additional layer to your existing workflow. If the browser doesn't support what you're trying to accomplish and you have the next best thing in effect, consider how the theories of design and the concepts applied throughout this book can help you use such tools. (If it's for an appropriate task such as providing video or audio, an example is shown in Figure 2-8.)

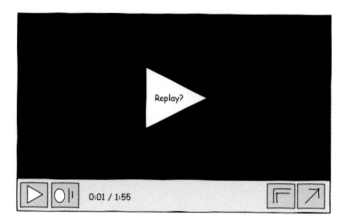

FIGURE 2-8: Using a technology like Flash, you can embed a media player that streams video.

Documentation delivery

On the web, it isn't always appropriate to deliver important documents in a conventional web page format. Perhaps it needs to be optimized for printing by removing all the visual flourishes that designers give their sites. Maybe it's a huge document that requires all the information to be joined together in one downloadable format. Or perhaps it needs to be made available for offline viewing. All of these valid publishing reasons guide you to consider using delivery formats instead of the HTML users expect.

Like with most things on the web, delivering a readable document requires the compatibility factor to rear its ugly head again! Sending someone a file that has been formatted in Microsoft Word 2010 when he or she only has access to the 97 version obviously presents an issue (if compatibility mode isn't triggered). Rendering such important documents requires a format that visitors' machines likely can recognize and use. The two most common formats on the web (as noted in Figure 2-9) are Microsoft's XPS (Open XML Paper Specification) and Adobe's PDF (Portable Document Format).

The justification for using these document formats rather than traditional HTML usually falls upon five factors described as follows. What's rather interesting is that the method used to design such documents has more in common with presenting and laying out print media than simply producing a traditional website on-screen (both in methodology and distinctive goals). Quite simply, it's like having a printed file outside your site's workflow and attaching it in a way that can be easily viewed or controlled.

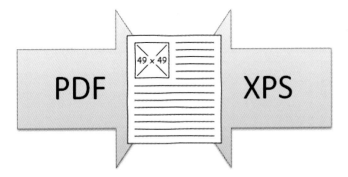

FIGURE 2-9: Two primary formats are optimized for documentation on the web.

The five factors that justify using these formats are:

> **Length:** You can have unlimited pages with better navigation aids.

> **Size:** Download the file and its assets all at once (or apply compression), and control the level of compression.

> **Quality:** Allows you to give pages a print feel, and you can focus on the content instead of spanning it over many individual pages.

> **Control:** You can add DRM (Digital Rights Management), password protection, copy protection, print protection, and other useful features.

> **Distribution:** Allows offline viewing and avoids accidental 404 errors if users attempt to continue reading after the website goes offline.

The web and print are indeed unique, and because of the way they are consumed they are not directly suited to simply converting one into the other with pixel-by-pixel precision. Document formats allow the structure, layout, and visual design of a printed product to be retained without suffering the formatting quirks of compatibility commonly found within many desktop browsers, though separate versions may be useful to optimize an experience for each device. (See Figure 2-10.)

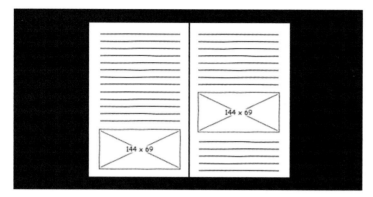

FIGURE 2-10: A document feels like print media because of its clearly defined page size and scale.

The benefits of this fixed and relatively unwavering layout style can be huge if you are try-ing to forge a stable content delivery method that carries a good balancing act between print and digital format. As such, document formats such as PDF and XPS provide you with an opportunity to engage visitors, offering a static distinction and feel to your content.

You could potentially use a Microsoft Word (.doc) document or another well recognized format, but it's arguably a better choice to use something more suitable for the web, such as PDF (the most popular one) or XPS.

Tip

At this stage, you are probably thinking that publishing everything in this format may be ideal if the noise ratio is minimized, but again we hit the same kinds of barriers that all proprietary plug-in functionality may have. Web browsers do not automatically embed a PDF rendering feature (with the exception of Google Chrome, and browsers with Adobe's PDF Reader installed), so compatibility is directly impacted.

To read one of the document formats mentioned (especially one that can be downloaded and redistributed), you will need to have a piece of software installed (or a service like Google Docs) that will display it. A PDF reader is free to download from Adobe and other hosts, but if one of your visitors has little experience with computers, the request for such a product can cause unexpected complications, since installing software can be quite a stressful procedure if a user has never done it.

If you need to host copy-protected content on the web, PDF works as a good solution. It has the capacity for DRM, password protection, copying restrictions, printing, and more! It's pretty great for sensitive files, though it's not bulletproof against hackers.

After saying that, document formats are great for what they do and are a worthy consideration within any design as long as you provide the obligatory fallback. For large documents like books and for material aimed at the print industry, they are unparalleled in their suitability. As you begin applying distinctive design principles to enhance your site, any that seem applicable to print will also work in these types of documents, so you can boost their performance, too. (Just make sure that you, as always, design with purpose!)

If you have files that need to retain their characteristics and formatting, these formats provide solid choices. Your visitors are likely to view such documents outside of the browser, perhaps by using an eReader or other PDF-friendly device. Other considerations such as accessibility can affect viewing. These formats are well worth investigating if you take the time to make sure that your distinctive purpose doesn't infringe upon visitors' needs to access the content that you put so much effort into publishing.

Design evolution

When you design sites, realize that many different layers contribute to how experiences can be portrayed. Creating distinction within a PDF document aimed primarily at print media (housed in a digital shell) will have different aims, objectives, and goals than your conventional layout. The scope of how you design for various situations is broader than many imagine.

Designers often find themselves limited to working within the constraints of standards, formats, and third-party components. Whether it's a browser providing the latest flavor of CSS or the visitor knowingly having Flash installed and active (thereby being able to take advantage of that wonderful montage video you've created), adjust your practices to take advantage of the features you're given. Experimentation is as useful to design as just being compatible, so don't let the ever-evolving standards bog you down into submission. Most technologies can be used in a design; it just takes the dedication and practice to cover your bases for that compatibility monster.

Distinctive design is about knowing what tools are at your disposal, what their benefits and limitations are, taking the time to implement them as effectively as possible, and doing so with consideration for less-empowered visitors. Making things look pretty but not useful is a bad idea, but turning that canvas into a clever masterpiece is something else! An example: In Figure 2-11, you could have the image link to an embedded PDF file, but provide an HTML or plain-text fallback using links below it.

FIGURE 2-11: Blending various approaches produces an engaging design.

It's important to emphasize how such implementations affect your work. A perfect design doesn't exist; you can never end up with something that works equally well for everyone (though that's not to say that you can't produce something that works beautifully for a majority). Building a website is like tackling a great engineering project. With the right materials, tools, and foresight, you can give an experience that is distinctive enough to gain attention but without user frustration.

Tip

Although you can be heavy-handed in your approach, doing so won't help your visitor's reading flow. Sometimes it's better to include some subtle elements that don't try to grab your visitor's immediate attention. Often, that attention is needed elsewhere.

Visually on the page, you have a limited amount of space to paint your words, images, media, and elements in a way that can gain recognition; you must always evolve your techniques and methods so they attract your visitors to what is needed to continue their journey. As the web evolves, the situation is only going to get more complicated. As additional layers are added to the features you create, distinction gains increasing importance.

The web design process has numerous layers:

> Content distinction through the portrayal of words

> Markup (HTML) distinction within the cascade

> Stylistic (CSS) distinction with applied emphasis

> Visual distinction using images and multimedia

> Scripted (JavaScript) distinction with behavior

> Extended (plug-in) distinction beyond the browser

> Assumed distinction through theoretical application

The web consists of various layers that you can easily see if you examine a website's source code. Several languages and formats can interweave yet still result in the kind of beautiful and distinctive layouts that many people crave. At this stage, you should realize that making the most of a layout isn't simply based on clever design tricks and theories; it's also about producing great code.

With a rise in Internet users and sites, there will come a time when having a single site isn't enough! Standing out from your competitors and getting visitors requires a need to be memorable, useful, and engaging—principles that make design distinctive. No matter the platform and however the web evolves, being distinctive (in any situation) is possible even if you reach beyond the browser and aim to provide some distinction in another format (perhaps by producing a custom smartphone application).

Applying Application Theory

With the smartphone revolution, the industry behind mobile apps has seen a significant increase in recognition among professionals on the web and desktop alike. It may seem rather strange at first to consider that a desktop or mobile app can be distinctive or have an impact within the web, since you are learning to design sites that naturally exist within a browser. But even with the simplest layout or interface you can still learn from the software industry and how a graphical user interface is engineered.

Whether an app is executable for a device or a desktop (via Adobe Air, which uses HTML, CSS and JavaScript), the capability to produce distinctive yet highly usable interfaces based on the existing web infrastructure is both important and relevant to the process of building a website. Many sites share common trends with apps, such as input elements for forms, as seen in Figure 2-12, and GUI conventions. Because of these similarities, distinctive software is worth looking at. If an interface has distinctive features, it could be used to inspire a lovely new website design, using features and techniques you hadn't considered before.

Contact Us

Department: Support (Technical Help) ▼

E-Mail:

Message:

Contact Us   Reset

FIGURE 2-12: Web browsers use input controls, just like you find in software products.

With so many different devices available, trends and conventions have formed upon the particular environment for which the app is intended. An app built for Apple products will usually be quite different than that of an Android, and both of those apps would be different than an app for a desktop product. These patterns are worth examining because as designers, you try to account for the variables that affect your work and reflect your efforts into a visual interface that users can adopt.

Important   Frameworks like Adobe Air (as mentioned) allow languages like HTML, CSS, and JavaScript to move beyond the web browser and give users something they can use on their desktops. This means that knowing how to apply distinctive GUIs for software could have real-world benefits.

Websites are usually a more open environment (because of the increased levels of flexibility in how content can be portrayed), so some rules relating to app development are not enforceable within the web. However, the techniques used in designing and implementing an app may give you additional insight into how to optimize any given environment to produce a unique, enjoyable layout.

Having control, understanding, and knowledge behind each action determines how productive and useful your services become, and knowing how to enrich an experience without causing detriment to the visitor aids your capability to give a memorable and distinctive experience. So as you progress through the ideals behind app design, remember that no matter your medium, only you know what works based on the knowledge you attain.

Tales from the GUI

Interfaces need to be tailored to the type of experience they provide. Although portable documents are visually oriented toward print design with a paper-like feel, and the realms of Flash lead to a world rich with varying levels of interactivity, mobile applications let web designers interact with their users in ever more unique, creative, and interesting ways.

It's not too difficult to see how apps and sites feature a range of common traits (as with Figure 2-13). Resulting from the wave of interest in low-cost (or free) widgets and apps that give a mobile phone or tablet device the functionality of a website aided by a few taps or pinches (and little else required), the merging of web services into desktop products has seen moderate success. As more and more services become part of the cloud (meaning web-housed), this interweaving with independent platforms will increase.

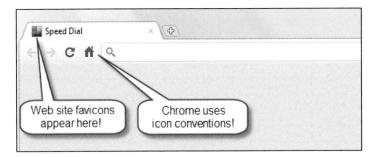

FIGURE 2-13: Apps use icons to distinguish themselves, and sites use favicons.

Clarifying the difference between the two is simple. Web apps are hosted online, and regular apps are installed to the device. Both have advantages and disadvantages, but the visual distinction that can be applied to the interface can be made to act quite similarly to each other. It's just the mode of delivery that plays a central part in how users interact with the content.

This brings up a range of benefits relating to distinctive design, since you not only can tailor the experience for that particular device (consistency is a big part of distinction, as is the clarity of the interface). You can also take advantage of a device's hardware in ways that a web browser does not allow, which may hold a range of distinctive performance benefits.

Tip

Unless you plan to use device detection (unreliable scripts that let you style or control a design based on the device or browser using it), one of the benefits of designing an app is that you have access to the native GUI controls of a device that the visitor identifies with and recognizes.

All things considered, providing the features of your site in a nice package that is tailor-made for a specific device sounds like a great idea . . . and it is! But fear not if you aren't the type of designer who likes to play with code! Although you won't get the advantages of the device's native hardware, you can emulate the feeling of a desktop product in the form of a web app. Even the look and feel of the window in Figure 2-14 can be replicated using imagery.

FIGURE 2-14: Desktop apps provide a distinctive interface, and that's something you want to achieve.

Taking this concept further, perhaps you are trying to offer a service, or you are at least testing the waters to see how you can make your content do more. That's great! Distinctive design doesn't just apply to how you can make your content more visually attractive; it applies in equal measure to app production for both the web and a desktop. Interface design is more than mere text, imagery, or even multimedia, it's about getting some attention where it's required within the app, the same ideal we hope for in websites.

Whether you offer services or just good content, the benefits of an app or experience catered toward such devices are without question. More and more handheld devices are becoming web aware, and the boom in Internet use on cellphones proves that this kind of experience won't be going away anytime soon. Coming to grips with the non-device-specific way of thinking is therefore more useful than ever before, even if you're giving individual groups a device-specific app!

Distinctive app design

The interface for an application is important, but how does this affect the average web designer simply wanting to portray content as accurately as possible? Well, the truth is that it depends on what kind of materials you host as to how useful the lessons from application design will be. If you're the kind of person who prefers feature-rich layouts that do more than just display content (like a social network), this methodology has value.

Distinctive app design isn't just about making the best out of the tools and space you have available to let your users reach their ultimate goal. It's about following the types of patterns and conventions forged through years of practice and training to help those who are using your work for the first time know where everything is. Part of your job is to adjust the learning curve so that it impacts the user as little as possible, and to ensure behavior matches experience (see Figure 2-15).

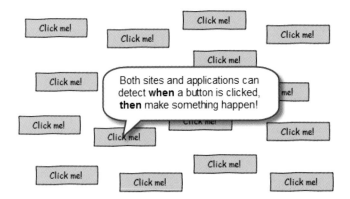

FIGURE 2-15: Most users know what a button is, and they know that clicking (or tapping) on it does something!

Within app design, the elements that make up an interface share common features with websites. Most apps have some kind of menu system that provides a list of options (websites portray a range of locations to visit; an example of this can be seen in Figure 2-16). You are also likely to find features such as an About section (or page, in the case of a site), and objects that can be clicked on (or tapped), moved, typed on, or animated. Some of these even have a web page-based alternative.

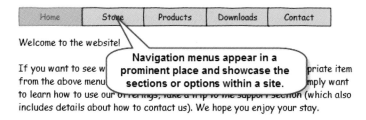

FIGURE 2-16: Conventions such as navigation menus work well with desktop, mobile, and web apps.

Modern app innovations are regularly being made so the sites' interfaces (for a specific device type) function and aesthetically match their desktop counterparts. Although there are benefits to having compiled applications (especially when connectivity is a factor), producing a web service that is as distinctive, recognizable, and usable as what you might find natively is more often than not possible to achieve (which is great for designers).

Tip

If there's one thing app design teaches us, it's that recognizable portions of a screen increase a user's confidence. If your visitors know what each part of an interface represents, they won't think twice about knowing a link or button can be clicked on (or tapped).

Experiences come in many forms, and because every web and app design is unique, the importance of taking some inspiration from sources outside of traditional web design is a lesson worth learning. Some desktop apps are really beautiful, and some mobile apps are carefully laid out. What separates apps from a website and its intentions to be distinctive is nothing more than what it's trying to portray and goals it tries to fulfill onscreen.

The web is becoming much more app-centric, and it's important to realize that an interface is more than the sum of its components. Whenever you apply the principles of design, you shouldn't discount the concepts aimed at the software industry to your sites. If you feel that one of your services would be well suited to such an environment, why not consider trying it? Building an app that's useful to people can get you some extra attention.

If not, don't worry. Just because you don't want to get waist deep in the development of some cool app doesn't mean that looking at others and how they are implemented won't give you some ideas. If you have a smartphone, get it out and look at the interface for the device. Compare it to the apps you've built. Some visuals will be more distinctive than others; yet, when you study what makes those UIs work, you get some transferrable ideas.

Going Beyond Digital Formats

Of course, there is more to life than the digital world, and many people still know the value of print mediums. Whether through books, newspapers, magazines, or something as simple as a business card, the capability to provide a distinctive interface through a physical product such as paper presents its own problems and complications (along with a range of benefits that won't match those found on a screen or electronic display device).

Because the print medium is very different than the digital world in so many ways, it's worth giving some attention to how such a format differs and relates to its online counterpart. Although many purists suggest that one is inherently better than the other, you need to recognize both as ways to provide distinction.

Note

The debate about web and print has been going on for many years. Check out www.cactusflower.org/the-web-is-not-print/, which explains quite well the basics of how they differ.

The traditional print concept can be taken to the web, and the amount of sites doing this is proof enough. Converting something into a digital format isn't an impossible act (as much as you sometimes feel it can be). The real difference and where distinctive design occurs is in the way people use such devices, and how they will consume, visualize, and interact with the content. So, you need to be sensible in your approach; don't simply guess what works and hope that your visitors take kindly to the format!

The process of converting to or from print involves:

> Moving the base content to its new location

> Styling distinctively to ensure that it's appealing

> Enhancing the material based on the medium

> Testing for durability, readability, and usability

> Publishing by using the correct output method

When converting something portrayed in print to a digital format, many designers make the common mistake of doing a copy-for-copy rewrite (which looks identical). Because people interact with the web medium so differently than traditional print, it's often the case that the change in format may not have the same impact after it's converted.

Implementing such types of experience really places demands on the subject being portrayed and how it should emote to visitors, and you need to first establish a knowledge of such an audience. Then you can use the variables and limitations (established previously) to decide what is possible or relevant within the requirements of your design. After all of these core elements come together, a beautiful website or printed (or even printer-friendly) document can be reflected and showcased with ease.

Print design

The concept of design and drawing a user's focus to the regions of a limited space may have evolved through one medium to another, but the realm of print design (and its many centuries of study and well-tested principles) remains as strong and relevant as in the past. Print may seem to be a primitive method of communicating ideas, but with different issues to contend with, designing such documents has become an art form in itself.

So why has print remained a consideration of such worth that it's included in this book? Well, as much as you might think otherwise, the web is still a relatively new method of communication, and although it has grown in many ways since its inception, the evolution of print design offers a glimpse at how conveying messages has altered over many more years than the web can offer, giving us insight into the future of the web. Figure 2-17 shows a printed business card with a simple design that maximizes space within a restricted environment.

FIGURE 2-17: You can turn a traditional business card into a website card (or vice versa).

Many of the principles that you apply to the web are drawn from the principles that apply to print (and face it, as print is a static medium, it's much easier to measure). Still, the web behaves differently, and some effects of print do not reflect well on the surface of the web (such as being able to control your layout and affix it in a finalized, non-editable format).

Tip

If you have any knowledge related to print design, don't discard it! Just because some principles don't cross over well to the web, it doesn't mean that the lessons learned are useless. Much applies equally in print and on the web, and those that don't can still infer practical lessons.

Within the scope of the web, much of the print medium's features still exist. The written word remains a prominent feature, and while media and imagery have their place, attracting readers' eyes to specific regions of a page is still the focus of many (as is the wish to be unique; thereby gaining attention like a movie poster). Ironically, with all of the extra tools that you have at your disposal online (such as the ability to markup headings with ease as in Figure 2-18), the level of noise and abuse has increased to match.

People choose to showcase their content in a number of ways, and within print this is not an exception to the rule. Just as there are hundreds of different types and styles of websites, there are also hundreds of types of printed mediums. The array of choices is like a rainbow of different implementations and reasons for being; when you think about it, it's quite striking that people can convey so many different types of messages through a restricted format (especially considering the web's flexibility).

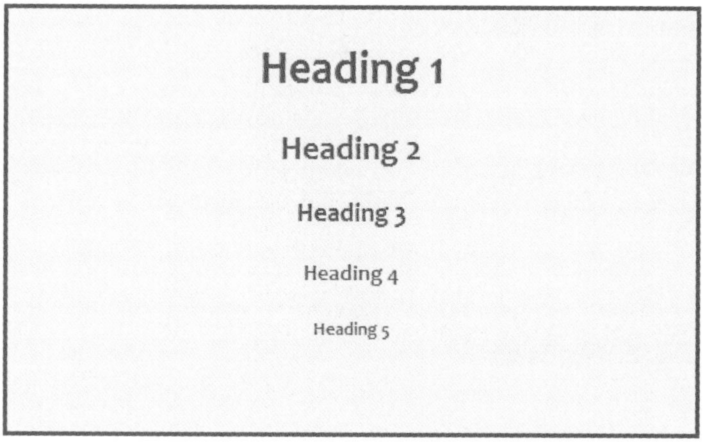

Heading 1

Heading 2

Heading 3

Heading 4

Heading 5

FIGURE 2-18: Distinctive elements like headings are used to make content stand out on a page.

The following examples have their own distinct layout requirements:

> **Print media:** newspapers, magazines, books, posters, greetings cards, letters, postcards, brochures, business cards, resumes, printed pages from a website, and flyers

> **Websites:** news, blogs, wikis, community, corporate, portals, e-commerce, business, personal, intranet, portfolios, and service websites (which focus on providing an app, rather than content).

A poster has different needs in showcasing distinctive elements than a business card, and the manner in which it is likely to be portrayed varies. Just as the information being made distinctive in one situation will differ from another, it's important to analyze what needs to go in the document before you make any decisions relating to drawing focus. What works in one situation and for one individual may inherently be flawed under different conditions (as with the web, size can be an issue). And as you will soon find out, the lessons print can teach you relate closely to its own limitations.

Tip

When putting a website together (or remodeling an existing one), put as much effort into making it "work" as you do in making it distinctive. Although there are many types of sites out there, sometimes you can get a bit crazy with the creativity (causing visitors to feel the brunt of it)!

With the formats that print can offer and its many lessons on designing good visuals, be careful to balance the uses of each equally. Sometimes, a concept may be better as a physical object; other times, it could work in a digital body. You can gain the user's focus and attention within any format, but it requires some savvy and understanding to make the transition. Be open to the concepts and theories this chapter explores even if they're not web specific, because the wonderful world of print design is a wise mentor.

Print design really plays into the idea of making something distinctive because you work with a much more restricted space in which to make your visual impact. There's no interactivity provided by clicking or gesturing, and no animation within the page; it's just valuable content waiting to be consumed and hopefully laid out in a readable yet interesting manner to attract readers. Making such a medium distinctive has been explored countless times with the goal to know how best to engage readers and grab their attention (newspapers tend to be alike as it's the optimum interface).

Important This section only skims over the relationship between print and the web because while it's an interesting subject, its application to what you're doing (in providing your visitors with something web-oriented) is rather limited. The lessons are good, but the journey is just a special bonus.

Some people think that down the line, the medium of print may completely disappear as the ubiquity of computers and their capability to replicate the printed word eliminates print's purpose entirely. Although this is a matter of debate, until the issues of web readability, accessibility, and basic content portrayal in a distinctive, useful manner , without the quirks of battery life are resolved, print and its durable, understood, hardened format will likely remain (and be treasured) in this data-driven society for some time to come.

Analog versus digital

The benefits of print design over digital formats mainly fall into how finite and steady the format actually is. When you print a document from your computer, there is no editing the layout or making tweaks to the content, and you won't find any way to switch off advertising or move things around the page. The simplicity of the format means that control is guaranteed visually.

On the flipside of this situation, the web is ultimately more durable because of its non-fixed layout and formatting. Having to deal with loads of different devices, browsers, and usage scenarios may seem like extra-hard work, but the payoff is that you're working toward a future where your content can be consumed by all types of wondrous electronic devices on demand, and you don't have those annoying post-printing mistakes that you encounter with paper (though printers do output content equally).

When the printed page is mass distributed and an error exists, a recall or a reproduction needs to occur to ensure that the quirk is resolved. Because of the web's update-friendly nature, you can rectify such problems without impacting a single existing copy (except in write-once cases, like sending an e-mail). This has implications in distinctive design because noticeable errors tend to distract visitors from the content's value.

Tip

Although this may be starting to feel like a rant on treating the two formats separately, the key thing that all designers should take from the world of print is that inspirationally, it's a great form of study. Never dismiss anything that can grab attention, even if it is paper based!

Distinctive design accounts for many factors that can impact an interface's performance, and society tends to focus on the negative and forget the positive. Even though this is a major problem for print to contend with, the printed document is still used widely among web designers and regular users alike. Many web designers (for example) prototype or draw paper-based wireframes to plan out their site's information architecture. To learn more about how this affects distinction, remember to check out Bonus Chapter 1 on the book's website. (Figure 2-19 shows a simple wireframe mockup.)

Some people doodle design ideas and sketches using tools like Adobe Photoshop, Illustrator, or a prototyping application, but many still feel the need to freely jot down ideas using a pencil and piece of paper. Eliminating the technical aspects of idea-forming keeps things simple, but as you have discovered, in certain occasions like with portraying content, a digitized version, like a PDF file, may also benefit the visitor.

The crossover between print and web options may prove useful if you're the type of person who wants to showcase your brand distinctively both using online and offline techniques. There's also no harm in applying principles of print or the web to their appropriate formats as you build your solutions. A classic example of allowing the web to transcend to paper occurs when visitors want to use a browser's native print functionality, something lots of people still do to this day, which really can't be helping the rainforests.

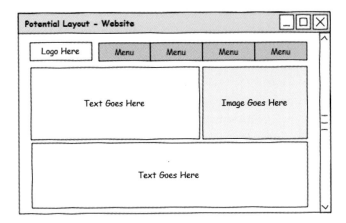

FIGURE 2-19: Designers who love paper might sketch a design concept using a website wireframe.

Perhaps one reason paper remains popular is that it offers accuracy and immediacy. No waiting, no apps, no learning curve; you just apply the pencil to the paper and create something that gives an impression.

Tip

The printed page has a lot to teach designers in showing restraint and attention to detail (especially when you have a small space to work with, like on a business card). The inspiration to turn your concepts into a physical piece of work, whether in a printed format or a web layout, should be based on how it works for the medium being used (not where it began).

The lessons to learn from printed media is that inspiration for the web can be drawn from non-digitized media, and you shouldn't be afraid to use the concepts of print design on your websites. In producing a distinctive design, it's certainly the case that as long as you ensure what worked for the print version also works for the web version (even if that means altering the design to make it compatible), you can have beauty both online and offline!

Cascading printers

Sending a document to the printer (or a website, for that matter) has been a time-honored tradition since the web first became popular. The web and print are two independent creatures with their own differences and quirks, which presents a slight problem. If you want to take your distinctive web design and make it look great when it reaches the printer, how do you assign appropriate changes to the file and ensure it's formatted appropriately?

The answer is simple and is powered by a clever element of CSS known as *media queries*. At their core, these elements of code allow you to assign styles based on the medium being displayed to the end user. If you use the @media screen selector, the code works only for computerized displays; if you use the @media print selector, only printers will be affected by the style (as you click the Print button within a browser, it will seek the selectors used by default). Using this, you can literally redesign a page to be printer friendly.

It's a great mechanism because you have the best of both worlds. Your screen gets that distinctive interface with all the lovely interactivity and visual flourishes (along with your content being afforded the space and positioning it requires). Your printer gets a layout that doesn't waste paper, is focused on only what's needed (if coded correctly), and will ultimately look great without needing a printer-friendly or PDF version of every page you have. Figure 2-20 shows a browser's default Print dialog.

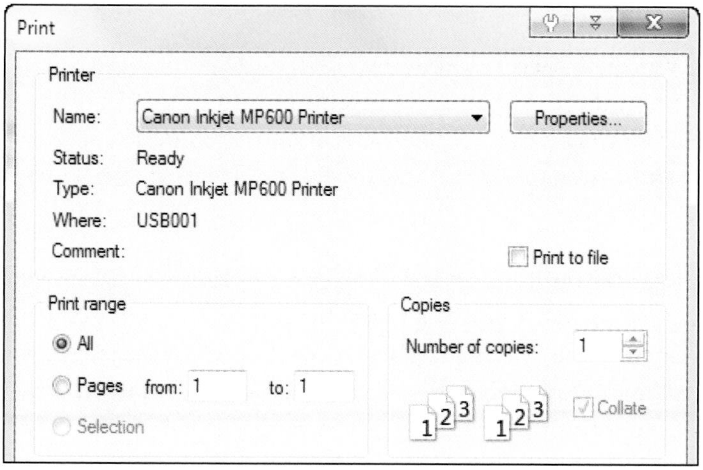

FIGURE 2-20: It's easy to take the print option for granted, yet it's important for your site visitors to be able to print their documents (so please don't attempt to cripple the functionality using a script).

In today's eco-friendly society, the need to avoid wasting your visitor's ink and paper is of critical importance. Ink and paper both cost money and environmental resources. Granted, the need to print things off the web may be minimized depending on whom you ask, but any savings you can pass onto your visitors will be appreciated. If that implementation focuses on printing only the content that matters and avoids printing things like unusable navigation menus (you can't click on paper and have it take you to another web page), then you have a more distinctive design as a result.

Print-friendly stylesheets follow the conventions of print design rather than web design because the goal is to output the document into something a printer can format, understand, and visualize on a paper. While less often used than seeing the page onscreen, some users do take advantage of printing a distinctive (print-oriented, formatted, and visually styled) layout, and that functionality improves their situation and gives them another reason to return to your site.

Note

Creating a printer-friendly page can be quite a challenge if you don't put much thought into how it will look on paper. For some basic tips, visit: `www.webcredible.co.uk/user-friendly-resources/css/print-stylesheet.shtml`.

Even with a print-friendly stylesheet; you may still encounter browser-enforced restrictions (like not printing background images because of the unnecessary waste of ink). You should still use the technique because it's one of the easiest ways to make content distinctive upon a printed format. (Figure 2-21 is a dramatic representation of how this could appear to users.) While the thought of optimizing websites for print seems limited, it's yet another way to target your reader's attention.

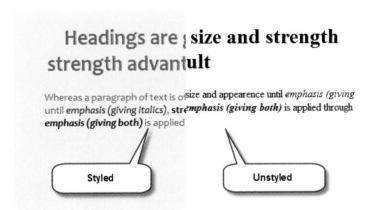

FIGURE 2-21: Comparing a generic site against a printer-friendly alternative can be quick dramatic.

Summary

So far this book has focused on various principles that outline distinctive design, and looked at the various factors that affect your attempts to build, implement, or cultivate a design (such as hardware, software, or even the browser itself). It's now time to move into something more practical (and this book's main focus): the factors that make a design distinctive, and what you can implement across the various forms of media (whether it's print, digital, or something else).

You are about to enter a world in which even the most basic choices that many overlook (such as what color to make your text or adding alternative text to images) become critically important. The world of distinctive design is focused around creating a balance between what needs attention and what doesn't, and a lot of tools help throw the focus in one direction or the other.

Part II

The Art of Distinctive Documentation

Principles of Information Design

The importance of valuing substance over style

PROVIDING YOURSELF WITH a distinctive design is important, but we need to give credit where credit is due. The content (with all the makeovers it's likely to encounter over its lifetime) represents the core component of any successful website. This chapter explains how information design underpins the importance of the content's role in a distinctive layout and how it helps make content in our layouts attractive.

Within this chapter, you learn about the relevance of research in your goals to produce a distinctive design in regard to your users, your competitors and your own inspirational concepts. I also highlight how the words you use (rather than visuals) create a distinctive layer of their own. I even explain progressive disclosure and the evolutionary style of content. Finally, because content isn't only about text, I take a good hard look at using imagery and media to make your content stand out.

Revolutionary Researching

Information design is, at its core, a skill that holds more relevance than most other aspects of distinctive design. It is about preparing your content so that visitors can use it effectively. The way you express your message and how you decide what information is relevant is critical to having a distinctive design, so you must ensure that you don't lose the message while you make your site eye-catching.

The value of content is undeniable. Search engines can't index websites without content. Without content there would be no explanation about what you're offering or selling, and the site itself would be pretty worthless and empty if it held a Flash presentation or image gallery with no fallback! Whether your site is (or will be) based on text, imagery, media, or something else, having that valuable content in some machine-readable format is critical. So we must now leverage the craft of information design to your advantage.

Tip

Designers whose websites are powered entirely by plug-in technologies like Flash are beginning to find out exactly what a content-free site can result in. In the age of smartphones, in which devices like Apple's don't support Flash, a site entirely dependent on Flash will cease to function.

Relating the value of content in distinctive design is simple. HTML code exists to be wrapped around your pages to convey explanatory meaning and to aid convention and style. CSS flows over the text and other components to turn the bland copy into something visually stunning. Finally, JavaScript allows you to lift the text dynamically from the page so that you can do more interesting things with the rest of the page. All three languages help your content get noticed (in ways that search engines can see). Figure 3-1 shows the binding relationship between code and content; they literally hold each other up!

```
1  <!DOCTYPE html PUBLIC "-//W3C//DTD XHTML 1.0 Strict//EN"
   "http://www.w3.org/TR/xhtml1/DTD/xhtml1-strict.dtd">
2  <html xmlns="http://www.w3.org/1999/xhtml" lang="en">
3      <head>
4          <meta http-equiv="content-type"
   content="text/html; charset=utf-8" />
5          <title>CH04-01 (516px x 650px)</title>
6          Code
7
8      <h1>Website Case Study</h1>
9      <p>Before redesigning a site it's important to che
   what works, what doesn't, what our    Content    nd ho
   our users interact with our content          een b
   to analyse the effects of a redesign and then to implement
   these changes. In total, this plan should take no longer t
   <em>28</em> days (approx).</p>
10         </body>
11 </html>
```

FIGURE 3-1: Web-oriented code makes your content distinctive.

Although designers spend much time reinforcing the power of the written (or visual) word, it's important to highlight that content on its own won't draw an audience without careful consideration. In addition, the content, visuals, and distinctive elements that appear on the page should be analyzed with research (over time) and through competitors' services. Such is the case that many website owners hire professional writers to help them produce the kind of audience-oriented copy they require to catch a visitor's eye.

The phrase "more than words" seems fitting to the issues you contend with, because making your content distinctive without justification becomes more of a hindrance than a help to the user. For example, you don't want a user becoming distracted by gimmicky messages that scream for attention. Having great content and an aesthetically appealing site for your visitors goes a long way to encourage them to come back, and knowing what your audience needs will help you make more accurate and prolific design decisions in the future.

Important

Every rule has exceptions, and there are sites that do not focus on content. Inspiration galleries, for example, depend entirely upon a site's aesthetics as the content for its visitors. Some portfolios follow a similar trend as well, because the imagery is the content.

If you've never taken the time to consider what makes a great site (or great content), now is the right moment to start accounting for this critical aspect of distinctive design. A lovely design with all the trimmings may draw your audience to your content, but, ultimately, what you decide to include and how you present it determines whether your visitors will find what you have to say useful.

Many different styles of content may appeal to your visitors:

> Content written by the owners of a site

> Feedback provided by users or members of a social site

> External content drawn into an experience through social networks

From what experience teaches us about creating a good design, layouts primarily focused on providing a high-quality, tailor-made experience for your visitors will ultimately become more successful than those built with a single end-user in mind. No matter what you put on the site (content, navigation menus, or something else), everything is accountable. (Even individual comments, shown in Figure 3-2, can make a difference.)

FIGURE 3-2: From the largest to the smallest item, consider its environmental impact on your site.

Before examining how to make content and the bulk of your site distinctive, it makes sense to find out how you can determine what your site really needs so that you can begin to reduce fluff and unnecessary content. Distinctive design isn't just about being unique and standing out from the crowd; it's also about making sensible design decisions that will ultimately allow end users to make the most of what you provide. Your audience is, after all, your ultimate critic!

The emphasis of implementation

Research is probably one of the least-favored disciplines in design because it requires thinking like a business person rather than a creative person. If you're building a design from scratch, it's likely you've already done this, especially if you looked to other sites for inspiration.

Sites that already exist shouldn't be exempt from research either. Just because a site is built doesn't mean that the work behind owning it is complete! Unlike print, the web is not a static and finite resource to be used and then discarded. A website should constantly be in the process of evolution and renewal. To remain distinctive and fresh, your site may need incremental improvements, and this is where research helps you succeed!

Note Regarding research, don't think about a professor sitting in a room looking over a bunch of numbers! Conducting studies is a great way to give your site some user-defined goals; look at other sites for inspiration while you start building a model in your mind. It can help — and be fun, too!

So how does research factor into your content and design? Primarily, it gives you some prebuilt solutions or ideas about how you can implement various elements. Secondly, it gives you an idea about where designs go right and wrong (from the third-person perspective). Finally, it gives you a platform to gain feedback, ideas, and any expectations of a chosen niche. So all things considered, those surveys, polls, and frequent visits to various sites aren't a waste of time; you can tell the boss that you're conducting some research! (See Figure 3-3.)

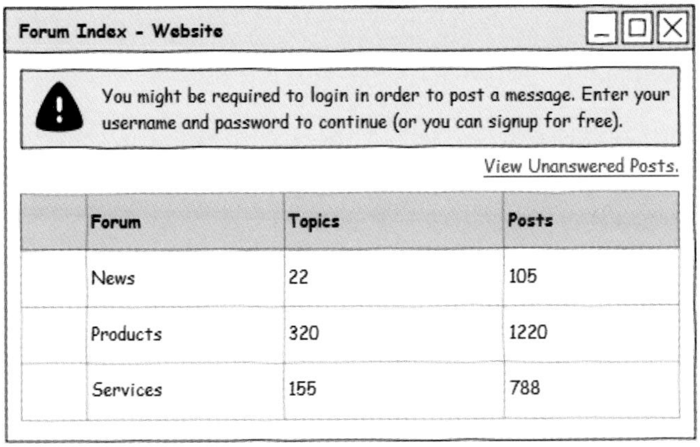

Forum Index - Website

⚠ You might be required to login in order to post a message. Enter your username and password to continue (or you can signup for free).

View Unanswered Posts.

Forum	Topics	Posts
News	22	105
Products	320	1220
Services	155	788

FIGURE 3-3: If your visitors request more interaction, consider adding a forum (prebuilt solutions exist).

One thing to remember as you research your competitors, or seek advice on how to go about improving your services, is to avoid reinventing the wheel. Instead, just improve it. It's likely that for anything you want to achieve, a site, implementation, or concept may exist that you can use to build upon your idea. Also, don't throw away your old designs and start from scratch unless you really feel it's necessary; perhaps you simply need to make some basic improvements to your existing site using the principles of distinctive design and research together.

Tip

Although getting feedback is a central part of improving a website to match your visitor's needs, it's important not to discard the negative comments. Being critiqued can be hard on the ego, but it's often the most useful in identifying critical faults in a site because it suggests areas for improvement.

Taking the time to seek out your visitors to ask them about recent innovations, trends, and their expectations might seem like a complex chore involving studies and talking to people, but doing so gives you the opportunity to continue to innovate and reach new heights. Asking for feedback doesn't take a lot of time, so why not give it a try, even if that critique is enthusiastically exchanged over an e-mail?

Put it into perspective: set yourself a plan and assign yourself a set amount of time to do your homework. Avoid getting inundated with feature and help requests related to complexities or anomalies in what you offer (keep in mind that some of your users will have migrated from another service, and every potential customer is important). Reduce the learning curve with some level of consistency to help your visitors, and as a consequence, distinctive content will be further visible upon browsing.

Distinction from competition

Because you want your designs to be distinctive, there's rarely a case where it could be said that research is unnecessary or adds cost to an otherwise fine project. The more you know about your visitors, the better you can optimize a design. The more research you do, the better you understand your site's market. It's honestly a win-win situation, and sourcing your data boosts your website's performance.

When undertaking research, adopt a spirit of inspiration and take note of the good elements you see that might benefit your project. Don't be afraid to follow in the footsteps of others (though it's worth adding a "don't outright copy them" disclaimer here), and never be afraid to put your questions forward to their audience. Getting firsthand experience using a service and understanding the people using it can really benefit you. Figure 3-4 shows just one method you can use to grab some useful feedback from others, and sites like Polldaddy can host it all for you.

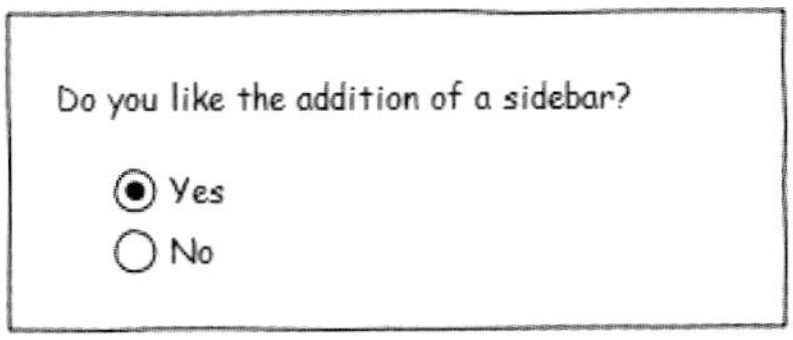

Do you like the addition of a sidebar?

⦿ Yes
◯ No

FIGURE 3-4: Polls can be a very simple, yet effective, way to measure your visitors' perceptions.

Within design, two approaches offer a way to target your research and get some of that primary feedback. Table 3-1 lists examples of both research sources. The first method is competitor-based research, which is centered on you poking around any competitor's or related sites to see what their users expect, which is great for new sites. The second is audience-based research, and this is generally a practice of talking to the consumers rather than studying the competitors, their behavior, and users for clues and ideas.

Table 3-1: **Approach-based research**

Approach	Methods
Competitor-based	Existing designs, existing products and services, prebuilt solutions, defined standards, software APIs (application programming interfaces), design conventions, design patterns, industry trends, development frameworks, published results, and content convention research
Audience-based	Observation studies, service feedback tools, analytics software, search results, social networks, user trends, usage patterns, accessibility users, usability tests, contact forms, experiments, spot testing, and simulations

Two research methods (referred to as primary and secondary) depict the way we undertake research. Avoiding all of the complexities, primary research is the study of data that does not yet exist (you actively collect and create it yourself); secondary research is the study of data that does exist (like articles on design trends or pre-existing usability studies).

Although secondary research sources can be found all over the web (especially on design sites and in books), you also should conduct primary research to give you a more personalized examination of how people and services implement functionality distinctively.

Sourcing data can be done either mechanically (like through computational analytics software, for example) or manually (via quantitative and qualitative research).

Tip

> If you plan to undertake research of your own, try to eliminate any visible forms of bias. The last thing you want is to influence your visitors' answers; that will give you invalid results.

Again, let's keep things simple: two forms of research you need to be aware of are quantitative and qualitative research. Table 3-2 lists research methods you should consider using, including the computational approach, which focuses on machine-generated data (like what you would find in analytics packages, for example). Quantitative research primarily focuses on solid numbers and measures hard data rather than personalizing the feedback (so you limit user choice to ensure the results are on track). Qualitative, on the other hand, serves the opposing purpose: It looks beyond the numbers to get feedback that is more "out of the box" and personalized so users interpret your questions and respond (such as a questionnaire).

Table 3-2: Research methodology variations

Approach	Methods
Computational	Simulations, statistics, activity mapping (heat-map tests, click-map tests, and eye-tracking), social trend analysis, automated tests (accessibility, usability, or content analysis), and traditional data mining techniques
Quantitative	Experiments, comparison (preference) analysis, site or social statistics, correlation studies, questionnaires, memory tests, and quizzes
Qualitative	User observations, field notes (noted trends), interviews (structured or unstructured), contact forms, open-ended questionnaires, focus groups, brainstorming sessions, user sampling, feedback (requested or not), usability tests, 5-second tests, A/B testing, surveys, and opinion polls

At this stage, it's worth considering how you undertake research, how reliable your insights are, and whether you can improve upon your project ideas. Drifting slightly away from traditional distinctive design (of a site's aesthetics in the purest sense), remember that gaining new knowledge and adapting one's skills is relevant both to anyone practicing web design and for site visitors who want more than a textbook design. Boilerplate templates don't impress anyone!

Important Get creative with any research you undertake. Using a good mixture of primary/secondary research methods and quantitative/qualitative analysis gives you a wider range of results to work with (and can help you better understand visitor needs), and don't forget what computers can observe.

Analyzing numbers is quite a simple act once you get used to the process, and you can determine from a large set of results what ideas particularly make sense. Quantitative feedback gives you controlled results in that you provide a variety of solutions and let visitors make their own choices. On the other hand, in qualitative research, visitors get to pick the route and answers they submit, and the capability to cross-analyze the data will be harder due to the range of results you may see. Computational research is the easiest of all because the machine does all the work and shows you trends; though as Figure 3-5 implies, mixing things up can benefit us further.

FIGURE 3-5: Balance research types to better understand user needs from multiple angles.

Of course, any research you undertake will be comprised entirely of theory, and there's no guarantee that the results will benefit your project. Just like with most feedback systems, you have to take the bad with the good. That said, if you can better understand how your audience thinks, you can make the final decision (rather than adding anything requested on the spot) and really improve the quality of service you provide. Take any results you get at face value, but don't dismiss their potential usefulness!

As designers, it's important that you put some focus on being practical, but you also must understand the theoretical components at work. While research may or may not provide you with some possible leads for functionality, the simple act of seeing how things function gives you the insight to improve upon the standards that exist.

Creating Content and Copy

Now that you have explored the realm of research and overviewed how important it is to consider outside influences on your site (such as your competitors and their users), it's time to focus directly on the internal influence that ultimately leads people to choose your site over your competitors'! Within the scope of information design and giving your distinctive layout valuable assets, it's important to carefully consider the content you choose to publish online.

If you examine every part of a website, you'll see that content comprises an estimated 90 percent of any site (of course the accuracy of this statistic depends upon the type of site). Your visitors come to your site to find details and information; they want to read text and look at images or videos, or listen to audio. It's critical to not only examine how content is visualized on the screen, but also how to properly maintain it, weeding out the unnecessary or what may confuse your users.

When search engines index your site, they look directly at the content you offer. The language you know as HTML exists purely to give your content definition, form, and factor. The value that content brings to a site is much more than just giving a lovely design something to keep visitors returning; its role as a forger of relationships with web-based services gives this communicative variable real power, distinction and sales influence.

The power of content has a ripple effect on other parts of the web:

> Search engines direct their traffic to appropriate websites.

> People in social networks recommend sites or promote useful resources.

> Sites gain inspiration or build services around your offerings.

People can be drawn to a site because of its inspiring and informative content. Just like with most things in life, humans care about substance over style. This (of course) doesn't mean that your design doesn't warrant any attention, but with 90 percent of a site being comprised of content and its value being greater than anything else held within the context of a site, how you treat this asset ultimately decides your project's fate, and its distinction.

Perhaps this seems overdramatic, but unfortunately for many designers, the failings of a site fall upon their consideration of content as an afterthought rather than a critical and essential page element. Undeniably, the phrase "content is king" matches the level of influence of your page's composition. One of the biggest mistakes leading to a project's doom (even above bad code) is not giving the content the attention it deserves.

Tip

Some designers use Lipsum or dummy text in site construction or placeholder pages to populate a site's index. Lipsum text is a type of filler content that has been used for centuries as a method to see what a design would look like once relevant content is added. Although this is fine for offline purposes, don't use it online! Unfinished sites don't look professional to visitors.

Carefully considered copy doesn't require you to be a perfect writer — some people find writing easier than others — but it's critical that you put as much effort and attention in writing your copy as you would for how your site will look when complete (it's just common sense). Ensure that what you publish, whether text, image, audio, or video (see Figure 3-6), is relevant and useful.

FIGURE 3-6: The three primary content types on a site are text, images, and media.

Within distinctive design, both information and content have their place. Although it may not always be the most glorified or visually entrancing, that About page or Product Guide can be designed and structured in a way that makes your visitors pay attention and take notice. (Content itself can be quite artistic. If you need an example, consider the value of typography or color usage within your design.) Make every word and sentence meaningful and contextually rich and you're sure to make a positive impact on visitors.

Note

In addition to About pages on a site, many visitors expect to see a wide number of other common pages. For a few examples of what you could include in your site (it has plenty of good ideas), read this article: www.brandbuildsell.com/top-25-common-website-pages/.

Because so much of a site is composed of content, visitors may be distracted easily. That risk is so great that you need to do all you can to ensure that you structure your assets in the most readable (and least intrusive) manner possible. When you visit a site, the content seems way more engaging if it's broken down into small, digestible pieces and it uses visuals, tables, lists, and more to explain its points. Sites based on a huge stream of plain paragraphs and reels of content simply aren't distinctive!

Arguably, the route for getting inspired to produce readable, rich, and engaging content is going to be different than following a bunch of design patterns. Turning a wild array of words and paragraphs into something both meaningful and distinctive (to the eyes and brain) is quite an undertaking. As designers, your job is to create your site so that it looks and functions at its best when users browse it at a comfortable pace.

The importance of terrific text

How you portray yourself, your products, and your services relies upon the text and content you produce. Although images and media have their own places within distinction in the scope of an experience, it's also important not to underestimate the value of the text you use to communicate with your visitors. Remember: Content is king (as is the context in which you provide it). If you want to maximize the level of impact of your site, you must use a distinctive approach to text. This isn't just about writing words; stylistic attribution (and even how it's interpreted by readers) is equally important.

When you apply text to the screen, give your readers something meaningful to take away from that experience. Making your content speak volumes in as little space as possible complies with distinctive reductionism and minimalism as related to any visual flourish. Think of where various websites would be if their value was entirely attributed to the design and not content. They'd offer nothing more than superficial beauty with little educational value!

Tip

Although text is important, specific sites do successfully rely upon the visuals rather than text. Sites such as the CSS Zen Garden provide an entirely visually focused experience.

History shows that knowledge is a valuable asset and that archiving and sharing it with the world makes society a better place. Your content's value depends on what you offer, but it should be useful to someone. Otherwise, its place on the web is likely to be a gimmick and won't sustain interest. Many blogs fail because they lack quality and updates (users may look for identifiable time references, as shown within Figure 3-7).

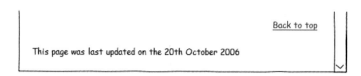

FIGURE 3-7: Dates play a large part in content recognition. If it looks out of date, it may be ignored.

Beyond the valuable knowledge you publish for public attention, you must take precautions to ensure that this knowledge isn't lost. So many computer users lose entire reels of history and their life in lost documents, pictures, and files. The same is true of the web. A site that isn't well structured or maintained can suffer catastrophic losses that result in extra work to restore your site's valuable assets.

Maintaining a distinctive approach to your content while ensuring its value also requires backing up your content and accounting for its sustainability. Although the subject of backups isn't entirely related to design (it has its place within information architecture) backups are an important variable that affects your site. Therefore, you should consider a methodology to restore content if it's lost or corrupted while planning the structure of a site. Backing up and archiving may be common sense, but people still forget to do it!

Important

Proper archival has a role in a site's professional appeal. If you redesign a structure with thousands of pages and a resource suddenly becomes unavailable (because of redesigns, file removal or other factors), the effect damages the integrity and flow of others linking to it.

As designers, your primary role is to provide visitors with an experience from which they gain something. Whether it's the sale of a product or a useful article on how to use the latest version of Windows, the way you portray your information and how you showcase your content gives your site the best chance for success and offers you an opportunity to be distinctive to an extent that visitors will bookmark or pass on the link to third parties using social networks. Text is the foundation of what people remember about a site; with that in mind, it's critical that you visually and cognitively showcase it with pride.

Readability evokes distinction

Within readability, the language you use plays an important part in how you portray your services (and yourselves). If you have a particularly content-heavy site (like a blog), this becomes even more important than sites that simply aim to provide non-content-focused goods. You must take the time to understand any language requirements your audience has (English doesn't work for everyone!) and if needed, provide suitable translations (tools like Google Translate can help, but they do not replace human translation).

Tip

Have you noticed how many websites use buzzwords like web 2.0? The problem with such terminology is that its meaning can be so broad that it really can't be used to define anything effectively (though that's not to say that it doesn't have meaning; you just have to be sure to explain its use properly). Dump any nonsense words from your prose.

As you might expect with language, if people don't understand your words, they will not be able to make sense of your message and the value of your content will be lost. (The same goes for marketing and technical jargon!) A common mistake many designers fall foul of is "optimizing" their content for search engine visibility. Although doing this with care can yield results, writing for the humans who'll actually use your site is far more important.

How you write content plays a significant role in its readability. Catering your text to the audience who will use it is preferential, and injecting tasteful humor, entertainment, or some other level of vibrancy can aid its distinction. (Beware: Some people don't understand certain types of humor like sarcasm, and it could backfire). Yes, it's true that some subjects require being serious and composed, but adding different writing styles when appropriate can make a dreary piece of copy something more interesting and life-like (Figure 3-8 has an example).

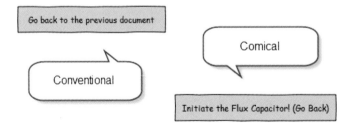

FIGURE 3-8: Changing the wording of a call to action is a classic example of humor interjection.

As you can imagine, ensuring your content is meaningful rather than full of big words, functional rather than superfluous, and empathetic to the visitor without diluting the quality of the content requires plenty of practice. Often, it's not what you say on the web that matters, but the way you say it. Communication is critical, and doing it effectively adds impact to your site.

Text is an aspect of design that can be used to work alongside your site's aesthetics. By following the distinctive principle of reductionism, you evade the dilution of your site's quality. If there's too much going on inside a page, you make it harder for visitors to find what they are looking for. Consider every part of your text, and if you can simplify or remove something, do it.

Important

Within reductionism, a common practice is to take any written document and attempt to reduce the length of that material by 50 percent. It's a hard task, but it's surprising how much content you can eliminate. Often, using fewer words, not more, brings into focus what you want to emphasize!

Although simplicity and reductionism purge a site of unnecessary waffle (which can only be a good thing), various factors within the text influence its readability. Consider how well your content is written and if it's overly technical. Jargon is fine if your visitors are familiar with the terms, but it immediately eliminates those readers who aren't accustomed to the sight of abbreviations, acronyms, or any industry-specific technical or legal terminology. Figure 3-9 shows examples of web industry abbreviations that many aren't familiar with.

HTML   SQL   XML
CONFUSION
JSP   JS   ASP
ALERT!!!
RSS   PHP   CSS

FIGURE 3-9: Web design is filled with abbreviations that mean nothing to the average consumer.

Beyond that, you must ensure that you use proper grammar and spelling in your text. Sites laced with incorrect grammar or misspellings immediately lose credibility (though all but the most crazed readers will grant leniency for the occasional mistake). Avoid using all CAPS (which is considered by many to signify shouting) or capitalizing the first letter of every word, not only because it annoys a lot of people, but also because it actually disrupts the reading flow.

If you keep your content error-free, condense it as much as possible without losing the integrity of the text, and avoid leaving the caps lock turned on, you'll have won half the battle. Remember also that the way you present your content also influences its readability. Use conventions like headings, paragraphs, lists, tables, and even hyperlinks to improve the organization and flow of whatever you're writing because they give the reader points of reference.

Attaining good content is much more than simply throwing text onto a page. To maintain a distinctive experience for your visitors, use the various writing tricks to highlight useful points, capture user's imaginations, and emphasize your aims. Because text isn't as attractive on a page than images or other elements, it's essential that you craft your content with great care.

Note

Many variables affect readability, some holding more weight than others. If you want additional advice about writing, you should read this great, yet straightforward, article. `http://whatever.scalzi.com/2006/02/12/`.

Progressive disclosure rocks

In some cases of information design, it may work well to remove the flood of content that barrages your visitors upon entry to your site. But in other cases, perhaps the level of content is just right. Overloading or flooding your visitors with an array of choices beyond what they can handle is a genuine risk of content (especially if you have lengthy pages), but the art of progressive disclosure helps resolve this issue.

At its core, progressive disclosure has the goal of ensuring that only relevant information gets the users immediate attention, thereby reducing the chances of visitors getting lost among the details. In the past, this meant simply breaking long documents into multiple pages, but with the advent of CSS3 and JavaScript (see Figure 3-10), you can rotate content on demand to make the experience much more engaging (and less cluttered in general).

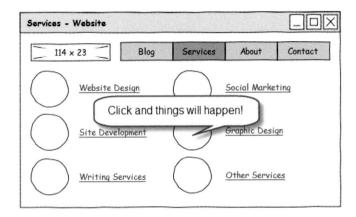

FIGURE 3-10: Disclosure works by targeting an event, then making content appear based on the choice.

As with all increasingly complex mechanisms, it's important to not only value your users' ability to choose what they read (and not force them through a process that absorbs their time and patience), but to also ensure that what you provide gracefully degrades. Yes, it may seem cool to hide certain pieces of content in a script until the More Information link is clicked, but in case people have JavaScript disabled, you need to ensure that content will be visible to visitors (as normal compatibility rears its head).

Tip

The CSS3 checked and target pseudos can style content and make it visible on demand (though browser compatibility may be an issue). Frameworks like jQuery and custom JavaScripts also perform this quite useful service. If you feel comfortable playing around with code, research the subject even further and learn how to wield these weapons for yourself!

The way that you approach designing content and the methodology behind progressive disclosure is in part influenced by how your visitors read websites. Most people who want to find a particular page won't read everything on every page; instead they use visual shortcuts by mentally scanning for references that might apply to what they seek, and then they filter those options to pick what seems most relevant (sometimes randomly).

Because of this natural inclination toward reading, how your content flows is important not just in how you visually represent that information, but also to distinctive design. If content is poorly mapped out and has too much white noise surrounding it, visitors will find their experience negatively impacted. To maintain your site's responsiveness (and avoid users having to work harder than necessary), implement your structure wisely. A sample of logical structuring can be seen in Figure 3-11, based on user assumptions.

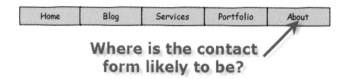

FIGURE 3-11: If you are looking for contact information, you're more likely to click on the About page.

Staging your text in a way that catches visitors' eyes and doesn't overload them is ultimately the aim of the game. Don't give them other places to look or make them scroll to great lengths to find what they need. Although outside influences (like a visitor's own particular method of browsing, seeing, or using the site) may affect the experience in ways you can't control, doing what you can to better your site is helpful.

Ultimately, your content is one of the most distinctive assets on the page. Your attention to detail actively promotes giving your content the appeal it deserves. Placing your content in distinctive, logical groups and promoting the most useful elements with the tools at your disposal encourages users to keep reading. Because being able to grab a visitor's attention with a sharp, snappy headline is very different than maintaining that attention consistently, your text had better be ready to win over your audience's interest!

Illustrative Visual Imagery

Perhaps as the most understated element, text does portray much of what visitors absorb online. The problem is that while text on its own can make a point, sometimes you can't garner the right kind of feeling or impact using simple words to visualize a point you want to make. This is where those great devices called images come into action. Sometimes, we use images as visual representations of objects, and other times images put text into a more digestible form (like a chart). In all cases, they can be very distinctive.

Perhaps it seems rather obvious that images play a role in distinction (as many designs use them as techniques to gain a flourish or certain effect), but it's useful to note that because of their form, shape, texture, and use of color, images often grab a reader's attention before the heavier and more generic-looking text that surrounds them. This visual effect marks a location of interest or point of reference, which can logically be useful if you're aiming to direct visitors' eyes to an important region of the screen.

Important

Images should ideally be self-descriptive and easy to recognize. The problem with graphics that require interpretation or guesswork is they can easily be misunderstood and misinterpreted, and individuals with low vision may be unable to decipher them.

As with the way you craft your content, you can build images that either ooze the feeling of professionalism or feel amateurish. A site filled with clipart images of dancing animals doesn't exactly give off the feeling that it should be taken seriously. Always consider how you will compose your images, what they portray and contain, and how they represent and supplement your text in a design.

With text, you're limited to just inputting the basic content and forming a structure around it. With images, it's rather more interesting. Images are, by definition, a static, pre-created resource for the page. This means that you can embed the items in a page or stylesheet as a decorative piece of art. You retain control over the final look, and can use a range of supported formats (like the three provided in Table 3-3) to ensure a balance among quality, file size, and other relevant variables.

Table 3-3: **Popular web image formats**

Format	Details
GIF	Lossless, 256 color palette, limited transparency, and full animation
JPG / JPEG	Lossy (degrades), full color palette, no transparency, and no animation
PNG	Lossless, full color palette, full transparency, and animation (APNG)

Creating high standard images is vital to building a complete layout, but you also need to take care in drawing a Zen-like balance between the ratios of images to text. Having too many unnecessary images quickly throws off the natural balance of a site, and the value of your text may suffer as a result. On the flip side, too few images can result in a bland or thesis-like feeling (a happy medium is usually the best methodology).

Of course, the production of images requires more creativity than just throwing something together and firing them onto the screen. To make the most of your images, account for variables like the composition (how the image is arranged) and the use of angles, color, and shape (much like in regular design). The way you produce the final image will differ depending on the type of image (such as a photo versus a hand-drawn doodle).

> **Tip**
>
> In addition to picking the right kind of image, the right image format is also quite important. Although all three formats are widely supported (except animation in PNG files), you want to analyze which gives you best quality versus size ratio (before committing to a particular format for an image).

Although many designers use tools like Adobe Photoshop to craft a mockup or basic visuals, there's essentially a lot more going on under the hood of an image than you find within text. As designers, you need to understand the power of images and how (and when) they can increase your capability to attract an audience. Although graphics get more attention than text on a page, don't just use them as a silver bullet for any situation needing some extra attention.

A picture says 1,000 words

Because images and traditional print design share many of the same principles (they are simply objects on the page), the principles that apply to elements within them (such as space, color and typography) apply in equal measure as they would to web design. Just as the web is a canvas to place meaningful dialogue, images are the same. As with text, they are communication tools to aid your goal of reaching an audience.

Pictures can evoke all sorts of responses in regard to their representation or intended meaning within a distinct design (in ways text perhaps can't express as easily), but not every visitor or consumer can do anything with web imagery. You need to add image alternatives to help visually impaired users, users with a text-based browser, or users with images disabled (as shown in Figure 3-12) access the content. Alternative content can also be helpful if you accidentally link to (or delete) the wrong file and no image can load within the page.

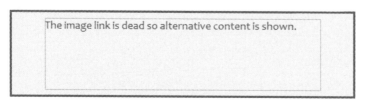

The image link is dead so alternative content is shown.

FIGURE 3-12: If an image is deleted on the page, its alternative content becomes mission critical.

Those reasons on their own are suitable expectations of a site because you need to think in terms of gracefully degrading code. The side benefit from having text-based alternatives for those images is the added context and value that are inherently made available. Although many users won't do much with the text, for those who do, that detail gives your images some distinction in ways they simply could not have if they remained in an unusable, unloaded, or unavailable state.

The art of using images distinctively relies on cooperation between text and image; they enhance each other. The visual literacy going on within an image gives your text added depth, definition and distinction. So if you use these images for added meaning to help the reader (and break down the blocks of text) you may find that individuals who look to draw quick insights into the content may turn to the images immediately.

Note

Visual literacy refers to the explanatory nature of an image and the content it aims to portray. If, for example, you have an image containing a triangle shape, people recognize and associate the image with the shape (and the content that links to the image should relate to this).

Being able to wield this tool, whether through textual images, or by enhancing your content in ways that it helps people understand your perspective gives distinction and attention to those regions of the page. The pages that take advantage of imagery will be easier on the eyes and more memorable, too!

If you can't produce images and graphics with ease, fear not! While there are plenty of tutorials and guides that can help you design images, paint pictures, take photographs, and use graphics software, there's also an entire industry built around stock images. You get a license for an image and use it within the license terms in your own work.

Note

Many stock photography sites offer a range of media, including royalty-free content (which means you only pay once to use it within your projects). One of the most popular sources is iStockPhoto. The URL is www.istockphoto.com. A free alternative can be found at www.sxc.hu.

At this stage, you may have considered that there are billions of images floating around the web; so why can't you use them? Without getting overly wordy, it's simply the law. Copyright is a big deal online (as in print), and although you want to be creative—and it's great that you've been inspired by someone else's work—get permission, get a license, or create your own work (inspired, not copied) from what you've seen. Essentially, be legal and ethical, because there are consequences for thieves.

How you should enhance content with imagery depends on the person who is reading the material. Sometimes designers see images, textures, colors, and flourishes as quick and simple ways to convey their thoughts and ideas, but not everyone is visually inclined, which can make interpreting the contents of certain images tricky. When being distinctive and implementing images, make sure it complements the work and benefits those who come to your site for answers. You don't want your images to make your site a valueless puzzle.

Content-focused imagery

Although traditional images depicting elements of the content can be useful in giving your content some added distinction, some of the more boring parts of content (like data or statistics) also can be made distinctive through the use of images. Placing an image that has meaningful content requires a fallback mechanism, but these content-focused images represent another excellent way you can boost the readability of your text.

A classic example of this text-within-images concept can be found in wonderful representations called *infographics*. These come in many forms, such as visualizations, maps, posters, signposts, and other explanatory graphics. (See Figure 3-13.) At their core, infographics aim to present pieces of content, ideas, or complex subjects in quick, digestible, highly visual formats. If you've ever seen one of those subway maps showing the rail line and its stations, that's an infographic!

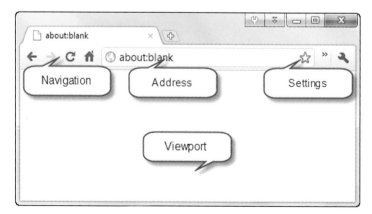

FIGURE 3-13: This infographic breaks down the various sections of a web browser.

The creation of sitemaps that show the potentially complex layout of a site could be deemed an infographic, as could a mind map or other form of information portrayal. Infographics come in many shapes and sizes, and although they all differ in how they look, the common factor they share is that they attempt to act like a cheat sheet giving valuable content distinctively.

As a distinctive designer, you know that you cannot simply rely on graphics alone to provide a great impression on the end user, and for accessibility reasons, it makes sense not to dedicate your careers to building complex infographics. That said, however, they do serve a noble purpose, and if you ever find yourself unable to get a point across through text and conventional images, some kind of infographic-style map could be just what you need.

Tip

Offering infographics attached to an article you've written or a service you've built could act as a handy cheat sheet or reference. Although it certainly won't be used by everyone, it could reduce the learning curve of an environment and make things better for adventurous beginners.

Although infographics can help you to reduce the complexity of a site's content (and the principles you want to relay to a consumer), another type of visual representation deserves to be identified individually. When creating web content, usually at some point tabular data or numbers will enter the equation. Representing this form of content using charts and graphs can help you underline the value of numerical statistics.

If you've ever made a direct comparison between a table or spreadsheet full of numbers and a graph or chart that gives a lovely visual rendition of the data, you know how much simpler it is when you know what you're looking at (see Figure 3-14). It's also easier to compare numbers in a graph or chart than it is in a table or spreadsheet.

Many different types of charts and graphs can be used to visualize a variety of situations (like the relationship between objects). Which one you use is entirely dependent on the type of information you are trying to portray, but all things considered the use of such visuals within a website can be exceptionally useful in helping your visitors make sense of something more complex (if left in its native form). If you find yourself having to present a bunch of data to your visitors, consider these useful tools in your work. For a quick sample of eye-catching graphs and charts, see Figure 3-15.

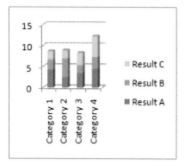

Sections	Result A	Result B	Result C
Category 1	4.3	2.4	2
Category 2	2.5	4.4	2
Category 3	3.5	1.8	3
Category 4	4.5	2.8	5

FIGURE 3-14: This comparison shows how much easier it is to read a chart than a table of data.

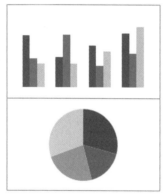
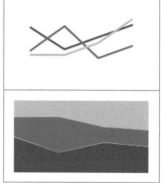

FIGURE 3-15: Graphs and charts in many forms are all useful content supplements.

So far, you've seen some representations of text within images through the use of info-graphics that try to simplify complex points, and charts that, along with graphs, aim to turn boring numbers into something visually interesting. Now you need to examine the third and final common implementation for using text within images for your website design. Prepare to enter the dangerous world of image replacement techniques.

Although the print industry has had the luxury (for many years) of being able to set typog-raphy and color in such a manner that no one reading the document can manipulate how it looks (beyond damaging the file itself), the web is an altogether different situation. With browser compatibility still being a very contentious issue, the need to offer a static implementation still exists for many designers who'd prefer attempting a pixel-perfect rendition and fallback rather than simply going with the user's own preferences and being more flexible. (Maybe things will change, but until then, see Figure 3-16.)

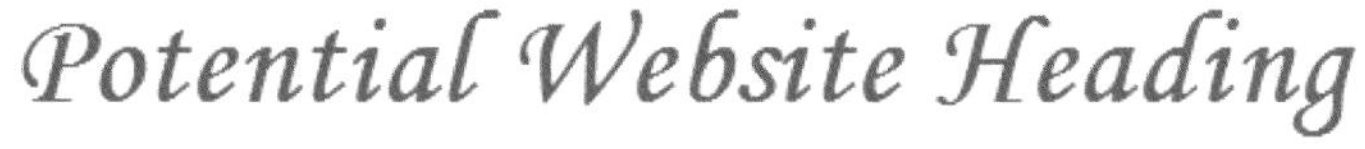

Potential Website Heading

FIGURE 3-16: This may look like an ordinary piece of text, but it's actually held within an image!

Although this isn't technically a bad perspective, as in most cases, this is simply an attempt to ensure your site looks and works beautifully for the widest range of people. It's important to reinforce the point that the web isn't a static medium (as much as some would like it to be). As an example, a designer may want to use a particular font in his site, but the visitor may not have that font installed. Rather than build an appropriate font stack, the designer simply uses replacement techniques to render a replica visual.

Tip

Font stacks are a list of typefaces (from the ideal one to the common fallback) that aim to give visitors a good experience even if they don't have a certain font installed. But when they aren't available, a number of web-safe alternatives exist as important tools in design.

In order to get that static (yet distinctive) visualization, many designers use images with the equivalent text printed. (In the case of typography, many designers wait for a CSS3 that's 100 percent supported, or implement a patchy workaround using Flash, SVG, or scripting.) Because the image is a pre-rendered object, when it appears on the user's screen, it will use the font they want.

This solution, like with all web images, requires a fallback. It also adds extra bandwidth consumption and HTTP requests to the website; so ultimately it's not a perfect solution (though no method is without flaws). But with images being able to maintain a distinctive yet static method of delivery that can display upon the visitor's screen (as intended), it will remain a solution designers use for years to come (and thereby worth considering).

Attention-seeking iconography

So far, you've examined a wide range of ways to implement your images to help you portray your content in more unique and distinctive ways. Although infographics, charts, and diagrams boost the amount of attention you can draw to the less interesting aspects of numerical data, one final and quite important aspect of distinctive design within imagery needs to be explored. This is the simple, yet elegant, attention-seeking medium of iconography.

Whenever you think of the word icon, most of the time you picture some little image that sits in a folder or on your desktop representing a document or application. (See those used in Figure 3-17, for example). Although this is an accurate portrayal within software (and to a certain extent, websites), the power of these small pictorial references that people associate with particular functions plays an important role in everyday life. Even when you're out and about, icons in signposts and other mediums grab your focus. Because these graphics are so influential, it's important to use them wisely on your site.

FIGURE 3-17: These icons within the Windows OS represent a folder, a browser, and a text file.

Icons within everyday life can be seen on signposts or even within maps. If you see the symbol for a gas station, you know where you can refuel your car. If you see a stop sign marked clearly on a post beside the road, you recognize that message and stop your car. This ability to associate is of great importance to graphic design because our ability to recognize shape, color and concepts allows us to decipher these iconic symbols. (We even associate with browser symbols; see Figure 3-18.)

FIGURE 3-18: Designers use a whole series of icon conventions to represent various browser features.

Although the use of icons may seem relatively straightforward, it's important to realize that icons only have meaning to those who understand their specific interpretation. You may see a sign of a red cross and think "it's for medical attention", but someone who's not encountered that symbol before could easily confuse it with anything relating to red and/ or a cross symbol, such as a calculator button. You need to decide upon conventions based on your audience's likelihood of recognizing the icons you implement, and you must also label them to reinforce the visuals and avoid confusion.

Clicking on links can lead to unexpected results (if labeled incorrectly, or not at all in the case of mystery-meat navigation), and although some icons are used merely for decorative purposes to gain recognition for something or as a reference to direct people's vision, those representing an action (like printing or saving) need to be as descriptive as possible. The results of such poor communication can be both misleading and counter-intuitive to the user experience.

Important

If your icons aren't self-explanatory, they will still emphasize the content but could cause additional confusion. As iconography is a subjective art form (like color), each individual gains different things out of recognizing such conventions on the page. You must therefore pay attention to the label you provide for your users and ensure that it's meaningful and useful.

One of the key points that allow icons to be so recognizable is their use of symbols. These devices are often easily recognizable (but sometimes misinterpreted) markers that usually resemble a convention or pattern. If, for example, you see a check mark character used in a page, you're more likely to associate it with the word Yes than No. Although *symbology* and its meaning is a complex subject (think the *Da Vinci Code*), the ability to express intent and tie symbols to words dates to the beginning of language. Figure 3-19 shows some basic symbols used to alert users.

FIGURE 3-19: Dialog boxes deliberately use a selected range of icons to represent types of messages.

The ancient Egyptians used symbols called hieroglyphics to draw written associations to objects and people, and after all these years people do similar things on the web (but with a well-formed alphabet). The ability to mark content or images with symbols (embedded at will) gives you a quick method to be more distinctive and creative in a design and to help visitors find what they want.

One common way people identify symbols and icons within the context of the web is through the use of mechanisms called *calls to action*. These representations dynamically express a persona of importance by pulling the visual out of the generic flow of a document and molding it into a common form such as a button or logo. (Figure 3-20 shows an icon used to identify a link.)

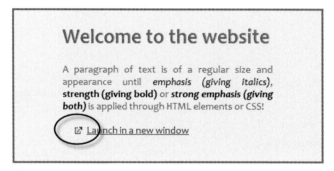

FIGURE 3-20: This web-based call to action recognizes that the anchor references launch a new window.

These representations that brand your goods and services (or guide people's eyes toward a point of interest or critical piece of the page) are usually both relevant and actionable (usually clickable). Calls to action are as much a part of interactivity as a piece of furniture is to a room. The symbol's job is to attract a user to the base of operations and then call the user to take action upon the particular role it has (such as clicking the Buy button or noticing the site's logo and name). They are small, but incredibly powerful.

Important

A poorly implemented button can be a dangerous thing. If users' eyes are drawn to the wrong part of the screen or if they miss an important factor, they could make a mistake that could cost them time, money, energy, or all three. Justify every call to action, and avoid misdirection.

These powerful devices, like most elements, should be used in moderation (and only when it's suitable). As with most aspects of distinctive design, excess use of attention-seeking components neutralizes their impact. When used appropriately, icons, symbols, calls to action, and conventions all play their part in drawing focus and distinction. Visit your competitors' sites; you may find some fantastic, recognizable examples to inspire your creativity.

Before moving on from the subject of icons, it only seems fair to mention the humble favicon (as seen in Figure 3-21), which has been gracing web browsers (and bookmarks) for many a year. Having a unique icon within the address bar, browser tabs, and favorite links or bookmarks gives visitors the capability to notice your site above those with a generic icon, which helps them avoid relying upon the text alone to find a page. The favicon is a small file that plays its part, and plays it well.

FIGURE 3-21: Favicons are 16x16 icon files helping users recognize a site. They're quite popular, too!

Because these unique markers have become so popular over the years, Apple, in particular, has shown a good level of grace toward the convention within its portable devices. You can produce a PNG-formatted icon (rather than or in addition to a traditional ICO file) that upon saving a link to the iPhone, iPad, or iPod touch's home screen (or desktop) you immediately see that icon appear in its place, just like a conventional desktop application, which could be useful for frequent visitors (as seen in Figure 3-22).

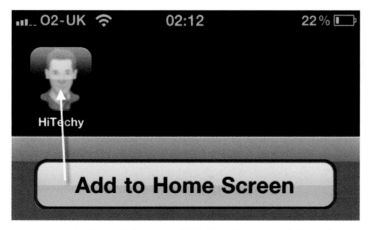

FIGURE 3-22: Apple touch icons are PNG files that act as favicons for your portable device's home screen.

Within the scope of distinctive design, the capability to use iconography gives you a whole range of techniques to enhance your content with references people will recognize and associate with. Although favicons (or Apple's alternative) help people identify your site against competitors' sites in a bookmark list, and calls to action draw on-page attention (usually toward another page), your capability to brand and use symbology to maximize your distinctive focus is worth investigation. A site could benefit from such simplistic, yet eye-catching, visuals—just don't overuse them!

Enduring Multimedia Magic

The roots of web media can be found in images via animations (animated GIFs are moving pictures and thereby could be deemed a type of silent movie, just like how frames of animation produce the effect of movement). These days, things have moved on from this silent format and people no longer rely entirely on plug-ins from video players. Many designers are sensible enough to make their content ubiquitous (or serve their content via an intermediary platform that's better supported, like Flash).

Important

You can still make use of embedded media players such as Windows Media Player, Apple QuickTime, and RealOne Player; however, you run the risk of partial browser support and require the software to be installed (adding another barrier for the user), so it's generally best to avoid them.

In terms of distinction, both audio and video have a range of advantages that can give your designs some added depth and influence upon your sites. Video is going to have the greatest impact because it's both animated (it will grab attention), and it's often interactive with menus and other controls (especially in presentations). With audio, however, the distinction is a lot more subtle because it focuses on auditory rather than visual senses.

If you want to include this magic into your site, your options include producing or buying (via a stock site) a video. Making videos has never been easier, thanks to cheap development tools; high-quality, low-price hardware (like webcams); and platforms like Flash that encourage ubiquity. As with all Flash or plug-in based development, you need a fallback mechanism (such as offering downloads in various formats and quality sizes and considering advances in technology like HTML5 and scripting).

Beyond that, you have option number two: audio. Again, the software is cheap, the hardware (like a good headset) can be equally cheap, and the quality can be very high. In the case of audio, you can either use it alongside a video or presentation or on its own (perhaps using Flash to stream it or offering the MP3 for download). Sites who offer music often include an optional on-page player (as in Figure 3-23).

You are listening to: Song Title - Artist
                        Album Title (2002)

FIGURE 3-23: Audio players should be simple to operate and should **never** automatically begin playing!

And finally, there are presentations. Presentations are in between video and the static web, because you can house an environment (like Flash) with its high level of interactivity, animations, and lots of other useful functions under the hood. Since all types of media aren't currently native to the web (HTML5 is changing this), you will need to provide alternative content like transcriptions to help visitors without access to the plug-in required.

Tip

If you want to host a PowerPoint presentation that can be viewed on the web, consider offering it within a technology like Flash or HTML5 mixed with JavaScript; you'll not only have more control over the progression, but also the animation (and yes, presentations are popular on the web).

All in all, it's a pretty dynamic way to get your website distinctive because you can engage visitors with the same level of attention and detail you would find on TV or at the movies. Of course, like all things, you want to ensure that you don't overstep the mark (no auto-playing media) and let the users access the attention-demanding content for themselves. But as a source of getting across information, it's a very powerful tool.

Vibrant media visualizations

Information design is important to both understanding how you build sites that grab your visitors' attention and making the experience of reading and viewing more interesting. The unique attributes that both audio and video have in giving a more centralized learning experience (by housing lots of information and progressively displaying it) opens up doors in terms of attracting your visitors' senses.

With distinction in video, the capability to give animation and added depth to a design with both movement and changing information allows you the benefit of transfixing your visitors' attention to a set part of the screen. Without the distractions of having to work their mouse and keyboard to navigate around a page, readers can more easily focus on your content. All in all, it has more power and influence than imagery.

Tip

The running time of audio and video can be just as much of a problem as with text and its length. No standard exists for the running time of a media experience, but avoid boring the visitor and ensure it doesn't take a full day to complete.

With audio, the focus is entirely dependent on stimulating the ears and getting attention through the use of sound. This level of distinction may seem more flawed than visual design, but it's actually a pretty good method of conveying information. Audio can be distinctive depending on the pitch, level of background noise, accent being spoken, and other factors.

Your ability as designers to portray knowledge in various digestible formats gives extra appeal to different types of people (Figure 3-24 shows the real difference in sensory awareness and usage). Some visitors prefer the idea of reading text rather than learning by visuals, while others may be the opposite and prefer visual learning to having to wade through a lengthy read. Other people may even prefer listening to audio or video that matches imagery, text, and animation fluidly to bombard the senses.

Ultimately, the power of your content depends on picking the right format for the right job and matching usefulness, suitability, necessity, and the reward gained from taking part in the experience. Although audio and video can indeed be powerful aids to giving your site's content added distinction layers, you need to consider compatibility and the fact that perhaps your visitors won't have speakers (or headphones) or be able to see the screen.

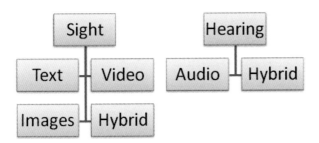

FIGURE 3-24: Each type of content attracts a different aspect of people's senses; all can be useful.

The most common uses for multimedia on the web beyond that of traditional education are through presentations, which act like instructional videos or slide show–based infographics on simplifying a subject to its essentials, or podcasts, which can either be radio shows that chat about a certain subject or videos (like a traditional broadcast).

Note It's amazing how many informative videos exist on sites like YouTube (even for technical subjects like web design). But if you're looking for something more in-line with a presentation or slide show, a perfect example of its implementation is `www.slideshare.net`.

Being able to emphasize your points using visuals and audio allows you to form associations and feelings, which is portrayed and reflected in the final production. If you find that the creative side of things is too complex, plenty of sites offer media that you can use within your product (on license) and give your attempts at building a broadcast that added polish and professionalism. You can even use Flash templates to ease the learning curve for beginners (so the sky really is the limit on using multimedia).

Essentially, making use of appropriate audio and video helps your visitors and gives them a more fun, interesting, and engaging experience. You need to pay careful attention to the quality of the material and how compatible it is for various devices (formats can prove to be quite tricky beasts), but this shouldn't discourage you from investigating how your site could benefit from the added interactivity that is likely to grab a user's focus quickly.

The pillars of digital endurance

A critical aspect of information design related to web media is the balance that needs to occur to make your distinctive layout catch the visitor's attention in all the right places.

Because some forms of media catch a user's attention more quickly than others, your content is taking part in an endurance race. How much stamina and sway a type of content holds reflects how it performs on the page against competing material.

Video, being the most dynamic and vivid form of content, holds the most amount of power in an interface (and thereby should be the least used). Next, you find that images take the silver medal in digital and aesthetic recognition. From that, it's likely that audio has the next highest amount of influence, simply due to its rarity and relative obscurity as to how it's used online. Finally, you have text, the backbone of a site and what should be in plentiful supply because it's the most widely supported (shown in Figure 3-25).

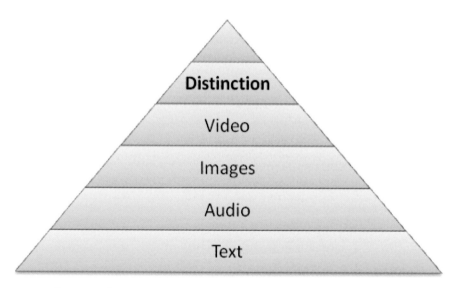

FIGURE 3-25: The various layers of content in order of their distinctive value.

Important   Earlier chapters examine the impact of hardware on a website. Because video and audio have special requirements and their output method goes beyond the monitor, you need to ensure accessible fallbacks like subtitles and transcripts exist to compensate for problems.

Summary

Information design is one of the most central and critical aspects of forging a distinctive design and is often overlooked by designers as an afterthought from the interface. A website in all its glory is dependent on the quality of the content to not only deliver search engine results, but also to get visitors to return. Although you can design your content in many ways, the focus should always be, and rightfully should remain on, substance over style. Consider this as you improve or build a site. Its future will depend upon it.

Design Concepts and Theories

Principles, elements, and ideas about design

WITH SO MANY THEORIES, ideas, and philosophies that make up design, web designers must know how objects make up a page, what visual effects implicate their effectiveness, and how to use the tricks of the trade for a polished result.

Within this lengthy chapter, you dive into the basic principles and elements of design that explain the aesthetic appeal and construct of visuals you produce. You also explore rules that many designers use to forge clean, balanced, beautiful designs. To round off the chapter, I examine the two most prominent figures in web design — color and typography. Understanding these fundamentals gives you the boost that you need to dodge basic mistakes as well as keep things cross-compatible.

Powerful Design Principles

Design wields its influence in almost everything web designers do — from the way you portray your content to the underlying construct of your site's architecture. Another critical aspect of distinctive design is the power of visual design and how your decisions impact a visitor's ability to find what they want when they want it.

Building on their artistic leanings, the many theories of design take into account the principles and elements that make up a distinctive interface. These rules are often flexible and apply not only to print and the web, but also to photography and sculpture. Yet, although they have a wide focus, the choices you make in your design directly influence and impact your visitors, so knowing these principles is useful.

Tip   Aesthetics make up a huge proportion of design work. While recognizing that content is ultimately king, know that the ability to visually catch a user's attention is the opening you need to seal the deal in visitor communication and to gain a competitive advantage.

Much of the theory of design can be broken into two general ideas: principles and elements. *Principles* relate to the arrangement of objects on your pages or within your compositions, whereas you use *elements* to build the pages. Principles give your design aesthetic appeal (such as position and direction); elements provide the shape and focus and enable users to distinguish a navigation menu from a search box in the header, for example. Figure 4-1 shows the trilogy of interface designing.

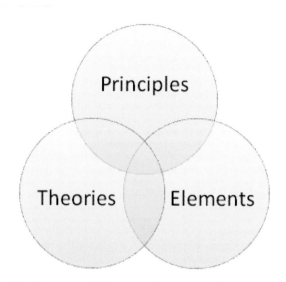

FIGURE 4-1: The principles, elements, and theories of design control how your final page appears.

Design principles and elements apply to a number of fields:

> Anything related to the production of items for the web

> Digital- or analog-transmitted data, such as photography or film

> Paper-based mediums, including newspapers and magazines

Although much of what this chapter covers is based on theory, the information is genu-inely useful for budding coders and portrayers of web content. The web is still a pretty youthful entity and is still evolving rapidly. Although designers are still learning new and interesting ways to use the medium, it's the design aspect rather than the web aspect that gives you the fundamental insights into how your visuals will appear on-screen.

Web design is a subset of the design industry, as are illustration and typography, both of which are transferrable to the web. Using the overarching truths of the philosophical methods that define the aspects of art and design, you can implement on the web centu-ries of craftsmanship, study, emotion, creativity, and attention that print has long enjoyed. You do so by understanding your medium and working it to your advantage. Begin by taking a look at the widely accepted principles of design, while maintaining the formula of enhancing a site's distinction.

Principles of web design

You can think of principles of web design as philosophies or theories that have stood the test of time. Unlike the elements of design, the guiding principles show designers how to work with multiple objects on a page, rather than breaking them down into their individual components. You take a quick look at some of these laws of effect so that you can see how they can affect your web pages.

The structure of a canvas or viewport remains worthy of inclusion. Websites are composed of shapes and a structure, known as a *grid*. These patchworks of aligned and organized components play a critical role in design. Depending on the reading flow, separation, or focus you aim to offer, a structural layout grid plays an important part. All things considered, no design would be the same without this grid. In simple terms, the canvas or viewport is best represented as the space in which a site appears (like a canvas being drawn on). The grids form little invisible "boxes" on which objects on a page appear. With few exceptions, most objects are rectangular, the same as you find in a wireframe sketch (as shown in Figure 4-2).

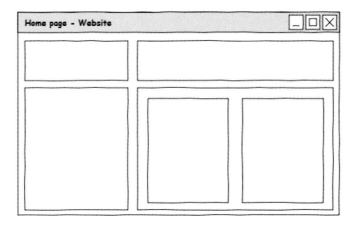

FIGURE 4-2: A site without a grid is like a fish without water! A site needs structure in order to survive.

This invisible structure plays a critical role in helping you to visually organize your site, so you need to consider it in your designs. In terms of distinction, you can do the following:

> Use a conventional "boxy" layout with containers of equal size. This layout gives a distinct impression of order and structure, like scaffolding.

> Avoid a traditional look by using images and visual effects, such as rounded corners. Grids are still used in this layout, but the effect is like an illusion of design using imagery and line tricks.

> Try a combination of different grid sizes to provide a unique but natural website interface.

Important

The idea behind grid theory is that everything on your site fits into little boxes. They don't have to align, but they do give you a framework or scaffold to build on, and their very existence is reinforced by the fact that elements in HTML are rectangular. Add a border to anything on a page, and it will naturally show you the top, left, bottom, and right sides.

Balance

The first principle to examine is *balance,* so picture a set of scales. Placing more items on one side causes distinction to tip toward it, but too much can break the scales and cause neutrality. This artificial form of gravity pulls and attracts people's vision or attention toward the distinctive parts of a site where the weight is. Leveraging balance can mean better focus to parts of a design. The weight doesn't have to be based on the number of items. It could be something else, such as color, which is distinctive or equally measurable. Figure 4-3 shows that proper positioning creates balance.

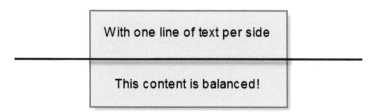

FIGURE 4-3: Symmetry plays a part in design, and balance is the principle that enforces it.

In design, four types of balance can occur:

> **Symmetrical:** This type of balance occurs when the weight of an object is distributed equally over a horizontal or vertical axis.

> **Near symmetrical:** Near symmetrical balance is having content that flows with a slightly uneven distribution.

> **Asymmetrical:** Asymmetrical balance occurs when your content is distinctively one-sided. Use this option with caution.

> **Disorientated:** Disorientated balance attempts are occasionally called *mosaic layouts* because of the way visual emphasis is broken into various defined segments, not linear to an axis, thereby pulling the users' eyes all around the window.

Rhythm

Balance plays a part in focusing vision to part of a page or spreading it evenly, and *rhythm* impacts the direction people look when reading. At their core, rhythms are a repeating element from which people draw a reading direction by moving through a process. For example, the way your text flows on a page has a rhythm to it that affects your visitor's reading flow by smoothing the transition between objects.

You can implement rhythm through the use of images, text, or another means. Here are the three types of rhythm:

> **Regular:** Objects are similar in size with set intervals, such as text or other objects that run in equal lines across a page.

> **Flowing:** Wavy lines in images are more organic and irregular with less equilibrium.

> **Progressive:** Think of the stages of a domino falling over or a sequence of steps from one point to another, using varying angles.

Because of the natural association these rhythm types have with progression, they aid your distinctive design work by allowing elements that break the rhythm to gain attention and force the visitor to react. A regular rhythm is easier to adjust to than a progressive one. Figure 4-4 shows regular rhythm: the text flows in equal, measured, straight lines. If regular rhythm "breaks out" (if the text gets bigger and then smaller again, for example), the content evolves into a flowing rhythm. Essentially, rhythm is all about maintaining the beat and flow of your content!

Content within a website flows from line to line.
This represents the flow of information.
People often read from the top-left hand corner.
And finish up at the bottom once they're done.
Though some nations read from right to left!

Figure 4-4: Has your page got rhythm? If you ensure that it flows to the beat, the page may become easier to read!

Movement

The next principle of design is deeply related to rhythm. *Movement* and a person's ability to interpret it affect many aspects of a site's level of distinction. Whether through the literal movement of animation (as depicted within Figure 4-5, in which the notorious HTML blink element, if used on a page, would cause flashing to occur when used upon objects) or the compositional movement of flowing text, you can alter the directional flow, the pathway of how content is read, and the orientation of a design.

FIGURE 4-5: If something flashes on the screen, attention is immediately pulled away from static content.

Rather than predetermining how people are likely to read the content or rhythm of your page, take the time to locate any naturally "active" parts that move or give the illusion of change (such as Flash or JavaScript interactivity or animated images). Consider how these active parts might affect their surroundings. Action can be useful in powering recognition, but when used in excess, it becomes a real distraction.

Proportion

Proportion compares the dimensions or general distribution of shapes in order to relate the differences among objects. Proportion has several applications, because it not only helps establish your site's visual depth, but you can also use it to gain insights into how symmetrical a layout is and where users' eyes naturally focus on the screen. You can measure proportion by using several variables, such as color and weight (as shown in Figure 4-6).

Headings are given size and strength advantages by default

Whereas a paragraph of text is of a regular size and appearance.

Figure 4- 6: Visually large items with strong colors always get distinction.

In design, if you have a few menu items on one area of a page and a whole bunch of pretty images elsewhere on the page, the proportionate weight falls in favor of the images. Their size is greater than the text. Put another way, if you have a large square with a bright color next to a small square with a pale color, the smaller square will fade into the background because of its smaller size and the weight of the color depth on the page. As a web designer, using such variables enables you to effectively place emphasis, attention, and focus on important objects.

Important Size can be a problem if a user is viewing your site on a handheld device. Because of the reduced screen size, body content and navigation items are the focal points with respect to size and distinction (rather than visual flourishes, such as oversized images).

Dominance

Although the weight of an object in your site is a mixture of proportion, depth, and scale, remember the value of dominance in your design work. A site relies on being able to put greater emphasis on content of value than on background noise. Emphasis (commonly referred to as *dominance*) is a principle of design, and although it comes in varying degrees of strength, its goal is to draw attention by exaggerating its worth. Figure 4-7 shows the effect of varying forms of visual dominance and strength.

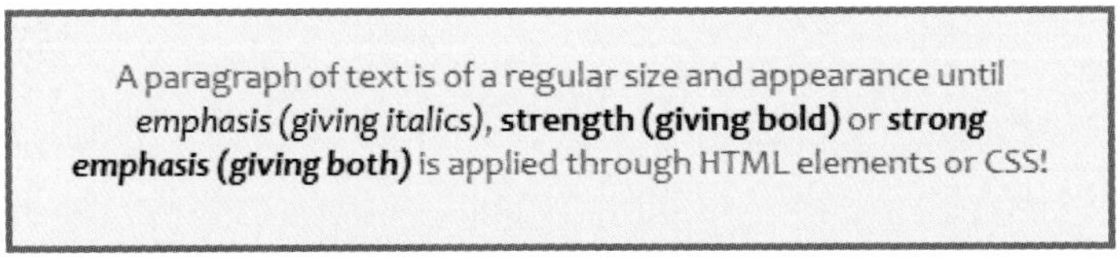

A paragraph of text is of a regular size and appearance until *emphasis (giving italics)*, **strength (giving bold)** or ***strong emphasis (giving both)*** is applied through HTML elements or CSS!

FIGURE 4-7: Add emphasis and weight to your content by using HTML code or CSS style.

Here are some points to keep in mind regarding the forms of dominance. Because of its bold appearance, strength has the most power; because it's normally represented by "italics," emphasis acts as a middleman between strong and normal (refer to Figure 4-7). As a rule of thumb, normal (nondistinctive) elements fade into the background and are the weakest, thereby ending up as the last ones to attract, withdraw, limit, or lose a user's focus. If something doesn't stand out, it usually ends up as a final consideration when the items most selectively noticed by the end user are read.

However, don't be fooled into thinking that you can apply emphasis only to text. You can also apply emphasis and strength in the following ways:

> **Object isolation:** Adding whitespace around an item gives it some level of emphasis. Because space has no visual emphasis or distinction, it focuses attention firmly on an object.

> **Contrasting proportions:** The size and scale of objects can draw emphasis, strength, and dominance to objects. Larger objects on a page receive more attention than smaller ones.

> **Object placement:** Even the position in which you place an object can give it greater emphasis than other parts of a page. Text at the top of a page "feels" more important than text in a footer.

Working out which form of emphasis to use may be a challenge, but doing so is worth the effort if it gets a user's attention, if only for a second!

Similarity

Another principle that is often not separated from its relatives but that is still important is the effect of highlighting. Highlighting is drawn from the principle of *similarity,* which highlights the recognition of objects joined by matching visual effects (such as how users associate links with their similar underlines and blue color). Highlighting is strongly related to emphasis and dominance in that it puts focus on a single aspect of a page. It also has the subtle ability to provide an "aura" (or focal point) behind or around an object. Figure 4-8 illustrates how highlighting can accentuate a word and, in the process, make it more meaningful on a page.

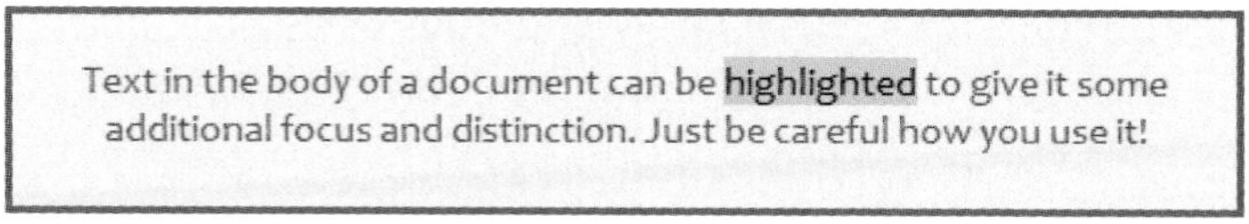

> Text in the body of a document can be highlighted to give it some
> additional focus and distinction. Just be careful how you use it!

FIGURE 4-8: Change the background color of a single word to give it added weight on a page.

You can achieve highlighting in design a number of ways. Color is an obvious route. In addition, the use of shapes such as icons, lines (for example, underlines, overlines, and strikethrough), or bold and italic typefaces can give a passage an ambiance that contrasts with the rest of the design. If something on a page needs attention, use emphasis. However, for a entire section, you may want to consider highlighting the background or using surrounding space to achieve the level of focus the objects require.

Tip　Certain browsers, such as Google Chrome, let developers define a custom highlighter color for selected text. This flexibility can aid users who want to keep track of where they are when reading your documents, and it's a fun alternative to the boring blue default many browsers use.

Unity

Unity in distinctive design allows you to see that everything you add to a page plays a role in the bigger picture. Every element must look like it belongs with the other elements and share a common relationship without suffering random or accidental occurrences. Breaking the unity within a page can cause friction, which in turn catches the user's attention. Balancing unity with *clashing* (when something needs to dominate) is critical in gaining distinction.

One key point of unity is that friction on the page draws immediate attention. Figure 4-9 illustrates a break in unity. Although the break looks messy, such quirks can override other types of distinction.

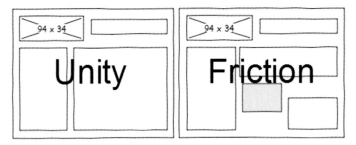

FIGURE 4-9: Objects that stand out from a page and look like they don't belong catch the eye.

Consider how consistently your pages join together and whether any breaks in the natural flow occur. Unity is an important part of an aesthetic balance. Perhaps also consider how the harmony among objects will be affected if objects don't line up or "fit" correctly in a scene, which could make people feel unsettled.

Proximity

The final principle of design to examine is *proximity*. Unity between objects on the page is important, but the amount of space, their placement and position, and how they relate have a great deal of power. Consumers are more likely to look at the text under a relevant heading than to scan down a page trying to match up text. Ensuring that related or similar items are placed in close proximity is a sensible option, and doing so can influence the final design. Figure 4-10 illustrates how the principles of proximity (position, space, relationship) add distinction to the single object in the left box.

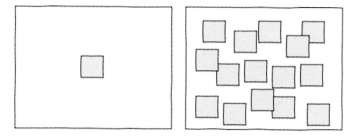

FIGURE 4-10: The closer objects are to each other, the less individualism and distinction they carry.

Using the proper amount of white space among objects forces you to choose the content carefully, as well as where it's located on the page. Because you have a limited amount of space, position is everything. Try to group the relevant parts of a page together. Give objects more or less breathing room, and reinforce your distinctive message with clear points of emphasis in the unified design.

Theories for design principles

A series of guiding principles exists to help you make wise decisions as you construct a site's layout and consider the effects. They can also help you control every aspect of your interfaces and experiences. You can use theoretical principles of design to supplement what you offer and give your audience a better experience. Although it may look like witchcraft to some, design theory is based on years of research and study.

Because design is an art and a science, it lends itself to being creative *and* controlling at the same time. The following theories are just that — principles that aren't as strictly enforceable as the general principles (discussed in the previous section). Don't feel obligated to strictly enforce the following, but do consider their worth.

Tip Even if you're designing an image, your composition will be forged from a number of objects positioned on the page, such as lines and shapes. Although much of what this chapter examines looks at the visual side of information and interface design, you can apply the information in a range of ways for specific needs.

Rule of thirds

The *rule of thirds* is a compositional rule stating that an image (or in your case, potentially a site) should be divided into nine equal parts with important aspects of the page placed along those intersectional points. Over recent years, this theory of balancing content has been adapted to web design, mostly because of its ability to displace content away from a central focal point. The general idea is that the content of each of the nine boxes should contain as much content as its opposing section. Major points of visual interest should match up with the lines that make up the boxes or their joining points.

As designers, you often have a limited environment in which to work, and you must make the most out of the space you have. Fixed-width designs create problems in resolutions larger or smaller than the intended target. By using the compositional rule of thirds (which expands or contracts based on the available space), you can produce flexible layouts that are fairly balanced in accordance to a page's scale. Figure 4-11 shows an example.

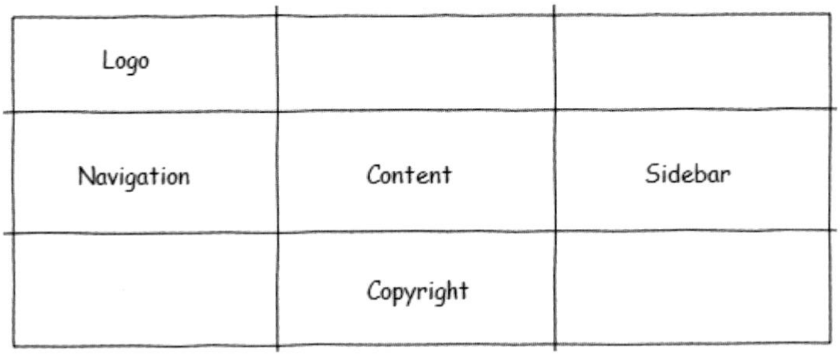

Logo		
Navigation	Content	Sidebar
	Copyright	

FIGURE 4-11: Although your content doesn't have to fit exactly on the lines, it may help balance the structure.

Maintaining a balance between various parts of the viewport allows you to ensure that every part of your layout offers something for visitors' eyes to revel in (for example, useful links or a great blog post). This kind of layout gives users a reason to explore the page and may encourage them to focus more evenly across the screen. Unless you want to deliberately limit a visitor's field of vision with excess white space to force a distinctive element to the surface, you may find the rule of thirds a useful neutralizer.

Iteration

The next theory worthy of consideration is the programming ideology called *iteration*. As you produce sites, you may feel the need to build once and stick with what works, rather than go for what works well. The process behind iteration requires you to keep repeating something, such as a design idea, with the aim of improving upon the previous build. Although this isn't reinventing the wheel, the idea behind iterating your design allows you to model your layout in various formats to see if you can improve it. Software and sites go through many iterations — check out Figure 4-12!

FIGURE 4-12: Iterative design goes through many phases. Websites don't just appear out of nowhere!

In design, reaching a desired result is always hard. You often have to compromise your ideals for such reasons as budget, consumer demand, and project scope. More often than not, you end up progressively enhancing your site's content and elements to match the way visitors use your goods and services. This form of iteration is highly desirable. Rather than continuing to redesign, recycling may be the best path.

Testing or analyzing your work gives you the opportunity to improve it, and iterative design is therefore a very useful tool to have at your disposal. Check out `http://en.wikipedia.org/wiki/Iterative_design`.

Reference

Iteration relies on your need to improve something and on the resources available for enhancing what you have. Perhaps your website already looks awesome or you're trying to think about what kind of layout to go with. Conceptual models such as wireframes, concept artwork, and prototypes can help you take something as simple as a search box and make it easier to use by adding useful features or by removing excess. To learn more about these models, see Bonus Chapter 1 in the companion e-book.

Iteration allows you to aim for the best of all worlds, but this isn't always possible so it requires a theory that allows a quicker method of getting your works online (with a distinctive but perhaps not as refined layout as before). In such cases, you may want to consider the theory of *satisficing* — merging satisfy with suffice, to end up with solutions that do the job without overindulging in complexity. At this theory's core is the strategy that having an adequate solution may be better than an optimal one.

Tip

If you want to get a website up and running as quickly as possible, begin by following the satisficing design theory by implementing the innermost core functionality required to do the task well. You can then upgrade and improve the service with flourishes after you launch it to your community.

It's probably a good idea at this point to state that when the iteration theory says "better" (regarding the progress it makes), it isn't referring to the overall design (optimal solutions will always be the pinnacle of a set goal); instead, it refers to the cost versus quality ratio. Simply put, if making a design that's so distinctively tuned takes extra time and effort, why not get 90 percent of the impact with something adequate and less than half the cost (in terms of iteration and resource usage) instead of the full 100 percent power drive.

Consider the following to determine if iteration may be needed:

> Do bugs, flaws, or issues exist that could affect the page?

> Can content on the page be made easier to understand or more accessible?

> Have multiple users requested something useful or clever?

> What can I add to make a site useful or distinctive?

Building a perfect design isn't possible. Although having something distinctive can be quickly achieved, designers may think that if it has everything thrown at it (in terms of its optimization), the excess in energy and effort will have been worth it. Aiming for the best site possible is a great thing, but there comes a point where you may find compromise and satisficing a good alternative. It wouldn't make sense, for example, to spend a week on a single element.

Performance versus preference

The next theory is commonly referred to as *performance versus preference,* and this theory plays an especially vital role in distinctive design because it's a user-centered approach. Logic tells you that more often than not, when offering content on a site, it's your job to get users to what they're looking for in the shortest possible time, as implied in

Figure 4-13. Making your site a good performer is a great ideal to maintain, but occasionally things aren't that simple.

> Home > Products > MyProduct > **Screenshots**
>
> Home > Products > Software > MyProduct > Tour > **Screenshots**

FIGURE 4-13: Which road would you prefer to take, the scenic one or the quickest and easiest?

The theory of performance versus preference states that although there may be a shorter route to a particular source of information, visitors will often go with a route they prefer or are used to, even if that route takes longer to navigate! This behavior may seem weird, but when you think about it, humans often prefer using a safe or known route to a particular place than going down an unknown path. This behavior applies to the web because users find comfort in knowing where their actions lead.

When you implement a navigation system on your site, try to reduce the click ratio (to a specific point) as much as possible. The three-click rule may seem outdated (thinking no more than three is useful to a user), but then again, perhaps it still applies. If you provide shortcuts that deviate from the common navigation system, keep the old routes open. Giving visitors a choice allows them to decide between preference and performance and also increases the potential for web window-shoppers.

Important

Usability research shows that although people are willing to make quick, judgmental clicks on a page to find what they need, they often aren't as willing to navigate a series of pages (such as search results) if doing so requires attentive reading.

Occam's Razor

Although reducing the barrier to navigation and offering choice through performance versus preference is one great way to obtain a distinctive design (where important content can be located quickly), another theory that can help the cause is commonly referred to as *Occam's Razor*. The theory behind this idea stands true today. If each option you have is of equal merit, the simplest one is most often the best. Note, for example, how a search box is simplified in Figure 4-14.

Keep in mind the central role that simplicity plays along with minimalism in the distinctiveness of a design. Simpler objects are easier to read, use, and digest. It stands to reason that if you have a choice between several good implementations, overcomplicating the process doesn't make sense. When in doubt, make simplicity the priority. Occam's Razor backs up this point and remains a tried and tested philosophy.

FIGURE 4-14: A search box that combines a button seems less disjointed than its separate alternative.

Distinctive designs require you to ensure that your work meets the user's expectations and doesn't lack necessary function. Simplicity doesn't mean killing off important stuff just for the sake of a reduction — it merely implies an agile work ethic. Following this principle requires you to ensure that your objectives are met. If an easier route of implementation exists (such as combining the search box and button, as many designs do), you may need to take that route to reduce the level of noise on the page and make objects function better.

Fitt's Law

Finally, look at *Fitt's Law,* which plays a role in the usability of your site by ensuring that important and distinctive content for your visitors remain within easy reach. Fitt's Law states that the time and effort required to reach a target is dependent on the distance and size of the object on the page. Within web design, this idea is emphasized by how humans interact with a computer. Consider Figure 4-15 in which a missing login button results in visitor confusion.

Because visitors use your site to achieve goals, you can reduce their confusion by offering a progressive and straightforward flow of relevant information. If the "I Accept" button of a license agreement is at the bottom of a 24-page document (without overflow in effect), the amount of time it takes to click the item is increased (because of the scrolling distance). If you have a mobile device, tapping a small button will be increasingly difficult. Reducing the energy or effort needed to perform an action decreases fatigue.

FIGURE 4-15: Connect related objects. Place a button with its box!

As you build sites, consider the principles that determine how you organize information on the screen. Unity plays a critical role in how easy it is to find relative information, and elements related to unity such as the proximity of objects forces you to consider these relationships further. Fitt's Law asks you to do what you can to improve the situation for your visitors. By making distinctive content visible and by reducing the time and effort it takes to actually get to that content, you achieve this goal.

The principles of design play a vital role in website production. Because you're aiming to get every mission-critical element of the page as distinctive as possible, it's important to know about proportion, emphasis, rhythm, and other "active" aspects of a site that literally hold the same sway in the online world as a force like gravity holds in the physical world. Consider every object on the pages of your site, the influence they hold, and seek existing research for best practices.

Elegant Design Elements

So far, you have read about a wide range of design principles that underline the manner of how you optimize your design distinctively. Although there are a few principles to remember, applying each of them in just the right way can really aid your design's elegance and readability. You now need to examine the second variable that plays a part in everything artistic and visual that appears on your page: the various elements of design, which take you to even greater depths as you examine the various building blocks of every object that appears on your pages.

The principles of design focus on the assumed knowledge (of the world) that guides people's ability to comprehend an interface. The elements of the design look at the components that help produce such effects as unity and proximity. Knowing the effects of using code and design is one thing, but knowing the elements that sustain a page or composition is central to your role as a designer. Without them, nothing on the page could even exist!

In most aspects of design, elements work in conjunction with each other to produce a desired effect. Elements can be added or subtracted and arranged in a specific fashion to give an object its visual characteristics. For example, the shape of characters, the focus (or blurring), the size of the typefaces, and the patterns or textures chosen affect the distinctive value of text. Elemental design is everywhere!

Elements of web design

Because every design is made up of elements, your awareness of these awesome components enables you to alter their inner distinctive nature. Depending on how they're used, you can produce a huge range of layouts. Although they can be isolated and defined, they carry a whole series of meanings and expectations and will literally structure your layout with a potential to make everything on the page distinctive. Recognizable patterns in these objects lead to distinction. Distinctive design relies on many different pieces working in unison. You don't need to be an expert in everything that touches the page, but knowledge of what can potentially be tweaked, optimized, highlighted, defused, or neutralized can guide you to decisions that give a design its subtle, yet distinctive, beauty.

Points

Of the many elements that comprise an interface, the *point* is the most simplistic. Formed of a single dot (see Figure 4-16 for an example of a point, which is enlarged for impact) with no trail or connectivity links, it can signify a specific target of interest, or it can be used in association with other elements to produce a line, shape, or other important aspect of visual interest. Your screen is made up of tiny pixels, and every visible dot has the power to work in association with others to form objects (if small enough, a single pixel may represent a point). In distinctive design, its value is absolute.

FIGURE 4-16: It may be rude to point, but directing a user's focus is the aim of distinctive design.

Applying points in producing a distinctive design is actually rather simple. A spot on a blank canvas immediately draws attention to that location. The very existence of an object, no matter how small, enforces a distinction between positive and negative space. The grouping of these points to build objects enlists psychology and the Gestalt theory (see Chapter 5 for more on the Gestalt theory).

Lines

The next element on the list is probably the second least complex aspect of a page you'll find. You know its many uses because you've probably seen it many times before. The *line* is an object that marks a distinctive rule between two points, offering both direction and a means of separating content on either side of the medium. Often seen in designs to mark a particular item (such as underlining links), lines add some distinctive value. Of course, they can simply be used for decorative or other effects (see Figure 4-17).

FIGURE 4-17: Lines can be straight, curly, or even wiggly! Artists commonly use them to outline objects.

Creating contours that separate objects is quite noticeable in design, especially if you consider the impact of borders. They create divides of no real value but offer a guiding limit to an object's physical shape and size so that site visitors can differentiate objects. Although lines do offer this breakup between objects on the page, they can also signify a visual process by following the point from one end to the other (such as directions on a map).

Shapes

Shapes are made up of lines that connect in such a way that they form a recognizable (or unique) pattern. Primary shapes that comprise most objects in some form are triangles, rectangles (and squares), and circles (or ovals). Shapes have significance in distinctive design, too. Figure 4-18 shows some very basic shapes (that could be used within an image on a website).

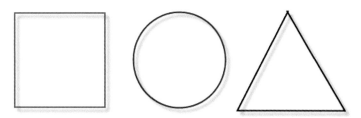

FIGURE 4-18: Shapes can be formed either by adjoining contours or through dimensions.

In Chapter 3, I mentioned the value of symbology: by providing small, recognizable objects that people identify with, you can add distinction to your website. In the same way, when people see a shape on a screen that they can identify with (such as the rectangle of a content box or a photo of a flower), they're more open to associating with the object. Try using shapes to identify a complete feature, point of interest, image, graph, or aspect of a page. However, shapes can be misinterpreted, so don't produce something that has no recollective value.

Tip

Symbols can be overpowering because visitors are drawn to them (if they recognize them). Consider the benefit versus cost ratio when adding a warning or attention symbol to a page. The last thing you want is to snatch away the distinction of other useful objects!

Pattern and texture

Now examine two complex concepts, *pattern and texture.* These elements allow you to take something with a form (or shape) and give it a tangible, physical, tactile surface. A background image adds noise to an interface, which reduces the levels of distinction of less critical content. Patterns employ simpler but repetitive, tiled effects. Figure 4-19 shows a chessboard, a very simple, recognizable pattern.

The differences between texture and patterns are rather simple. Patterns promote a flowing effect on the page (or object), using a repeating (usually *ad infinitum*) mixture of various lines, shapes, and points. With textures, the surface that's produced emotes a particular feeling of a real-world object, such as grass, carpet, and so on. Both are usually applied to enhance a bland or overly spacious environment!

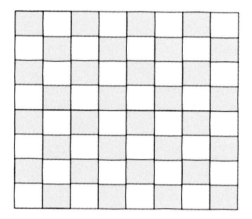

FIGURE 4-19: The chessboard is a simple example of a pattern that repeats a consistent visual style.

Diffusion absorbs the design that a texture inherits and provides a sequential pattern or style. The reader's viewing experience is similar to viewing a flat screen. The contrasting medium can simulate a real-life object or add depth. However, because of how they impact the screen visually, textures have to be used with a degree of caution because they can add noise to your projects as well as a sense of realism or authenticity.

Tip

Many stock image sites offer textured patterns that flow seamlessly, offering a cool way to gain an "infinitely" large background. Using a wooden texture, for example, can give a natural feel or emotional feel to a site.

There are far fewer elements in design than principles, primarily because even the most complex of objects, when broken down into their simplest form, are made up of several components. Some people like to have space listed as an element of design (and in some ways, it qualifies), but because it lacks physical, visible form, the most you can do is either extend or reduce it.

As you get used to these elements or space, consider how the lines, dots, or shapes play their roles in your design. Anything that exists on the page has an impact and leaves a trail that can get a user's visual attention. Even white space can attract visitors' eyes, if they're after some breathing space or feel that what exists isn't quite as interesting as the background aesthetic. You want to ensure that your site doesn't have too much of either. If empty space looks good, something went badly wrong!

Theories for design elements

With the principles and elements of design established, are you looking for something extra to help turn your site into a distinctive design? Here is your chance! Following are a few of the cool theories that are closely tied to choices of shape, line, and anything else that consumes elemental space on your site's pages. You may want to consider them as best practices.

These theories may not hold as much weight as the raw principles and elements do, but research and study suggest that if nothing else, implementing these useful components can give you a better interface and may help improve the distinction of your site; which is ultimately your goal. So pick what you want to take advantage of, but consider these philosophies carefully.

Important

Even though theories are laid out in this book, it doesn't mean that you should simply accept them or avoid any other research. Test the validity of your choices in each site's environment.

Picture superiority

The first element-based design theory is called *picture superiority*. The concept behind this theory is that no matter how much textual content is showcased on a page, an image will always dominate the landscape and be easier to recall. Although this theory isn't true in every circumstance, it plays a role in the psychology of memory and how you can ensure the awareness of users. Figure 4-20 showcases how the size of an image dominates the landscape and its surrounding text.

The effect of this theory requires the individual to be able to see pictures on the page, which in some circumstances, such as problems with accessibility, might be an issue. However, if images are available and you can use them to illustrate important points, you can give those special sections of your page some distinction. Images draw focus toward them.

FIGURE 4-20: Pictures speak louder than words, but mainly because they visually absorb screen space.

If you have media on a page, it grabs attention because of the experiences it evokes. Your use of shape and movement must be planned in a way that directs the visitor in the right direction. There's nothing worse than flashy fluff that bloats your screen.

Remember that not all media is appealing to users. Always avoid using it to dumb down a point, and always treat your readers at a level appropriate for them, while understanding their needs.

Tip

Form follows function

Of course, although directing and grabbing attention with vivid shape and image use is a surefire way to get something from the user, building your design in so that it is the natural selection of appropriate choices is always useful. The next theory, *form follows function,* is used regularly in architecture to denote that the shape of an object should be based on its intended function and purpose.

Putting this into a more web-orientated role, base every decision you make on the needs of the content, from what gets emphasis on a page, what should be placed where, and even to the wireframes that denote the shape of sections of a page. People visit a website to read content and use services, so a beautiful but useless layout that scatters content everywhere isn't going to help users get to their final destination. Sitemaps, such as the one featured in Figure 4-21, illustrate form following function.

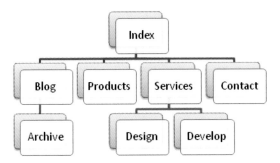

FIGURE 4-21: A site map's shape is defined by its hierarchy. It looks distinctive and serves a purpose.

You are accountable for every design decision that could impact your site and its pages. Taking the time to carefully structure and plan everything saves you time in the update process and ensures that important content is as visible as it needs to be. Many websites aren't very organized when it comes to having a sensible layout. As a distinctive designer, you must take it seriously.

Entry points

The next theory to examine is the theory behind *entry points* (which facilitate calls to action, like the one in Figure 4-22). These parts of a page attract a great deal of immediate attention and the visitor's focus. Entry points are usually the most prominent aspects of a page, such as content placed in the upper-left corner of the screen — a logo, for example.

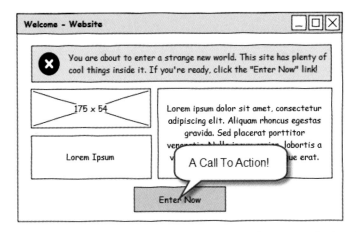

FIGURE 4-22: The "call to action" is visible because of its distinctive color (matching the header).

To produce an entry point or call to action, you simply need a single item with an attention-seeking nature (such as something big, bold, colorful, or animated) that eclipses most other aspects of the page. While producing an entry point to begin grabbing a user's focus, decide if it should be a primary (immediate) or secondary (delayed) visual point.

Note Primary focus points are defined as the very first thing your visitors should be drawn to, and secondary points commonly draw focus immediately after the primary point. An example could be how a user's eyes jump from a logo (immediate) to a menu (delayed).

An entry point's role in distinctive design is considered absolute because you're stealing the focus away from everything else on the page, so handle entry points with care. However, if you have something that demands a visitor's attention like nothing else (such as an advertisement, a new product, or a download), entry points can guide your users to quick decisions. Examples of these entry points can include "calls to action," header passages or introductions, and even lightboxes, as shown in Figure 4-23. A *lightbox* causes the surrounding content to fade into the background, forcing the user's attention to a central location.

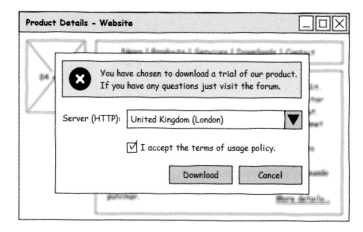

FIGURE 4-23: A lightbox, with surrounding content fading into the background.

Field of vision: the fold

Another theory worth considering is the idea behind the *field of vision*. Traditional print and web design can both utilize a few of this theory's elements. The first of these is the *fold.* This principle works great in traditional print design because if something is folded, part of it is no longer directly available to the eye (consider how newspapers are folded in half to show only part of the front page).

On the web, the concept behind the fold still works in terms of visibility (scrolling makes content farther down the page visible to the eye — see Figure 4-24), but it's less of an issue because users are more willing to scroll in order to locate potentially useful content. They're also usually willing to jump between pages to continue from a point of the page they left off, even though this breaks the reading flow. So the fold concept still exists on the web, it's just more flexible or unpredictable.

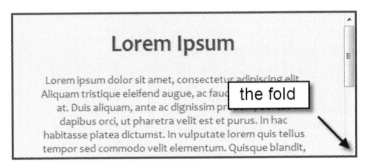

FIGURE 4-24: The fold exists on the web. It's simply the dynamic point at which scrolling must occur.

Field of vision: overlapping

Although the fold is an important aspect of the field of vision theory, the idea of positioning is also quite important regarding how people read content. *Overlapping* is a well-known technique in which objects are carefully layered over something else to achieve an effect of joining forces. Overlapping must be done with care to prevent reducing the content's readability, and the fold can be considered for finding the initial points of reference. Don't avoid scrolling for the sake of the fold, except when both horizontal and vertical scrolling occurs at the same time. Contrary to myths, users do scroll pages.

Important   Just because the fold or field of vision appears in one place on your browser doesn't mean that other users will experience the same thing. Resolution, window size, monitor size, DPI, toolbars, sidebars, and a range of other features can affect the fold's relative on-screen location.

The 80/20 rule

Next up is a common theory that rings true to the average user of both websites and software. The *80/20* rule states that, in essence, 80 percent of those using what you offer will make use of only 20 percent of the functionality. If you consider a piece of software like Adobe Photoshop, you can probably understand how this may be the case. It is full of functionality and complex elements that allow you to achieve the most amazing things, but the average user of the program isn't going to use everything on a regular basis.

Taking this concept to the Internet, this theory is true for web applications (especially those of increasing complexity). The more features and depth you provide to a program, the lower the percentage that users are likely to employ on a regular basis. Figure 4-25 shows the learning curve, core needs, and feature factors involved. If you build something that offers plenty of functionality, keep in mind that, although useful, some of what you add may clog up an interface. Consider enabling it on a needs basis.

FIGURE 4-25: Applications with fewer options are statistically more likely to have those options used.

Mozilla Firefox takes advantage of this rule by providing extensibility in which people add features as they require them. This approach tightens up the size of code required for the product and helps avoid bloat. In a normal site design, you can implement this concept by reducing the number of visible objects on-screen. Remove any unused sidebars, secondary navigation menus, and pages that aren't visited often.

Note

An extension is a piece of code or useful functionality that can be plugged into an interface or application. Often developed in coordination with APIs, they aren't limited only to software applications. The popular CMS product WordPress allows for fast, easy extensibility, too!

Elements play a huge role in design because every object added to a site uses elements in some form. Much like abstract art, every composition (or layout) you produce will be composed of the points, lines, shapes, textures, and patterns that form all objects in a real or virtual world. Consider real-world objects such as a table, a chair, or even a human. They are made up of shapes! Applying these elements enables you to keep the layout distinctive and to arrange your content in carefully structured grids and blocks.

As you can see, the theories presented so far blend the principles and elements of design in elegant ways that you can use in your work. What separates an element and a principle doesn't matter that much (they work in unison and blend together well), but the fact that these principles, elements, and theories exist means that you need to spend a bit of your creative juices deciding how to best communicate your message to users and visitors.

Targeting Color Theory

You now have explored plenty of principles and elements of design, and you may be thinking that nothing else can possibly be added to help evolve your design's distinctive nature. However, you would be wrong! Although all design features play a part in the overall appeal of a site, color is so distinctive and powerful that it deserves its own section explaining the theory behind it.

More studies and research have been done on the effects color than on any other distinctive element or variable in the scope of design. Sometimes people pick colors to evoke emotion or to reflect a physical object; other times they simply want to give a certain impression and use color to reinforce that effect. Choosing a color in your web design does just what painting a room does: Color can evoke feelings of warmth, neutrality, or even emphasis (if you go with neon, for example).

The types of research undertaken on color include the following:

> How various colors can influence or affect human behavior

> The problems of color in disability (such as color blindness)

> Human perceptions of color and optical illusions it causes

> Associative links between color perception and temperature

> Best practices for color use with various ages and genders

> The sociological and cultural impact of color perceptions

> Trends of color use in various sites and why they are used

Color use is subjective and its distinctive value is without question, so consider the variety of colors that are available, the issues with mixing colors (such as contrast), and how you can implement them on the web to give your content the appeal it deserves. Color can be a complicated subject, especially because it's so versatile and has more variables than do proximity or emphasis.

Color use in design usually falls into the realm of communication (how it speaks to and influences people through psychology) or application (how you use it to improve your designs). Color can be your most powerful asset, if used correctly. So, as a designer, you need to understand the various aspects of color, which are based both in theory and in practice. If you've built a site in the past, you've probably considered color on several occasions. But why is it so critical in your mission to attract a visitor's eye to your important content? You find the answer to this question in the following sections.

Characteristics of color

Color is the label applied to how people's eyes perceive varying degrees and spectrums of reflected light. Considering how different an object looks during the day than it does in the dark of night can help you differentiate your perceptions of color. Regarding color in the digital form, depending on the medium you work with, one of two systems will almost certainly influence color use: CMYK and RGB (see Figure 4-26). CMYK primarily orients toward the use of color, as depicted in print; RGB orients toward screens or other digital displays, which use the less permanent form of light emission.

The CMYK mode uses ink mixing and is aimed primarily at print. It uses cyan, magenta, yellow, and black (a key color because the other three are aligned to the black plate) to get the rainbow of colors people see on a printed page. CMYK is a *subtractive* color system because it mixes the ink to get the right hue and then adds black as required to deepen the shade or uses less black to lighten the shade.

For screens and other digital displays, designers use RGB (for red, green, and blue). Unlike with traditional print on paper where you start with white, adding black to deepen the shade, pixels on a digital screen illuminate. RGB color is accomplished by using the light emitted from pixels on the display, either superimposed from a black screen or reflected from a white one. This illumination is the result of colors being generated by spectrums of light that cross each other to create perceptions of colors. For that reason, this system is referred to as an *additive* color system.

Figure 4-26 shows the two color systems side-by-side.

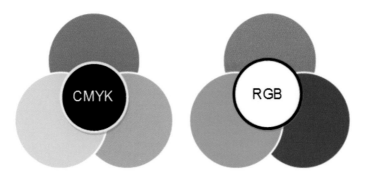

FIGURE 4-26: The CMYK and RGB color systems.

In terms of color, be aware of the following:

> *Hue* describes the color or combination.

> *Chromaticity* describes how pure a color is — having less black, white, or gray clouding the primary color mixtures that are used.

> *Value* describes how close to black a color is (making it darker) or how close to white a color is (making it brighter).

> *Saturation* describes the strength and relative brightness of a color under certain lighting conditions (for example, during the day or at night).

Reference If you're finding the process of building color palettes difficult, some prebuilt apps may help. ColorSchemer Studio (paid), Color Cop (free), and Adobe Kuler (web-based) are your humble author's personal recommendations. You can even find color pickers for mobile devices.

By mixing the primary colors (red, green, and blue, or in the case of print, cyan, magenta, and yellow) and adjusting the value and saturation (or brightness) of your color, you can create an entire rainbow of colors to make your designs as beautiful as you want. With the aid of color picker tools, you can grab a shade you like from an image or digital source and convert it into something usable on the web, such as the HTML hex value. On the flip side, having so many choices can make picking a palette difficult.

I need to mention the color wheel. If you've never seen one, these devices provide a method of combining or analyzing colors (such as the wheel shown in Figure 4-27). Using the color system of your choosing (for example, RGB), you position the primary, secondary, and tertiary colors in the circle. The primary colors consist of red, green, and blue and can't be mixed. The secondary colors consist of green, purple, and orange and are made by mixing two primary colors together. The tertiary colors are made by mixing primary and secondary colors together, producing even more colors.

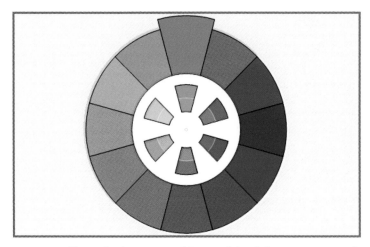

FIGURE 4-27: These wheels are pretty things, and they help you compare and contrast a range of colors!

In addition, you can expand your color choices even more by mixing a range of colors with the two monochrome baseline colors: black and white. If you mix a color with white, you get a *tint*. If you mix a color with black, you get a *shade*. And if you blend a color with gray (or mix shades and tints), you get *tones* (see Figure 4-28). Color wheels give you the opportunity to use all these tools to produce dynamic and beautiful colors to give your design some extra distinction. Because software can provide designers with color wheels and tools to help build palettes, it's probably worth your while to use them.

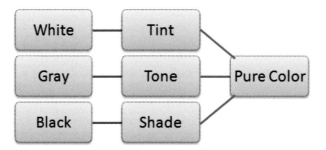

FIGURE 4-28: Tints, shades, and tones may sound similar, but they all change a color's appearance.

On the subject of the color wheel, consider color harmonies, shown in Figure 4-29, which help you find suitable choices for your palette. *Complementary* colors oppose each other on the wheel. (They stand out, but clash!). *Analogous* colors sit next to each other on the wheel and blend well, but need contrast. *Triadic* colors are like complementary colors (but from three opposing points, not two). Of course, you can build other color harmonies, but these color harmonies along with *monochromatic* colors (which consist of blacks, whites, and grays) are the four most popular ones!

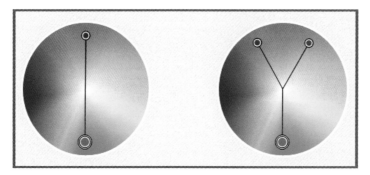

FIGURE 4-29: Using a color wheel, you can identify various types of color harmonies in action.

You can easily add splashes of vibrancy to your text, images, or multimedia by applying color. However, be certain that the color reinforces the consistent look and feel of your layout and content and works with the principles and elements you are already using in your designs.

Now you are armed with the theory behind color and should understand the three primary variables: *contrast, harmony, and distinction,* which help you use color in a distinctive manner on the web.

The most obvious color-related variable is contrast, because it allows you to differentiate among background, foreground, and elements that comprise your content and thus its visibility. For an object on your page to be visible, you need to establish a solid level of contrast between the object and the space around it. The more contrast you have, the stronger the lines separating your objects. As an example, yellow text on a white background is much harder to read than black text on a white background. Color wheels can help you evaluate contrasts.

Tip

Applying a high level of contrast to text may reduce the distinction, and therefore attention, that other parts of the page wield. In addition, if the text has a low level of contrast, the words may be hard to read. Achieving the right level of contrast is a balancing act that designers must consider.

Harmony relates to the way color interacts with the visible objects on the screen. As with everything in distinctive design, an immediate need exists to ensure that content requiring visibility gets bold, distinctive, vivid colors so that it stands out. And, of course, lesser content should "fade" with a lower contrast. Maintaining this balance requires a keen eye to avoid overcooking the most dominant colors, because if everything becomes too vibrant, the emphasis may be neutralized.

Creating distinction with color is a pretty cool technique! Not only do you have a wide range of choices, but also, the sky really is the limit on how you reflect your text and images through vivid visual representations on the screen. Color is central to everything you host on the web, and your site will be boring without it. Mixing colors, contrast, and harmony gives you many choices for making your design distinctive.

Compatibility with colors

You can use the core principles of color, balance, distinction, and contrast to make your layouts unique and different. The final aspect of color that you need to understand, however, is *compatibility,* and it can ultimately affect how you use color in your design. Perhaps you'd love to use colors without question and implement them with little more than a dash of code, but the compatibility issue (as with many web features) rears its ugly head again!

As technology has evolved, so has the computer's capability to render an ever-increasing array of colors on desktops and handheld screens. Some time ago, the average monitor could render only black and white. At one time, PCs could render a maximum of 216 colors (although computers could actually display 256 colors, some color space was reserved by the operating system to avoid dithering). However, as various computer platforms evolved, it became necessary to develop a set of universal colors, referred to as *web-safe colors*. The web has evolved around the need to cater to less advanced technology, and so the need to be *web-safe* with color choices has also emerged. Figure 4-30 shows the spectrum of color choices between old and new.

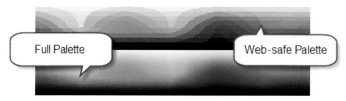

FIGURE 4-30: This before and after shot underpins the depth of color you can now use.

Plenty of users still employ old hardware, and a number of people want to access the web using their limited technology. So, when you apply color to your site, be sure that a limited color palette won't get in the way of readability, checking that non-safe color usage won't affect the visitor! The practice of using only web-safe colors (or just using black and white) has mostly died out. Using the more expansive web-smart palette (4,096 colors) or having your color schemes gracefully degrade should be a more acceptable compromise.

Of course, hardware isn't the only problem. Human vision can also be a tricky issue, which can affect how distinctive your content will appear when you use color. The first example to examine is the concept of "clashing." This primarily occurs when complementary colors are placed next to each other in their most vibrant state or when discordant clashing colors are mixed together — the result can be quite shocking. Figure 4-31 not only highlights clashing, but also the need for strong, stable contrasting color.

FIGURE 4-31: If your eyes don't hurt when seeing this on a screen, you might be superhuman.

These breakdowns in visual harmony result in what is commonly known as fatigue clashing, color discord, or vibrating boundaries, where the two clashing colors are seemingly trying to force their attention on the user (both at the same time), causing visual disturbance (that hurts your eyes). Figure 4-32 shows an example of visual distortion. All things considered, avoid all types of visual clashing on the web.

FIGURE 4-32: Stare at the image for about 30 seconds, and then look at a white sheet of paper!

The case of fatigue clashing is interesting because exposure to the colors for a long period of time (staring at the image or text) and then navigating away to a blank page leaves a residue in your vision, and you may see a phantom outline of the image. This effect is mainly a result of your vision being fatigued by the hue's persistence, and the lengthy exposure forces your vision to adjust. (This effect is only temporary, but it's not helpful to the eyes if you need to read a long page, because the phantom can affect legibility.)

Another example of how vision can distort your perception of color (and this is of particular relevance to distinctive design) is a common disability, colorblindness. Colorblindness affects a fair proportion of the population. Those with this usually genetic deficiency cannot distinguish between certain hues or colors. In such cases, color becomes less important than contrast. Colorblindness affects not only the ability to see all color, it can also limit a person's ability to see certain variants entirely, such as red, green, and blue deficiencies, as well as reduce color perceptiveness to varying states (see Figure 4-33).

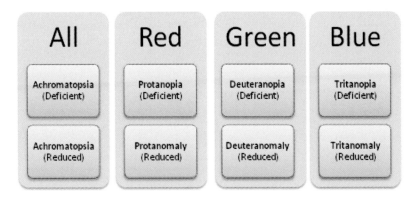

FIGURE 4-33: This graph highlights the eight different variants of colorblindness.

Although catering to this type of audience is important, problems usually occur when low-contrast colors are placed together, meaning that people who can't differentiate between certain shades will be unable to physically see the change on-screen. If you have red text against a green background, some individuals may be unable to read or perceive that any content exists in that location, which isn't great for distinctive designing.

Reference   Testing a website for colorblind-friendliness requires a little bit of mechanical help (most people can't simply filter out or diffuse the red, green, and blue on their screen without difficulty). This site may be just what you're looking for: `http://colorfilter.wickline.org/`.

Now that you understand the theoretical compatibility issues of color, it's time look at how implementing color on the web can affect distinction. You can use several forms of notation to reference an item's color or background color in CSS. The methods include named colors (by the W3C HTML color standard or x11 standard), the system color palette in use (although this is now deprecated and may not be supported), and the usual hex denotation (such as #FFFFFF) alongside RGB (CSS2) and HSL (CSS3, again if they are compatible with your browser) color models (with or without alpha transparency).

A couple of other color features worthy of note are *transparency* and *opacity*. A cool way to add layered color effects to your design is to fade less important content into the background (using partial opacity or transparency) and give content that requires distinction a 100-percent opaque appearance. The issue is that opacity and transparency both have browser compatibility issues, and older browsers may need extra code to ensure that it functions properly (but that can be achieved). When used correctly, transparency and opacity are great tools to help neutralize or enhance your content's visual perception.

Tip   Internet Explorer 6 supports only single-layer transparency levels (such as that in GIF files and PNGs set to 8-bit mode). If you want the full spectrum of alpha transparency in your designs (to give your work that extra special look), you'll require a hack or a better web browser!

Whichever model of color you use (notation, opacity or transparency), check that your color use is as consistent across web browsers as possible. Some browsers may not support CSS3 color functionality or the capability to use transparency like opacity, especially older browsers like IE6. Follow the same protocol as when you examined how the web has changed, and use whatever tools are at your disposal with care and attention. Your colors are only as distinctive as they are visible and supported. Although tools such as proprietary code can assist, they are not effective, long-term solutions.

The theory of color requires more than this book can cover, but the value you get from sensible color choices is worth the time and effort you initially invest. Color touches pretty much everything you throw onto a page, and your website designs will greatly benefit from its careful use. Part of being a designer is ensuring that your colors account for compatibility needs, and that they set the mood. Another part of the job is using this medium to provide a level of distinction and focus to the elements of your page that demand the immediate attention of site visitors.

Targeting Web Typography

Just as color has earned its place in the field of design, so typography deserves a place in the scope of important design aspects (you can also refer to Chapter 3 for my earlier comments on typography). This subject is often contested, with plenty of people willing to argue in its favor. Consider this: If up to 90 percent of the average site consists of text, then the art of portraying type onto a page is very important.

Some people dedicate their entire careers to this aspect of design, because the creation and implementation of type has not only existed for hundreds of years, but also it (like color) is one of those subjects with endless facets to explore. As designers, you aren't expected to know how to produce fonts, but you are responsible for the fonts you use on your site and how those choices affect a user's experience.

Tip

Typography isn't just limited to the text that appears in your source code; it also plays a role in any textual components of your images and even your videos (if you include such content in them). However typography appears, its presentation and substance are important for any website's purpose.

A lot of work and dedication are required to ensure that your content and copy is accessible, readable, and useful to the visitor. By employing all the factors discussed so far into your design, you increase the level of distinction and readability in your content by reducing the clutter on pages and making the useful bits ever more visible. It would be a shame if your efforts to write great material were wasted by presenting it poorly online. Enter distinctive typography, the artistic expression of words!

As with most things, distinctive typography is about paying attention to the small details that could snowball into a bigger problem. You owe it to your readers to avoid presenting something that diminishes their reading pleasure. By using the right font or style for the right job, you can improve readability, reduce complications of finding useful information, and ensure that your content is distinctive so that the content on the page becomes useful to your visitors.

Important Content is about communication, and your website represents the body language of your copy. If you don't put the effort into presenting your wares in a manner that is appropriate for the situation (such as users' needs) or you consider text as an afterthought, your mission for success may fail.

You can design and compose text in such a way that it becomes artistic. Many typefaces have visual flourishes and can emit feelings that influence the reader. Although designers are more restricted on the web than in other mediums with regard to how text can be visualized, the text that appears on your screen can be designed in a way to make your site appear unique.

Before moving into the fundamentals of typography, one recent trend in design has been to use nothing but fonts and perhaps a few splashes of color to forge a beautiful layout. It may seem strange that a site can survive without any imagery or media, but sometimes this subtle yet quite remarkable use of basic typography can become the crux and central focus of your work.

An anatomy of type

Often, the terms typeface and font are used interchangeably by designers, but these terms actually are distinct from one another. Keeping things simple (you can see visual examples in Figure 4-34 of these definitions), a *font* is a specific weight or style. If you consider the well-known typeface Arial, its font children include Arial Regular, Bold, Italic, Narrow, Black, and so on. You generally trigger the variants of typefaces by clicking bold or italic in your word processor, but they are different files (unless the system has to try to render it manually because no actual font variants exist).

A *typeface* is the name for a family or collection of fonts. Using the Arial typeface again, the word typeface applies to the collective of Arial Regular and its many fonts, such as Arial Bold. Another term that tends to trip many designers up is the word *glyph*. Inside a font, you find a range of characters, including representations of letters, numbers, and various symbols. These representations are referred to as glyphs (think of Egyptian hieroglyphs).

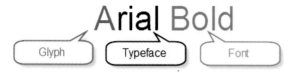

FIGURE 4-34: The difference between a typeface, font, and glyph can be showcased visually.

Browsers tend to render font styles and weights as defined by the system, so it's pretty safe in a web-specific scenario to use the terms font and typeface interchangeably. This is mainly because we reference fonts and typefaces in CSS by their family name (such as Arial). Designers should use the right names for them, but it will rarely affect your work.

Another important element of the typeface is its letterform. Every typeface has an anatomy (just like a human) that is made up of various parts, such as the ascender, descender, arm, counter, serif, stem, and stroke. Hundreds of names exist for the bits that make up a font, but the only part of the letterform that most designers need to be concerned with (apart from height references) is the serif, which relates to the use of font families.

Reference If you want to learn more about typeface anatomy, you can buy the Typography Manual at the Apple Store (it has the most detailed list your humble author has seen) via http://typographyapp.com/ or visit this site for a good, free guide: http://typedia.com/learn/only/anatomy-of-a-typeface/.

Typeface classification on the web is a pretty big deal. Matching similar looking fonts gives you the opportunity to provide fallbacks in case a visitor tries to load a page using a typeface that isn't installed on that user's device. All typefaces fall into one of a set number of categories that define their presentation and visual appearance onscreen.

The typeface classifications you encounter most frequently include sans serif, serif, monospace, cursive, and fantasy (see Figure 4-35). Because of their relative simplicity and readability, you'll probably end up using serif and sans-serif most often. Many sites like to style (in-page) code using a monospace font to give it distinction and character, and the cursive and fantasy families are best left alone (unless you know what you're doing!).

Monospace
Cursive Serif *Fantasy*
Sans-Serif

FIGURE 4-35: The difference in the styles and appearance of these typefaces is visible to the eye.

A longstanding debate exists among web designers as to whether serif or sans-serif should be used in body text — the bulk of your content. Some people believe that serifs help to emphasize the letters of small print, and others say that it just adds clutter and added complexity because there are fewer clean lines. Although there isn't a guaranteed solution to this debate, the recommended way to ensure your text's readability is to use trial and error. See what looks better to you.

Every situation is different on the web, and no "one size fits all" for the best font or classification. Most people shun the use of Comic Sans in general, because of its inappropriate and ubiquitous abuse throughout history! As you produce your designs, use fonts wisely and avoid abusing the life and emotion they bring to your content. Of course, you have plenty of other ways to maximize your typography and give your content added distinction.

Tip

A great way to decide between serif and sans serif is by sampling them. Using two identical versions of a page, apply a serif font in the body of one page and a sans-serif font in the body of the other one. Decide for yourself or test with users to determine which font works better.

Legibility is an important aspect of typography. Organizing your content into lines of text requires you to apply distinction. If you just paint your content onto the screen without structuring it in a way that people can negotiate, the text won't get as much attention as you want it to. Patchy and inconsistent applications of text won't give you the professional appeal that well-structured blocks of organized, effective content provide.

The capability to structure your content is important for ensuring that the text containers are distinctive and visible to the naked eye. One useful method you can use to form virtual grids around such content is the concept of *alignment*. The margins of space that define a reading area can be structured in many ways, and the components of your site can orient in a certain direction. If you left- or right-align your text, eyes will naturally rest in those margins. If you center-align content, the focus is drawn to the screen's midpoint. Left and right alignments cause text to fill to the left or right gutters (the left and right margins) of a page. With justification, the spaces between the words expand or compress so that the text spreads to the left and right gutters. Figure 4-36 points out these different alignments.

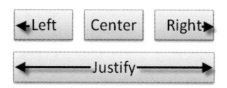

FIGURE 4-36: Aligning and justifying text alters its appearance (and potentially its location) onscreen.

If outlining your boxes by using blocks of text needs something a bit more substantial than simply drawing the eyes to a region on the screen, text justification can help. Because justification forces text to space itself between two margins, you don't get ragged edges; justification defines the outline of your text better and may be considered "cleaner" looking. However, justified type can create big, odd gaps (often called *rivers*) between the letters of a word or between words within sentences and paragraphs, so take that into consideration.

In addition to structure and text alignment, you need to consider distinctively visible scale and size elements. It doesn't take a rocket scientist to determine that larger text has more impact and emphasis than smaller text does. Consider scale in regulating how much visual control particular passages of text have on the screen (control gains essential status if small screens are involved). Headings are, for example, traditionally larger in scale than body text, acting as visual separators between content subjects and as focus points to draw targeted attention. The text size shown in Figure 4-37 holds more dominance than this paragraph.

Can You See Me?

FIGURE 4-37: Larger blocks of text like headings grab the visitor's attention before the body text.

Two additional ways to gain distinction through typography are spacing and indentation. As you may already be aware, white space is a useful asset in making your content distinctive. Giving your text some breathing room and avoiding cramming too much information together improves the readability of your material and gives users visual reference points to separate your paragraphs, headings, and other content.

Tip

The idea behind "breathing room" is to offer your readers an opportunity to pause in their current position and return to that section when they are ready. (Chapters in books are a great example.) The logical power of white space is that people use it almost like a bookmark for finding a breaking point.

The web offers a range of methods for adding spacing to your content, such as *margins* and *padding* (space between text and other elements on the screen). At this point, I will avoid the complexities of the CSS box model and just say that padding refers to any space between an object and its border (if it has one). For now, just note that the CSS box model defines how an object's scale is calculated (shown in a very rudimentary example in Figure 4-38). Margins, on the other hand, act as space from the border and its boundaries.

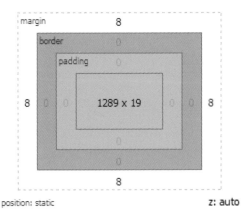

FIGURE 4-38: The "Box model" accounts for an object's dimensions, padding, margins, and borders.

The positioning and floatation of objects on a page can affect spacing, which can allow you to create equally positioned and well-defined spacing and overlapping or layered design features. Many designers use positioning and spacing, but they often forget that they can also indent text, limit the line length, or add word and letter spacing, as required.

At times you will not want to make the area around an object more distinctive which is what spacing does, by drawing focus from the space to the nearest object. You may, instead, want to apply emphasis directly to words, paragraphs, or aspects of a web design in order to force attention to them. Or you may want to give an object strength, perhaps with some careful outlining. However you go about the task of improving your typography, be as engaging as possible (see Figure 4-39).

Normal / **Bold** / *Italic* <u>Underline</u> / ~~Strike~~

FIGURE 4-39: Emphasis, strength, underlining, and strikethrough: all cogs in the distinctive machine!

Consider how much of your text looks identical; this can be frustrating if you want to pull attention to a particular part of a paragraph! One method of gaining that attention and attracting the user's eye is through the medium of color (for example, highlighting). Just remember that color use may be limited to (or by) certain users of your site. If you want a foolproof way to emphasize content, think about using the typographical conventions of bold (strong), italics (emphasis), underlining, and even striking through text!

Although using these "tools" to apply distinctive style to your text (from size to strength) can be helpful, it's important to realize that such conventions hold power only if you use them with constraint (recall the earlier subject of distinctive neutrality). Whether you design for the web, print, or another medium, using all your tools effectively makes good sense. Emphasis and strength are intended for visual effect.

Tip

If you plan on applying styles to your content, be sure that they don't conflict with anything that requires your attention. You don't want to lead visitors into thinking a visual reference signifies something it shouldn't (for example, an anchor link, by replicating the blue underlined effect).

The way you portray your text can have adverse effects on its readability. Using uppercase letters in all your text (see Figure 4-40) can seem like shouting, and although this may seem useful, if you want to shout, doing so may be deemed unprofessional. Coincidently, placing all initial letters of a word in uppercase has the effect of messing with a visitor's mental logic of pausing at assumed important words. As people visualize words based on shape, they are forced to pause and inspect those words independently.

TURN THE CAPS LOCK OFF

FIGURE 4-40: Using all caps (or uppercase letters) may be deemed a sign of abuse or shouting.

Web typography touches every page that you create and is one of the most useful arts that a designer can use. A few guidelines that may aid your decision-making include honoring content over the more than visual appearance (substance over style), always reading what you design to ensure legibility, and ensuring that what you design reflects your audience's needs and has been visualized in a way they can enjoy using.

Wonderfully web-safe

At this point, I'm sure you understand that compatibility is a huge part of web design. Because the web is such a dynamic and flexible medium, it also imposes limitations, which can create situations that users don't expect. Within design, you need to take such problems into account to ensure that your careful distinction plan works (and isn't lost because of some glitches). Unfortunately, on the web, with typography, the issues keep coming!

The first issue is the problem of being web-safe. Earlier in the chapter, you took a look at web-safe colors, where the issue was mainly restricted by the type of display used and the capabilities of an OS. Typography, on the other hand, depends on your browser and OS rather than on hardware. This issue arises because typefaces (unlike colors, which are standardized objects) are physical files requiring installation. So in order for browsers to use a particular typeface, it must exist on any computers being used.

Computers, and certain applications, come with a default set of typefaces known as *web-safe fonts,* some of which are shown in Table 4-1. You may think this provides some kind of standardization (in a way, it does), but the problem is that pretty much every font can be removed from a system by the end user. Reasons for doing this vary, but the potential for a font not being available is actually widespread, especially in less common typefaces (such as those you purchase or download on demand).

Table 4-1 Web-safe Typefaces

Font Family	Typeface
Serif	Baskerville, Big Caslon, Cambria, Cochin, Constantina, Didot, Georgia, Hoefler Text, New York, Palatino, Palatino Linotype, Times and Times New Roman
Sans-Serif	AppleGothic, Arial, Arial Black, Calibri, Candara, Corbel, Franklin Gothic Medium, Futura, Geneva, Helvetica, Helvetica Neue, Lucida Grande, Lucida Sans Unicode, Microsoft Sans-Serif, Monaco, Optima, Tahoma, Trebuchet MS and Verdana
Monospace	Andale Mono, Consolas, Courier, Courier New & Lucida Console
Cursive	Century Gothic, Comic Sans MS and Segoe UI
Fantasy	American Typewriter, Apple Symbols, Chalkboard, Copperplate, Herculanum, Impact, Marker Felt, Nyala, Papyrus, Segoe Script, Symbol, Webdings, Wingdings, Zapfino and Zapf Dingbats

As designers, you need to offer a layout with a relevant look and feel. With the potential for fonts not being available, you currently have two options. Either you can gracefully degrade your fonts using a *stack* (basically, a CSS font family containing a list of similar and increasingly common alternatives) or follow the dicey route of *type embedding* (which has other implementations and compatibility issues).

Font stacks

The font stack is the most compatible and widely used way to apply great typography in a design. You begin the stack, which is a list of typefaces, with the font you want to use, hoping your end users will also have the font installed on their computers. However, if your users don't have it installed, it's not a problem. The list includes a second, similar-looking font, followed by a web-safe alternative (or two) that the user's browser will be able to use. These alternatives include fonts like those that come with an OS or popular software products, such as Microsoft Office. An example of a font stack might include the font Candara, followed by Tahoma, and an alternative such as Geneva.

Reference Creating the perfect font stack has become a bit of a science. If you are feeling lost and need help picking the right typefaces, consider visiting either www. codestyle.org/servlets/FontStack or http://font-family.com/.

Every font stack should end with the font family it belongs to as a final note of compatibility — just in case all else fails. If failure occurs, the stack drops back to the system default, which you have no control over. Although the list of fonts considered as web-safe is fairly sparse, the stacking method gives you a chance to provide a similar (or fairly similar) experience to a greater number of visitors.

Embedding

Embedding occurs when you host a physical font and reference it within a font family using CSS3 (the @font-face selector produces the magic behind this code), as denoted within Figure 4-41. Doing so, however, comes with a lot of potential legal issues if you don't have distribution rights on a typeface (but foundries that make the typefaces we know and love are becoming friendlier about this practice). In addition, the embedding technique can vary according to the browsers being used (some need unique file types). Although currently not an ideal option until such issues are addressed, embedding is set to be "the future" of web typography, so don't rule it out entirely.

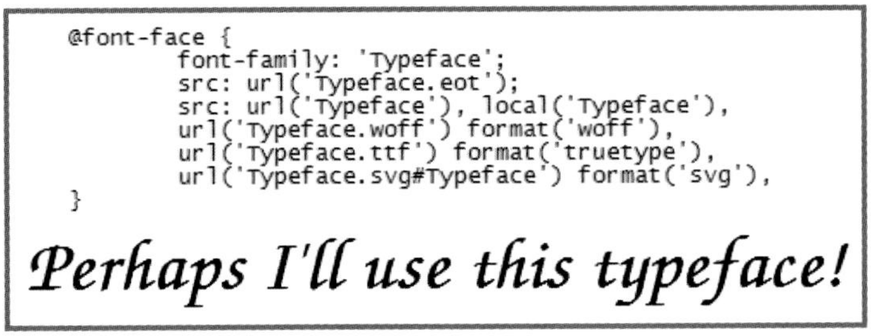

```
@font-face {
        font-family: 'Typeface';
        src: url('Typeface.eot');
        src: url('Typeface'), local('Typeface'),
    url('Typeface.woff') format('woff'),
    url('Typeface.ttf') format('truetype'),
    url('Typeface.svg#Typeface') format('svg'),
    }
```

Perhaps I'll use this typeface!

FIGURE 4-41: Using the CSS3 @font-face selector, you can embed any font you are licensed to use.

In addition to embedding, various techniques have been developed to offer a more compatible and equivalent method of viewing custom typefaces (through *font replacement*). These techniques may seem like ideal solutions, but they often rely on SVG, JavaScript, Flash, or other applications that end users can disable; they can also increase the stress to your site's rendering efforts (it's working with other materials, too). That said, font replacement techniques do the job and, more often than not, gracefully degrade when scripting or the required aid is disabled, so they can be simple, effective patches.

Following are a few common image replacement techniques:

> SIFR (Scalable Inman Flash Replacement)

> FLIR (Face Lift Image Replacement)

> Cufón (Mixture of scripting, SVG, and VML)

> Typeface.js (Script Powered Replacement)

As though compatibility (and the availability of fonts) isn't enough concern in regard to the use of cool and expressive typefaces, another issue recently appeared right at the forefront of font rendering — the problem of *font smoothing*. Anti-aliasing, or *rasterization*, acts as a mechanism for minimizing distortion, smoothing or softening the physical appearance of text to make it easier to read on a monitor.

Because anti-aliasing aids the legibility of text, its usefulness is without question. Compatibility problems occur when visitors try to view rasterized (scalable) typefaces with their default font-smoothing technology turned off or unavailable. In Windows, for example, the default anti-aliasing solution, ClearType, may not be enabled by default, which means some visitors using Windows may suffer illegible text full of jagged edges! Figure 4-42 shows a basic example of before anti-aliasing and after anti-aliasing, although be forewarned that the effects can actually be worse than shown in this example!

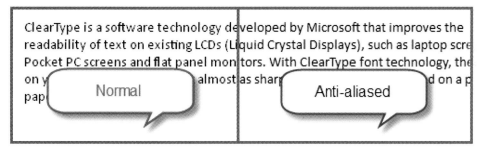

FIGURE 4-42: Anti-aliasing smoothes the typeface into something more readable.

As it stands, Safari is among the few browsers to contain its own anti-aliasing method for font smoothing. Although this capability may seem like a good thing, because each anti-aliasing method has its own standard for smoothing and means of undertaking rasterization, text usually ends up appearing different, depending on how a visitor consumes the medium. How do you avoid such an issue? Unfortunately, you must either avoid fonts using this kind of aid or use them and hope everyone's anti-aliasing mechanism is turned on.

Units of Scale

The final issue needing attention is the problem of *scale*. CSS provides useful measurement units to control how large and distinctive your text becomes, but some units are better suited to the web than others. Because the web is a dynamic medium, layouts relying on fixed physical units aren't going to help much. Although included within the CSS specification, some units of measurement are best suited for use within your print-friendly stylesheets! The CSS specification provides more detail on the meaning of each unit's value, but for ease of reading, Figure 4-43 divides the units into three categories. You'll need to know these units as you code!

Web	Print	Other
• %	• PX	• DEG
• EM	• IN	• GRAD
• EX	• CM	• RAD
• REM	• MM	• TURN
• VW	• PT	• MS
• VH	• PC	• Hz
• VM		• kHz
• CH		

FIGURE 4-43: The best unit of measurement depends on the output medium it's being used on.

The unit of measurement you choose depicts the flexibility of your design. In addition to the issues of fixed physical units, you also need to avoid using the PX or pixel unit on text (though it's fine for use on things such as images that have specific and static dimensions). Letting users resize text within a browser can give people with vision difficulties a way to make your content visible; unfortunately, the "text resize" menu in Internet Explorer refuses to scale PX-measured text.

Important Zoom isn't affected by the PX unit factor in the various incarnations of Microsoft Internet Explorer, but it's worth highlighting that Internet Explorer 6 doesn't support zooming at all. Therefore, if you want to ensure compatibility, don't use PX for text (it lacks alternative options).

Summary

Distinctive design has many facets, and it's critical that designers know how these essential components come together to produce the final result that visitors see on-screen. By applying the elements, principles, and theories of design (including color and typography), you can optimize your site's appeal to a user's requirements. There's nothing like having a beautiful, polished layout, so consider how design can help the distinctive experience.

Design includes as much theory as practice. People spend plenty of time thinking about what does and doesn't look good, what's accessible, and what's just plain annoying. When placed on the web, a whole exciting array of design options are presented (designers are spoiled when it comes to choices). But with so much variety, it's the hard work and energy you put into building your unique designs that gives you something in return. Your aesthetics are important, so don't let them be wasted; make them distinctive.

Part III

Implementing Design Theory

Introducing Design Psychology

Understanding how design influences the human mind

DISTINCTIVE DESIGN IS more than just an art; it's a science that has gained widespread recognition, accounting for and acknowledging fields such as psychology, which influences every page and every user who takes advantage of our services. Users interact with your services. Sometimes, users behave irrationally and erratically when negotiating a site's structure, and understanding how they think, react, and feel is as central to design as is the creation of content. Without knowing your users, you cannot hope to design for them.

In this chapter, I underline how behavior affects users' perceptions of sites, examining how ethics come into play and how you can responsibly produce safe, objective, unbiased layouts that don't inhibit users. You also read about aspects of psychology, such as the nature versus nurture debate, and the two conditioning models (classical and operant). Then you examine user emotions and expectations, the psychology of color and type, and information on empathy and empowerment. Finally, I round off the chapter by having you look at the Gestalt theory, perception theories, and how memory plays a central role in the ability to engage with a site's core layout.

Of Ethics and Objectivity

Given the range of design theories and elements covered in earlier chapters, it's important to note that a design exists far beyond the confines of what may be physically attached to a page. Your work may be composed of cool objects, awesome code, and a bit of magic, but a design means nothing unless the user connects with the material, understands its context, and behaves in a way that responds to such needs. Your work needs to use some psychology!

The idea behind using design psychology may seem obscure, but this science focuses on understanding human behavior, which matches the aim of designers! You try to match your designs to your audience's expectations (and keep the path as smooth as possible), yet without knowing how visitors will react or perceive your work, you have no hope of achieving such objectives. Understanding how visitors are likely to act (or react) and make decisions allows designers to provide the optimum experience in which barriers to entry are minimized. An example of manipulating decision-making — design psychology — is shown in Figure 5-1.

> Click me! You know you want to!

FIGURE 5-1: Impulsive people may be willing to click a mystery button just to see its consequences.

The goals of distinctive design are to be noticed in the right kinds of ways and to lead users in the right direction (which can be tricky if there are distractions). You need to leverage users' behaviors in a way that causes them to subconsciously go through the paths you set and reach the destination you intend (instead of using blatant and hard-hitting messages that create a "spammy" impression).

Important Note that psychology covers a broader range of fields than this book includes. Because the web is such a diverse and interactive medium, don't underestimate the implications of behavior, interaction, and memory within your projects. The human mind is complex, and as a designer, it's your job to try and promote the behavior you like.

Attention goes hand-in-hand with distinction, but it's worth highlighting that sometimes the distinction can be just as effective when done without going over the top. If this subject were to have a motto, it would be "distinction in moderation!" Sometimes in an effort to get a user's attention, designers can get a bit crazy with the over-engineering or crudeness of their site's layouts. Be responsible and (if needed) conservative with your design choices.

Important Because psychology (as a subject) delves into users' minds, you must tread with caution. As a professional, it's your responsibility to ensure that you produce nothing that may harm your users. Manipulating users without regard to ethics will surely guarantee that any trust or hope of success will fly out the window. Psychology is a powerful tool that can give you some useful insights, but as a web engineer (of sorts), you need to remain objective and ethical in how you practice. This message also applies to every aspect of the work you undertake.

Designing responsibly

Because psychology has the power to influence people and alter their perceptions, highlighting a designer's responsibilities is important. To start, don't put people off by toying with their emotions in your design (although you can use psychological techniques to help visitors), and be aware of potential abuses. Even if you don't actively employ psychology, your designs can affect a visitor's behavior. In fact, in many ways, it's nearly impossible to entirely avoid influencing behavior.

The first aspect worthy of your attention is the responsibility of practicing design ethically and morally. Although manipulating users into doing something may seem like a good idea, you need to carefully consider your implementations. If you decide to place something on a page, first determine whether it's justifiable and ethical and if it's worth any potential downsides.

Important   A lot of vulnerable people have access to the web. Although no strict ethics exist on what marketing techniques or influences you can employ within a website, strive to be as transparent and trustworthy as possible. You will become more trustworthy as a result.

Manipulation, trickery, and trust-breaking unfortunately occur regularly online. The dangers of such "radioactive" (making people glow with anger) design such as pop-ups, deceptive advertising, spam, and so on are profound. Without trust, visitors will abandon you for your competitors (or become one), or they may trash your brand on review sites, articles, blogs, or social networks, which could result in the loss of repeat customers and sales.

A poor reputation can destroy a venture or business overnight, which, of course, you want to avoid. One of the critical aspects of the web, related to trust among users and providers of a service, is the controversial issue of privacy. You want to gather information only on a need-to-know basis because if users don't feel they can trust you, they'll stop spending time on your site.

Tip   Distinctive websites always do things in moderation. Never force people to hand over information in order to access certain pages of a website (unless payment is part of your system). If people aren't willing to pay the price, your content loses its value.

Another aspect worthy of mention is the need for control or constraint over your users. Because site content is openly accessible to the world, many designers want to control or enforce a strict viewing experience. Whether through trying to prevent content theft or attempting "pixel perfection," the ability to enforce control over a user's setup is neither desirable nor possible. It simply cannot be done!

Your visitors ultimately have some power over you in that they can always choose to leave your site and look elsewhere for what they want, so it's important to be fully transparent with your practices and to avoid undermining users (in their choices, their rights, or their ability to access your services). As a designer, you have a responsibility both to any clients for whom you design a site, as well as to their visitors. Honor this role.

Keeping your concepts clinical

Decisions you make and the rules you enforce on users directly affect their willingness to return to a site and discover your wonderful content and to continue browsing to find it. A distinctive design will encourage visitors to continue browsing and will allow them to follow the trail and use their knowledge and skills to easily flow among pages. Be scientific and methodical with your approach, and always try to look at every situation from both sides.

Two primary aspects of design can influence how psychology aids your methodology: subjectivity and objectivity (see Figure 5-2). *Subjectivity* means looking at things from your own perspective and is thereby open to bias, yet many people rely on subjectivity as the determining factor. *Objectivity* in design means totally removing yourself from the picture and focusing purely on the collective needs of an audience.

FIGURE 5-2: Subjectivity and objectivity influence the decision-making process on many levels.

As you produce your sites and take into account all of the theory and practical applications of design, you will base many decisions — such as what language to use, how visuals should look, and what content to write — on your own observations and ideals about what you want on the page. This is subjectivity in action, and as you create websites, this subjectivity can give the sites a sense of identity, personality, and uniqueness.

Of course, subjectivity can be a bad thing, too. Because people have their own ideas about what works and what doesn't (what looks attractive and what looks garish), at some point, your own biases toward particular styles or techniques may hinder your distinctive design. Yes, it's important to express yourself in the design, but it's more important for those using your site on a regular basis to feel as connected to the finished product as you do, in terms of both authority and the feeling of being in control.

Important If you have an important decision to make, subjectivity and objectivity can become tricky because you want to do what's best for those who use the site. As a designer, you may want to conduct a series of tests, opinion polls, or other type of research to ensure that the decision and outcome are the ones that best serve your users' needs.

To ensure that your expression, creativity, and ideas don't hamper the design's capability to function and be used, follow the principles of objectivity. At its core, objectivity simply asks you to place your perceptions or assumptions aside as you consider what's measurable or factually accountable. For example, don't assume that your visitors are a certain age unless you can back that up with facts. Keep your mind wide open and don't jump to conclusions or form inaccurate opinions about users.

Keeping your site as clinical as a doctor's office will be time-consuming and may not even yield conclusive results, so it's not a tool to deploy in every scenario. But having a good mixture of subjectivity and objectivity to cover the basics should hold you in good stead with your site's users.

Developmental Behavior

Among the many aspects of psychology that influence your designs, the study of how humans behave within a digital environment plays one of the biggest roles. The study of memory and emotion has its part in the scenario, and the ability to leverage a visitor's natural instincts toward becoming a customer is powerful. Encouraging certain behavior traits has always been a controversial subject, but because everyone is influenced by design, it makes sense to ensure that you encourage the right kinds of behavior from the start.

Tip

A classic case of behavior at work in design is the fight-or-flight mechanism. When someone encounters an issue with your service, the natural instinct is to either give up (flight) or struggle on (fight).

Interestingly, the power and influence of a design and how it's perceived depends on a number of variables. You can find some of these variables in Bonus Chapter 2 in the companion e-book (namely accessibility and sociology, which includes group behavior dynamics), but right here and now, follow how your visitors (as individuals) may associate with the layout put in front of them. Think of this relationship between each unique user and your site as an *evolutionary* dynamic.

Following are a few aspects of personality that can influence design effectiveness:

> Openness to experience (conformist, independent, or practical)

> Conscientiousness (careful, compulsive, careless, or disciplined)

> Sociability (extrovert, introvert, privacy aware, reserved, or interactive)

> Agreeableness (trusting, suspicious, skeptical, or vulnerable)

> Neuroticism (calm, anxious, self-satisfied, secure, or paranoid)

The extent to which you can influence your visitors depends on a variety of factors, and there are no guarantees that your behavioral aids will get any visitor attention. People react differently to stimuli. Unlike the principles and variables of design, this science is harder to measure, and perhaps more importantly, you don't have a golden rule to continually follow.

The value of design is reflected in what you offer and how you portray that information. The study of behavior allows you to better understand your users and to make choices based on empirical research from which users can benefit. Essentially, your visitors make the final decision, and no amount of psychology can force your users to do something they don't want to do. But you can play on visitor expectations and habits to make their experience better.

Using nature and nurture in design

To better understand how your users evolve their patterns of site browsing (they behave according to what they know), examine the nature versus nurture theory. This fierce debate puts forward two perspectives in an attempt to calculate the relative influence of someone's inherited qualities (nature) versus the role of personal experience (nurture) on his or her behavior. Although it's likely to be a mixture of both, the concept of learned versus inherited behavior affects the way your design may be consumed or appreciated.

The idea that nature and biology can influence human behavior is best showcased through inheritance. Genetic characteristics are passed from parent to child. It's also well known that some behavioral characteristics may be passed on (such as vulnerability to depression). Of course, a child may learn to use technology to overcome challenges of an inherited disability (for example, see Figure 5-3). Inherited characteristics can influence or affect individuals' online behavior (for example, having depression may reduce enjoyment or fulfillment from participation in online activities). So consider these issues and how you can reduce negative effects (for example, if you put visitors at ease and don't aggravate them, their anxiety may be reduced).

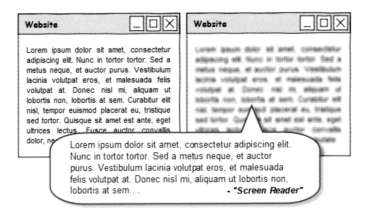

FIGURE 5-3: People who suffer blindness interact with sites differently than people with sight.

The case for nurture follows a similar pattern of pinning behavior on a specific influence; however, in this case, I'm talking about outside influences rather than inherited ones. Although you can do little as a designer to reduce inherited behavior, you can help nurture visitors by influencing their decisions using aids such as engaging content, useful navigation menus, and product tours. Figure 5-4 shows a product tour in the form of an online video, which gives individuals an opportunity to learn how to use a service through a particular method.

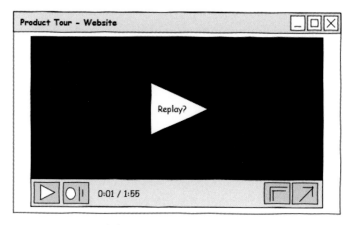

FIGURE 5-4: To nurture behavior, provide the right kinds of tools such as a learning aid.

Generally speaking, in terms of web use, the balance between nature and nurture isn't equal (using a computer is an act of nurture). However, the two perspectives can directly affect individual perceptions of your sites, as well as affect users' characteristics in a way that influences their use and interactions with your sites. In a nutshell, every person is unique and can be influenced differently by your decisions, so consider those choices carefully.

Tip

Although many of your users may have something in common (such as enjoying your content), don't perceive them as being too similar. Every person has his or her own style when browsing the web, so don't take their relative uniqueness for granted. What may work well for one person could be hell on earth for another!

Your ability to change perceptions, opinions, or even your content in a way that gives your visitors the best opportunity to find what they are looking for is limited. In fact, designers often introduce features to a site in the hope that it will attract a certain type of person, only to find that it occasionally misfires. You cannot get inside your visitors' heads and view the world entirely through their eyes, and the closest thing you have to *reactive design* is through research and constant vigilance (reactive design means changing appearance based on behavior).

Users will behave differently based on previous sites visited, technologies used, and familiarity with the tools that they interact with (such as browsers). Certain tools may confuse some visitors, whereas other visitors will be able to use whatever is provided with ease. All things considered, measuring user behavior is a tricky goal (studying usability trends can help). Consider how people may react with your site and its functionality and ensure that the site complies with their needs. Doing so will help you remain ahead of competing services.

Conditioning user behavior

Behavior has many facets, and as a designer, you need to guide people to making the right decisions, decisions that will serve their best interests. Although additional methodologies exist, the methods mentioned in this section have simple but useful practical applications within design that can enhance the goal of influencing users and training them within a beautifully designed environment. Two primary methods are used within psychology to challenge behavior, if not change it successfully: classical conditioning and operant conditioning.

Although often viewed in a negative light (such as peer pressure, for example), situational conformity and simply following trends (see Figure 5-5), patterns, and conventions can be beneficial. Your ability to change a visitor's attitude on a particular subject is the primary aim of a site (you want to sell a product or a concept). If trends are established and followed, your interfaces become self-explanatory and the design will guide user behavior, irrespective of the content, while meeting user expectations. So encouraging users to follow accepted routines isn't a bad thing!

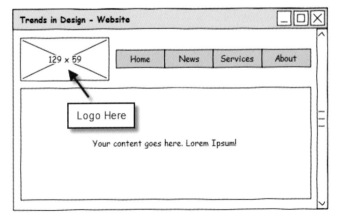

FIGURE 5-5: People expect to see logos at the top of a site. Trend expectations are a type of conformity.

The aim of this behavioral engineering ideology is to get users to conform to a practice that makes their browsing experience easier. The two primary ways of encouraging a user to follow such roles are *classical* and *operant* conditioning. In both cases, the aim is to implant predictable behavior that can be measured as a response to the stimuli provided. However, you must acknowledge that outside influences may challenge both.

Classical conditioning

In classical conditioning, you try to evoke a natural reaction from visitors so they respond to specific events. When regularly exposed to an event, people associate and perceive the two variables as related. An example of this is a pop-up window. Because of the amount of spam received through pop-ups, many people have developed the automatic response that all pop-ups are bad, closing unexpected ones without viewing their contents.

Tip

The best way to leverage classical conditioning is to make your site take advantage of preexisting learned or natural responses. Teaching users to act in an unnatural way takes more effort and time than relying on a previously built behavior pattern.

One popular method of implementing classical conditioning (at a functional level) is through the stimulus response, or its opposing position, the stimulus-stimulus, theory. At their core, they focus on the basis of associating a stimulus (an action or object) with a response (or another action or object). A classic example in web design that people have become receptive to is the padlock icon located in a browser window's address bar (as a condition of safely navigating within a site); in effect, the padlock equals security.

As they're trained to recognize objects and associate them with features (such as RSS feeds, media players, and site maps — because they're routinely implemented in websites), people become sensitized and receptive to those objects. Figure 5-6 shows this free-form association in action. This sense of association is how fraudsters use fake warnings to trick people into installing malware. Users associate a warning with a good, helpful action, and by being receptive to its use, they may click the provided buttons and install the dangerous application.

FIGURE 5-6: If people see a button, their natural reaction is to expect an event to occur when they click it.

You can also desensitize people when you flood them with stimuli (such as Google ads). If too much stimuli is visible on a site, the stimuli loses its potency and psychological distinction, resulting in users ignoring it (Figure 5-7 shows an example). This is called the *zombie effect*. When shopping in a store with which you're familiar, you generally pay attention only to aisles stocked with what you want, losing touch with your overall surroundings. This works to your advantage when you need to achieve a goal quickly in a place you recognize. However, stores fight against this behavior by offering you new things to buy so you are forced to reassociate stock with locations.

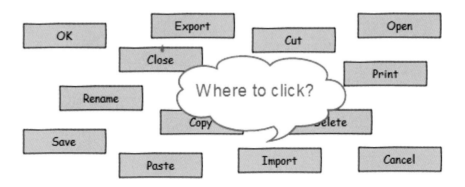

FIGURE 5-7: Too many buttons on a page make users less likely to click a button.

Operant conditioning

In operant conditioning, rather than focusing on changing primal behavior (as classical conditioning does), you aim to alter choice- or thought-based actions. You can modify voluntary behavior by providing or making visitors aware of consequences for doing things the right or wrong way, or by reinforcing a user's current behavior by adding or removing beneficial stimuli. This behavioral engineering is more direct and easier to implement on a site because you train a user's memory, rather than change their basic thought process.

An example of implementing operant conditioning within a site is to offer your regular members something free (such as an icon pack, e-book, or discount coupons). In this way, you motivate users to join a community and also encourage regular interaction to ensure eligibility. But the effects may wear off once the promotion is no longer employed.

The two primary methods to achieve operant conditioning are through reward and punishment, and the theory of *reinforcement* (both *positive* and *negative*). Reinforcing behavior is preferential to reward and punishment in producing long-term results. While rewards (see Figure 5-8) and punishments give quick results, they can have serious side effects on user expectations. Rewards and punishments usually result in a temporary shift in a user's behavior because the incentive to behave in a certain way disappears when the justifications end. When applying this method to distinctive design, promoting good actions and avoiding punishing mistakes is considered the better practice.

FIGURE 5-8: Giving users a list of benefits could alter their decision about joining a community.

Rewarding users gives them a temporary feeling of satisfaction (such as offering a one-off deal on the site), but such brand loyalty will eventually expire. Punishing users also has a temporary effect; it may discourage interaction and encourage complaints, or it may hurt feelings (even causing you to lose customers), but the effect usually wears off (unless someone holds a grudge, which can happen online!). If you want a good, lasting impact on users of your site, avoid short-term deterrents or incentives, and reinforce consistent behavior instead!

Visitors hold a lot of power over a business's reputation, especially when it comes to the web. Consider punishment only as a last resort — for example, if a user's actions are harming the entire community by doing something like hacking.

Reinforcement is the ideal method if you want your design to have a lasting behavioral effect on your visitors. Rewards and punishments offer some quick and dramatic results; reinforcement differs by offering or taking away something, so the effect will be beneficial to a user's long-term behavior. For example, offering visitors a way to contact you is positive reinforcement and may encourage them to purchase from your site (if you respond). Giving visitors a strongly worded notification that they require a password to enter a member's area is negative reinforcement. Simple!

Emotional and Influential

Distinctive design is a methodology that focuses a great deal on implementation as well as the motivation behind the choices we make. People's behavior can take form based on preconceived practices or perceptions taught over a lifetime, such as how to use or navigate a site. Every site users visit will have some influence on their assumptions and requirements for yours. For example, if users spend time on Amazon, they may find Craigslist a stark contrast. The web is joined at every level, and your job is to match associated experiences with a well-rounded, recognizable interface.

Reinforcing good behavior and helping people avoid making mistakes is part of your job in creating a good interface. In distinctive design, if you don't provide relevant details to help your site's visitors make appropriate choices, then you risk leaving them in the dark and unable to browse your site (which could mean important pages are lost). High-quality content and a well-produced aesthetic can help your site, and wielding these behavioral tools can, too.

Tip The behavior of a website should not be exempt from the confines of psychology. Just as you must conform to the restrictions of your user interfaces, so a site must conform to user expectations. Treat your site like a person and consider how it expresses itself!

Of course, not everything that's related to the psychology of design is associated with actions that result from human behavior. People's emotions and their ability to empathize with others by drawing upon previous experiences also play a role in distinctive design. Giving your titles a large font and bold weight makes it appear visually distinctive, but the way you emote a feeling or show images, by association, has a powerful influence on users, too. If your content emits feelings of happiness, users may be more receptive to influence. In contrast, users who suffer negative feelings toward a design may reject conditions of usage. Table 5-1 describes types of positive and negative emotions.

Table 5-1 Emotions Can Influence Perception

Type	Emotion
Positive	Affection, appreciation, attachment, awe, craving, compassion, curiosity, desire, ecstasy, enjoyment, empathy, envy, euphoria, gratitude, happiness, hope, interest, kindness, love, lust, passion, pleasure, pride, respect, satisfaction, surprise, and wonder
Negative	Aggression, anger, angst, annoyance, anxiety, apathy, apprehension, awkwardness, betrayal, boredom, contempt, crises, denial, depression, despair, disappointment, disgust, distress, distrust, embarrassment, fatigue, fear, frustration, grief, guilt, hate, helplessness, horror, hostility, hysteria, jealousy, misery, pain, paranoia, pity, rage, regret, rejection, remorse, resentment, sadness, shame, shock, shyness, sorrow, stress, terror, tiredness, dissatisfaction, and worry

Emotion affects people in many different ways. And, ironically, the feelings they possess can affect their behavior and even to a certain extent their physical abilities. People sometimes may suffer stress, which makes them more likely to give up on a particular task. In another example, anger could make them less patient, lowering their sociability (and increasing their awareness of small quirks). Considering your visitors' emotions is an empathic job, and some may find it difficult, but it's part of the ethos of design.

A design that uses flashing content and vivid colors, for example, may heighten the heart rate or stress levels of an onlooker. Content that uses soft pastel colors, friendly images, and inviting content with positive language may act as a calming influence. Your site portrays its own body language, and if you give off the wrong impression or a design doesn't fit the purpose, you could alienate your audience (or increase the amount of negative emotions they suffer in a vicious cycle).

Color and type psychology

The influence of behavior and emotion within design has far reaching implications in how your distinctive designs will be perceived. Earlier chapters examine the value of color and typography within the process of building a distinctive design. Now, it's time to attach the use of color and typography to relevant aspects of psychology that guide it. If you didn't already know that psychology had its claws within color and typography, you'll now be waist deep in it!

The first aspect of psychology that lends itself to color is association. Color is a very rich material that has context and hidden meaning associated with it. Consider the color red. Most people associate it with passion, fire, blood, anger, or stopping. Users may associate the color yellow with a sunny day, a happy feeling, or a shiny image. You may associate blue with the sea or royalty (or a number of other things), and green is often correlated with wealth and being close to nature. Every color has a persona and evokes emotion. In Figure 5-9, you can see a few visual perceptions that can be associated with colors.

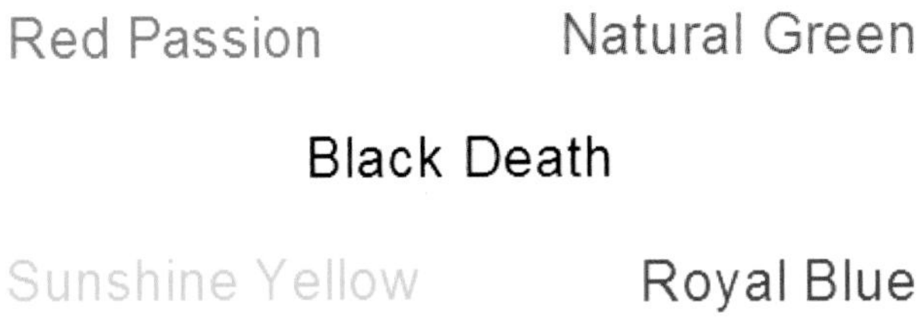

Red Passion   Natural Green

Black Death

Sunshine Yellow   Royal Blue

FIGURE 5-9: Color evokes emotion, and you can use it to invoke a certain emotional response.

Color means different things in different societies, so your choice of color may need to differ depending on your audience. Personality types, any meaningful associations to the visitor, and perhaps simple preferences can alter a visitor's favorite color choice or what that person deems suitable. If you want another fine example of color taking effect, use temperature. Often, blue emits a cool feeling (of things like ice), whereas red emits a hot feeling (for example, of fire). See Figure 5-10.

Hot Color   Neutral   Cold Color

FIGURE 5-10: Giving off an impression of temperature could be useful, for example, in a travel site!

The symbology of associating color with objects, temperatures, memories, or meanings is common throughout the world, and implementations may influence a user's perception of your site. If you use cartoony, vibrant colors, for example, people may not see the site as professional in comparison to one using white and silver corporate colors. If you use color in your website, consider how people might psychologically perceive your palette.

Note There are far too many cultural and global ideas about what color means to different people to mention in this book; however, one site does a great job of showcasing how people associate color with emotion: `www.sibagraphics.com/colour.php`.

If the influence of color and how users perceive it isn't enough, typography can also have a range of psychological impacts upon visitors. Consider the style of typography you use. A typeface such as Comic Sans may be perfect for children or some sketchy diagram (like those used in this book to give a sketchy contrast between things hand drawn and computer aided), but it won't emit a professional feel on a business site. Another example is the Impact font. It stands out by giving a feeling of strength, but it isn't suitable for subtle text. In fact, many fonts give off some kind of impression; Figure 5-11 shows a few examples.

FIGURE 5-11: Typography expresses emotion! If you don't believe it, check out these images.

The way that you use typography and color influence how people perceive your content and messages. Color could potentially influence the mood of your site's design (and its visitors), and using the right font stack could dramatically affect the visual emphasis, strength, personality, and other distinctive variables. If you want, for example, to reflect a soft and beautiful feeling, you could use a calligraphy font with a pastel pink color. For a feeling of passion and love, you could employ a smooth, elegant typeface with a fiery red color!

Empowering performances

Behavior may be an important part of understanding your design through the eyes of your users, but its critical function is to empower your visitors and let them achieve their goals by making your content as flexible, visible, and usable as possible. Empowering people gives them control over how your site is displayed or served to them, but you must keep an eye on visitor feedback and do some analysis to understand the problems they suffer.

Websites help people achieve their goals by giving them new information or offering them a useful public service. Distinctive design focuses heavily on aiding this philosophy by making content easier to read, navigation easier to browse, and by avoiding nasty surprises by playing to the visitor's behavior. This joint design and psychology effort aims to help users get the most from an experience and to improve your ability to serve them.

Tip

Without being patronizing, encouraging users on the page can be really successful in making a visitor want to return to the site regularly. Friendly messages on their progress through a purchase or within tutorials help visitors retain a sense of power and control. However, it's worth reinforcing that welcome messages are considered both wasteful and unnecessary by many users, and thereby aren't a welcome addition to a new website.

This is where Abraham Maslow's famous hierarchy of needs theory enters the picture (you can find a picture of this pyramid of human motivation and requirements at en.wikipedia.org/wiki/Maslow's_hierarchy_of_needs). Maslow's theory aims to describe the things every individual requires before being able to progress and move forward onto other needs (such as safety before self-esteem). Relating this to web design, you can attempt to help your users achieve a sense of growth, trust, and safety, which in turn makes people more willing to participate frequently and return or shop with you regularly.

Prioritizing your visitors' needs (or that of your website) is subjective and requires solid measurement and research to account for your visitors' own needs. Adapt your site to take advantage of the theories that may apply to your users. If you haven't already, start planning and testing! A website's hierarchy of needs differs from an individual's hierarchy. In Figure 5-12, you can see an example of what could arguably be a web equivalent.

If there's one skill within design psychology that will help you more than any other, it's the somewhat underrated but critically important emotional tool called *empathy*. Websites expect much from the average visitor (let alone the designer). Which pages people need to visit, where they find answers, how a new web app works, and many other factors get thrown into the cosmos daily. Knowing how your audience feels is central to this process. Without understanding users' needs, you cannot hope to succeed.

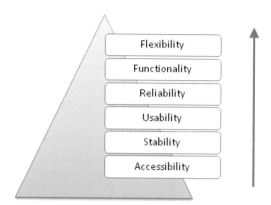

FIGURE 5-12: Users have a hierarchy of needs; if those needs aren't met, the site will fail them.

Empathy has a central role in design, because you build sites for your visitors, not for yourself. If you're the kind of designer who doesn't know what visitors need, ask them! But if you can sympathize and empathize with users and portray those emotions in your sites (even if it's just technical support), your skills can go a long way in building rapport with your clients. You could even become quite good at predicting, or even recognizing, behavioral or emotional quirks or trends in designs and be able to pass on that support to users.

Important

When (and if) you provide a method of contact in a site, be sure that you actively respond to users' requests for support or feedback. One of those users may uncover a design glitch that causes you to lose customers or that needs its distinction redefined. And if a user's mail remains unanswered, his or her trust in you may be reduced considerably.

The last things related to emotional design are the two theories (yep, more design theories) that can help your decision-making process: Hick's Law and performance load theory. *Hick's Law* describes the amount of time it takes for users to make decisions based on their available choices. Within design, this theory actively encourages applying a reductionist methodology to navigation menus (as an example of reducing user choice) so that decision-making is easier. Labeling the menu well also helps to aid recollection. Figure 5-13 illustrates how the more options users have, the more difficulty they face when making choices.

FIGURE 5-13: The more options you provide, the longer it takes users to make an informed decision.

Beyond clearing out unnecessary choices or options (be it links, text, or something else) to help people make decisions, also consider the theory of *performance load* in your designs. This theory states that the more effort required in undertaking a task, the less likely it'll be completed successfully. As you can imagine, this makes sense: Users can be fatigued by complex, annoying sites (think of when you've given up on a site), or layouts that implement overly complicated routines to get anywhere (like the left form in Figure 5-14).

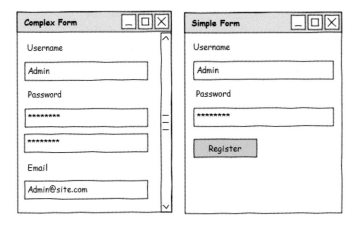

FIGURE 5-14: A complicated registration form is less likely to be filled in correctly than a simple one.

Empowerment and empathy are great tools to help your visitors accomplish certain tasks and goals. Such emotional design can be provided by tours that point people in a direction, by friendly reading material, or by the way you portray your design visually, thereby appealing to their sensitive side or triggering thoughts and feelings (good or bad). Design is subjective, and emotion is basically at the core of everything people do.

Cognition and Perception

Another aspect of psychology relating to distinctive design is based upon cognition and how human brains memorize distinctive, well-formatted content (and how they actually interpret and visualize that information). This aspect involves more design theories and elements (in Gestalt theory) that are just as prevalent as shape, texture, or lines. As with all theories, implement them when (or if) they become useful; just try to be as distinctive as possible.

The most obvious aspect of perception within distinctive design relating to cognition is a site's aesthetics. Putting it simply, people love pretty things. If you craft your site with the care and attention it deserves, you should have something pleasing to the eyes, which may encourage visitors to explore what else the site can do.

Tip

Personality guides the natural aesthetic. If your site looks beautiful but matches another in terms of its visuals, then yours will have less distinctive impact (thereby being less memorable in regard to individuality, but not so much perhaps in recognition) than one that is totally unique and quirky and that retains memorable, trendy eye candy.

Because so many designers put their time, money, and effort into the eye candy of a layout, the principle itself is a well-founded one. People associate professionalism online with the visuals or depth and technicality of content. Of course, just because a site has some good eye candy to catch new visitors doesn't mean the eye candy should appear without quality content. After all, content is king, and without it, a site won't impress!

People come into contact with new sites all of the time, and the exposure to this stimulus forces them to react and adapt their perceptions of a website's layout. By compromising and consistently adapting to different environments, your users can explore some of the most poorly designed websites (just with a little extra effort to achieve the goal). The human mind's ability to logically process what sits in front of it is remarkable.

Important

Associations are formed through memory, so if your site isn't distinctive enough to be memorable, then it won't likely become successful. Allowing users to invest time in customizing their experience (say, with a profile) could aid commitment to memory.

People learn by association, and they're perceptive to behavior, emotion, and their own cognitive functions. In this section, you explore elements that help reduce a design into digestible blocks. Although the idea of tapping into one's memories to use a site may seem invasive, the ability to recollect and use experiences from the past makes for adaptive, well-adjusted visitors (as they learn from what the web throws at them). Without cognition, the learning curve would be too much to take!

Gestalt and design theory

Although color and typography play their part in distinctive design, Gestalt theory (a branch of psychology) also needs to be acknowledged. This particular approach of design allows you to perceive the overall picture rather than the individual parts that comprise an object. Just like a movie requires more than actors (a director, producers, technicians, and others), you compose your site using a composition of multiple objects all working in harmony (at least, that's what you should be hoping for).

Gestalt theory works on the principle that a complete, working composition has more value than an object that remains in pieces. A completed jigsaw puzzle offers more than the its individual parts because the finished composition has a cool picture displayed upon it. Likewise, the *Mona Lisa* is a much more valuable object than the paints used to create it. Arranged properly (in a digital format), the Gestalt of your site adds value to your work.

Note Your project's Gestalt will be the website itself, composed of objects (and pages) all fitting together to engage the user with an experience. This literally meets the definition of a composition in which the whole is greater (has more value) than the sum of the individual parts (components).

Figure and ground

The first aspect of Gestalt theory is referred to as *figure and ground* (or the Prägnanz principle in design circles). The term refers to the weight of the item in the foreground (the central figure) against those items that fall to the background, yet still contribute to the overall effect of the picture. Consider a landscape painting: A figure standing in a field could qualify as the focal point, whereas the field gives ground value as the background. If you want a very simple example of this, see Figure 5-15.

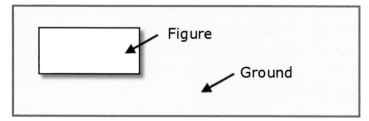

FIGURE 5-15: An object that is clearly visible against its surroundings (the ground) is called the figure.

This concept applies to design principally by the manner in which you construct a site. Designers regularly use a mixture of foreground and background images to add stylistic emphasis to page content. In addition, site visitors like to encounter an interconnected experience that ensures everything on the page flows correctly. If you've ever used a textured background to add to the impression or impact of a design, that's also figure and ground.

Similarity

Similarity is the next principle of Gestalt theory. This principle highlights the tendency for objects sharing characteristics such as shape or color to be compared and thought of as related when structured in close relation to one another. If you take, for example, a series of dots and place them next to each other (see Figure 5-16), the result almost forms a line that, while not directly interconnected, draws your attention and assumes that the relationship has meaning (such as, the dots equate to a completed line).

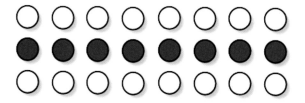

FIGURE 5-16: You can tell which items are similar because they share the same color and form a line.

In web design, similarity plays a critical role in transition among objects. As readers of a site regularly scan a page to find the content they desire, designers often tie certain types of information together using visual hints and similarity to make them easier to distinguish. This is why most sites group navigation menus close together and use similar shapes or sizes to strengthen their graphical relationship.

Tip

You can use several associations within scanning, including, but not limited to, a border around several objects (joining them with a visual ring fence), a background color or texture (associating them in a room), and space (giving proximity to other objects).

Proximity

The next Gestalt principle is *proximity*. It simply means that the closer the objects are to each other within a design or composition, the more likely they will be assumed to belong together (visually and psychologically). Scale within any composition is important, and the capability to order or structure objects within your page gives you the ability to influence how objects seemingly relate. In Figure 5-17, you can see how the dots appear to relate as they form a shape (from proximity). Perception of objects and how they interlink (or seem to interlink) can lead to distraction or confusion upon the page if you don't treat them properly.

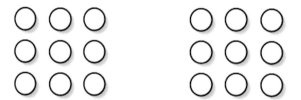

FIGURE 5-17: The items in this menu show they belong together because of their close proximity.

Take, for example, the case of a navigation menu. The reason items in a drop-down menu system appear to relate is because of their proximity to each other, and this is reinforced by the behavior of the menu items both appearing and disappearing in unison. You can control proximity through the use of block colors to separate objects, white space, and even through the use of shape (by containing menu items within a box), thereby improving the readability and relationship of your content.

Continuity

Although proximity plays its role in joining the physical space between objects, the principle of *continuity* focuses a user's attention on the object, thereby causing the brain to make assumptions about the form of shapes on the page and what actually comprises those objects. (Figure 5-18 shows the cognitive process of joining lined objects.) Humans try to relate objects on the page in the simplest way possible, letting them focus their attention on deciphering the object's visual context quickly. It's a straightforward mechanism that can be tricked into assuming it has multiple meanings (as you'd find in optical illusions).

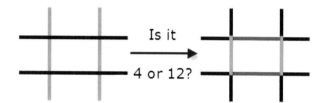

FIGURE 5-18: This may look like four lines interconnecting, but it could also be 12 lines!

If you see overlapping objects on the screen, you assume it to be a single shape made up of two adjoining lines rather than being made of four lines that connect in the middle. In reality, it could actually be either! Be mindful about how your shapes can be perceived on the web. If something looks like it's joined, people will naturally assume it is. Diagrams provided on your website may be wrongly interpreted if they aren't labeled effectively.

Note

This breaking down of visual information is almost like a cognitive form of reductionism. By making the weightier objects less complex, the brain can more quickly analyze the contents of the object and more quickly define it (or its value) by those characteristics. It's the brain's way of coping with lots of structure (and it actually helps in reading text).

Closure

Another psychological aspect of Gestalt theory is the principle of *closure*. Just as people mentally try to form shapes from interconnected objects in an attempt to reduce the complexity of information, they also try to fill in the gaps when part of an object is missing (if they can envision the shape being attempted). A cross made up of dots that don't join can still be perceived to be a cross (see Figure 5-19), even if information is absent and it's intended to be just dots, and nothing more. Isn't the human brain clever?

FIGURE 5-19: This showcases a cross made of dots and how closure aids human vision.

When designing a site, take advantage of closure to work on people's assumptions of object connectivity. Because the human mind naturally reacts to patterns that seem familiar, it has the ability to form an object using the existing sum of its parts. Have you ever stared at a cloud and noticed it looks similar to a certain object? This experience is similar, because your brain perceives an object based on the data available and tries to make sense of what's in front of you.

Area

Relating to the concepts of figure and ground is Gestalt's *area* theory. This principle of design states that if you have two objects, one small and one large, the smaller of the two will naturally assume the position as the figure (or foreground object) and the other one (if overlapping occurs) will default as the ground or surrounding element. Although this does give the impression of foreground objects being on top, color can reverse the effect, giving the perspective of a hole in the ground (as though something is missing rather than added). Figure 5-20 shows how area can be perceived either as addition or removal.

FIGURE 5-20: On the left, the square appears to overlap; on the right, it looks rather like a hole!

Relating this to design, CSS positioning allows you to alter the location and priority that objects on a page should hold (refer to Chapter 2 for more on CSS). If you use the CSS z-index property to overlap design elements, the effect of area theory could be met. When you use overlap, the relationship among the objects on the page appears to be carefully thought out. The effect of having an overlapping object draws your visitor's focus away from the intended target, which could affect a design's distinction.

Tip

Your ability to determine scale and position within design affects this principle. If you make use of fixed positioning within a design, the Gestalt theory will increase in its distinction because the object gains added attention by not moving with the scroll. This also gives an impression of the object overlapping (as other content usually appears under it).

Symmetry

Finally, consider the principle of *symmetry* in design. Overlapping objects can potentially draw focus away from the design, but it's also true that the act of obscuring elements of a design can manipulate the way the object is perceived on the page. Consider two circles (or rectangles in the case of Figure 5-21) overlapping; you could either notice it as a single shape formed of two objects or three very odd shapes! It's all about perspective.

FIGURE 5-21: Objects can be broken down by the number of shapes that can be formed from them.

You must consider the effect that objects have on each other (and how you can obtain harmony among them) if you're ever to understand how your designs will be perceived. If a conflict arises between two parts of a page, users become confused about what's being shown, which adds to the user's stress. If confusion occurs, spend time trying to untangle the mess. It's worth making your website's layout as clear as possible.

In many ways, Gestalt theory follows the similar force of reductionism, which concludes that by breaking down an object into smaller pieces, you can better understand the nature of the composition. The art of Gestalt theory in your design isn't simply that a site is built from a wide range of objects; it's that you should acknowledge every component that makes up your site, tweak the design until it looks perfect, and give pages added contextual value.

Cognition and perception

Perception is a critical part of cognitive function. It allows people to distinguish the many objects on a page and associate words or images with meaning. Additionally, it allows people to recognize what areas of the page are important and how an interface should be used, and it even plays a part in associating those visuals that play to emotions and memory. Without perception, users wouldn't be able to understand how to read your site.

Designers have to battle against various objects vying for attention (such as advertisements); therefore, a basic knowledge of how people perceive, see, or react to your pages and content for the first time is essential. A great number of factors can influence perceptions or people's ability to distinguish objects on the page (some previously examined), but a few deserve some added attention because they play a central role in distinctive design.

Important

Designers have the perceptual ability to determine how distinctive an object is, which plays a part in the whole design process. When people see an object that stands out, they value its level of attention based around the other visible objects on the page. This capability can also work against you, because knowing an object's function gives you a cognitive and visual advantage over your users (you may know what features do, but they may not).

Attractiveness bias

The first of the perceptive theories relating to web design is known as *attractiveness biased*. Although many people like to think it doesn't affect them, humans are naturally inclined to be more trusting or willing to pay attention to attractive objects or people. If you walk down a street and see an attractive person, you're more likely to gaze in his or her direction. When shopping, you're more likely to buy an attractive product. Aesthetics and visual beauty play a fundamental role in design and put people at ease.

Within the web, beauty does play its part, but just like in the real world, its uses are still limited. If you see an attractive website, you are less likely to navigate away immediately (the visuals will entice you into the environment). This makes your site more perceptive to those who may want to uncover more within your site (exposing your content). But this is where the benefits end, and it's also the reason why content is more important than design.

Tip

Sites built entirely using Flash (in particular) suffer from this problem. Although the issues of Flash aren't strictly limited to compatibility, sites that primarily function using the tool tend to gravitate toward using interactivity and visuals in preference to good, static content. This isn't to say that all Flash sites are bad (the same goes for other styles of design), but you must ensure that the eye candy isn't the only on-page value.

A beautiful site with no content is shallow and will have no redeeming qualities except as an inspiring work of art. Without substance to give your visitors a reason to return, your site is doomed. In a best-case scenario, aim for a mixture of a beautiful interface (to catch the user's eye) and great content (to entice them to visit again). As with the preceding analogy, you may feel inclined to talk to an attractive person, but if the person is boring and shallow, the relationship won't last. (It's a case of substance over style.)

The reading flow

The next theory is related to *flow*. People's eyes naturally move through a design based on their ability to scan and pick out areas of interest (and if you're creating a distinctive design, you should have great visual distinction within your pages). To aid this readability and to take advantage of the way eyes naturally glide and gravitate through a design, make use of flow patterns (for examples of the three most popular reading flows, see Figure 5-22).

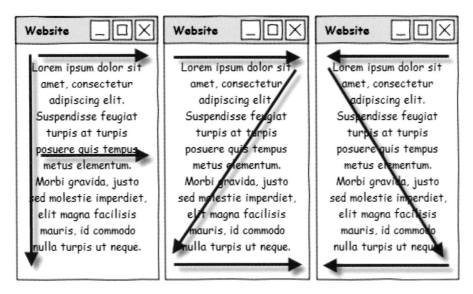

FIGURE 5-22: The most commonly accepted methods of flow or scanning are the F, Z, and S patterns.

At their core, flow patterns identify ways that people choose to read through a page (not only by reading across the page, but also how quickly they gravitate down a page and use scrolling). Much of this research has been based on eye-tracking studies and could be useful in your distinction goals. The first route eyes may take is the classic F pattern, which starts along the top, works down the left side, and then ends by scanning the middle.

The second flow pattern is the Z shape, which signifies the strict spanning of the top-left to top-right side and then veering diagonally through the page to repeat the effect at the base. The third of these patterns is the S shape, which mostly occurs in eastern nations where reading up to down is more common than left to right (consider it as the reverse Z pattern). Use of these patterns varies depending on the audience.

As a quick test, see how your site's distinctive elements hold up against this scrutiny. If you find any barriers that might visually conflict or block the scanning patterns, resolve the issue immediately. In order to make your site as efficient as possible and allow distinctive design elements to get attention, the reading flow should be clear of wasted energy or barriers that could break the visitor's concentration (a capital sin in regard to content readability).

Tip　As with all psychological perspectives, the theories behind them are subject to further testing, refinement, rejection, or acceptance. Don't qualify a particular perspective as factual unless you can be sure that the evidence supports that theory (in its context).

Cognitive dissonance

The final theory is *cognitive dissonance,* an uncomfortable feeling resulting from holding two conflicting ideas in equal regard. An example of how dissonance affects people can be demonstrated by how consumers purchase something but then feel the need to justify their actions about a product's functionality to satisfy an uncomfortable feeling that their purchase may not have been the ideal decision (commonly known as buyer's remorse).

When dissonance occurs, people naturally feel that they must deal with it. Some methods used to resolve such conflict include changing or altering beliefs (to fall in line with the constant variable), justifying one's actions, or even blaming and denial to remove the self-questioning that results from such conflicts. In design, this can be a particularly troublesome issue to contend with. Although you cannot directly prevent such problems from occurring, you can strengthen a user's justification for picking your products and services with good sales pitches, useful content, incentives, and prevention of any time-wasting.

Making memories

Memory and how human minds adapt to learning new things (and of course, how to use that lovely new website design you put together) is interesting. Memory is formed of both short-term (useful for small details that don't need to be permanently stored) and long-term (useful for information that needs to be recalled and stored over a long period of time) components.

Memory is based on experience and the ability to recall things you've seen, said, or done. As designers, you aim to produce memories and forge places of wonder that inspire and give your readers what they desire. You, therefore, have a responsibility not to overload your readers with too much information. The point at which a user is unable to cope with the level of content or detail (visual or otherwise) on-screen is called *cognitive load:* A breakdown of memory (or retention loss) occurs beyond a certain point.

Important
Stress plays an important role in memory, and its effects are profound. If people are stressed, they may find retaining thoughts or recalling events under pressure difficult (which is why exams are tricky)!

You can use several methods to reduce users' stress, and by doing so, help them to easily remember your content (memory under stress degrades). Rather than critique the abundance of content you usually find on a page or focus on how much can be remembered (it differs among subjects), a few principles can guide you to making your distinctive designs memorable. And if a user remembers your content, it gains distinction beyond the page!

The first method is to take advantage of devices known as *mnemonics*. These tools refer to any learning technique that aids a user's ability to memorize information. Common types of mnemonics in use on the web include *chunking* (grouping content in a way that makes it easier to recall) and *confirmation* (asking users to acknowledge a choice they have made, such as delete, thereby forcing them to at least pass a basic test to gauge attention).

Reference
Many techniques aid a visitor's memory. To learn more about mnemonics, check out the article at this site: `www.k8accesscenter.org/training_resources/Mnemonics.asp`, and to learn more about priming, visit: `http://en.wikipedia.org/wiki/Priming_(psychology)`.

The second method relies on a technique called *priming,* meaning to expose someone to something that will help him or her recall an event or object (for example, if you say the word "moo," the response is likely to be a cow). This type of suggestive memory aid prods existing knowledge to aid users. It's a useful tool in design (for example, using words like *site map* for navigation in which people may think of other maps that identify locations) because simplifying an association leads to faster recalls.

The final methods are based on two effects of design, accepted as helpful for making the information easier to recall. The first effect is called the *serial positioning effect*, which in basic terms states that the first and last items on a list are more memorable than those in the middle. This process (illustrated in Figure 5-23) makes sense because it involves the first thing you commit to memory, as well as the last thing you see on the page, which has a level of importance in and of itself.

FIGURE 5-23: The first and last items in a list hold the most natural distinction, so choose them wisely.

The second effect of memory (known as the *Von Restorff effect*) states that if something on a page stands out like a sore thumb, it's more likely to be remembered. This should interest you as a designer in particular because it's precisely what distinction is about. Without this effect, your content will not get attention (through the eyes or the memory). Humor, bizarreness, and oddity influence your work, tickling the senses and gaining remembrance.

Summary

Psychology plays an important role in design. It takes into account how people see the visual stimulus on a page and turn it into memories (which makes them return to a site) and how experiences evoke emotion (helping visitors bond with and trust a site, creating brand loyalty). Psychology is such a detailed subject that this book covers only the basics. But plenty of theories that could aid, influence, or affect distinctive design exist and may be worth researching further. It's one of the few design subjects that keeps on evolving!

Sculpting a User Interface

Practical applications for distinctive design theories

WITHOUT CODE, DESIGNS cannot exist online. HTML, CSS, JavaScript and other languages, frameworks, techniques, and best practices turn sketches and artistic creations into something that you can render within a browser. The ability to build increasingly difficult, unique layouts that interact with users and provide them with the functionality, content, and experience they require has become the passion of many. So, you need to be able to create and implement your creations in a way that sculpts a beautiful interface.

This chapter examines how you can work with HTML elements (also known as tags) and microformats to promote distinctive, rich layouts. You find out about the various properties within CSS that help turn your aims for a design into reality, including how you can target devices for specific types of style. Then you move on to providing interactivity through JavaScript and frameworks such as jQuery to promote a more feature-rich, depth-loaded experience. Finally, you read about the rich history of code and how it affects browsers, how to debug, and how future standards will affect your ability to add distinction to your pages and to give users the best possible interface.

Markup and Microformats

All aspects of design revolve around the concept of giving visitors an experience. Although user-interface design has the same primary goal (to provide something useful), it's important that your interfaces reflect your hard work and turn all of the theory and fanciful thinking into an implemented solution that users can enjoy. Don't ignore the distinction that real-world coding provides.

Distinctive design doesn't just sit on the back bench providing you with an assortment of theories that preach design best practices! It gives you ideas and examples of how things appear on the screen, how your images are portrayed, and more importantly, how you can (with a bit of code applied carefully) turn a dull or less than sensitive layout (or one that's overly excited) into something beautiful, elegant, and useful. That said, ideally, you will take advantage of the theory provided; code provides just one method for doing so!

Note   There is a debate as to whether designers should know how to code (opposed to just providing the aesthetics). Because you are providing materials for the web, it seems natural to learn how to code (to take advantage of everything the medium has to offer). After all, if you don't put all of these variables to work, what's the point in learning them!

So how can you give a site some distinction right away (with nothing more than some well applied code)? The answer is clear-cut! Craft your interfaces using languages like HTML, CSS, and JavaScript, and that's precisely how they're delivered. This chapter examines each one of the languages, looking at what they offer the distinctive designer. Rather than just focusing on contextual value, it examines how the languages add distinctive flourishes to your pages. Figure 6-1 shows that before such languages evolved to the extent they have (for various platforms), the ability to give your site a unique look was limited.

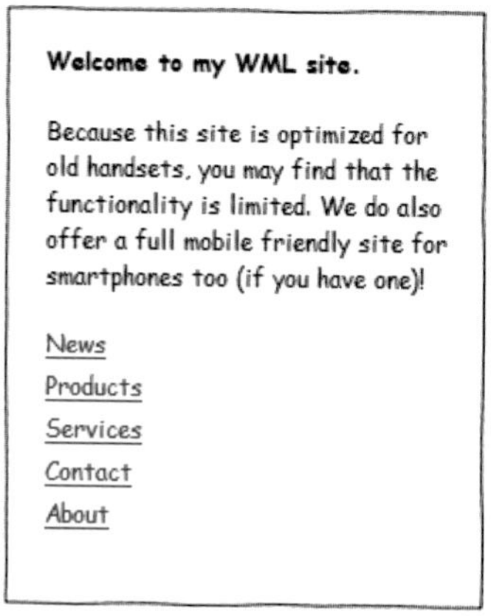

Welcome to my WML site.

Because this site is optimized for old handsets, you may find that the functionality is limited. We do also offer a full mobile friendly site for smartphones too (if you have one)!

News
Products
Services
Contact
About

FIGURE 6-1: Before the smartphone era, mobile devices had WML, which wasn't very distinctive at all!

Before you examine how HTML can supply distinction (and before moving on to the other useful and distinctive inducing languages), it's worth giving a "shout out" to the designer's nemesis, compatibility (refer also to Chapter 4 for more on compatibility in web design). Although HTML4 and XHTML 1.0 do have a decent level of support, certain devices and web browsers have little support for HTML5 (the latest version at the time of this printing) or have a preference for restrictive mobile profiles or WML (a language designers should all fear because of its limitations).

If you're looking for comfort about which languages to use for a cross-platform and user-friendly experience, eliminate XHTML 1.1 from your list. It's not compatible with Internet Explorer 6 through 8. Tread carefully if you want to use HTML5 or CSS3. Remember that not all devices or browsers are born equal. For distinctive designs, visibility is critical (if people can't see a site because of rendering quirks or failures, your visitors suffer), though designs can work if you provide good fail-safe fallbacks! Keep this in mind as you move forward.

Important   With modern standards such as HTML5 and CSS3, there's no escaping the need to tweak your code for specific rendering engines. CSS3 has a bunch of vendor prefixes (which can degrade gracefully). HTML5 often needs added markup and scripting to do the job. Although getting it right can be tricky, getting a beautiful interface has value.

Elements dictating distinction

Although *structural languages* such as HTML may not seem to be involved in your site's distinctiveness, their role is more central to the process than most people realize. CSS has the power to paint your site's canvas with visual flourishes commonly associated with the design, but a site's structure says plenty about the relationship and influence of content within the page. Don't dismiss a structural language's importance in distinctive design. You may discover that in certain circumstances, the code makes all the difference.

One of the most overlooked places for distinction is a site's header (the document head). Consider TITLE, which is one of several HEAD elements. Within a browser, this element holds emphasis by giving the window where your site resides a unique label that can be easily read. Figure 6-2 shows an example of identifying a page among a range of other tabs or windows. Such conventions may not seem influential, but they can increase visibility and reduce the amount of time a visitor must spend navigating while multitasking. Choose your titles carefully, keep them descriptive, and don't make them so long that they are trimmed by default!

FIGURE 6-2: Represent your site's pages with a short, distinctive title in the tab or window.

The TITLE element isn't the only header tag that can place a distinctive mark on your site. The LINK and STYLE elements can aid your site's distinction and appearance by referring a browser to CSS code that needs to be rendered to give the layout its unique experience. In addition to those two header tags, you have the SCRIPT element, which refers to the JavaScript code executed (and that can impact the visuals if used for such a purpose). Your site's "thinking" code literally has a visual impact of its own forging! For example, take the use of a jQuery carousel. With it, you can provide a rotating slideshow, and it's interactive, code-based, and even gives your content an animated edge.

Although using CSS or JavaScript with the appropriate tags is an obvious example of HTML's effect on your design, giving a nod to the browser is worth your while — the browser, by default, gives code some raw, basic visual style (if no CSS is present). This default styling provides a base level of distinction that you can either take advantage of or overwrite. It provides a solid place to begin styling, with guaranteed distinction (the only issue is that each browser has its own defaults, which lead to CSS resets and a few rendering quirks along the way).

Tip Although the style and script tags do give you an opportunity to embed distinctive objects in pages, separating style, structure, and behavior to take advantage of caching (saving bandwidth) and maintainability (less work to edit code) makes more sense.

Beyond using those elements to give your layout a bit of additional distinction, the head of an HTML document also allows you to reference favicons (short for *favorites icon*) and Apple Touch icons, which give bookmarks a quirky little image that provides a bit of subliminal distinction from other bookmarked links (see Figure 6-3 for an example). If you haven't put much thought into the header section of your pages (in terms of distinction), now is the time to examine cool assets you can include. Small details give your site a polished feel and a more distinctive, visual identity. If they aren't invasive, they may be worth having!

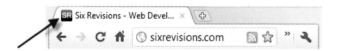

FIGURE 6-3: Icons may be small, but they give bookmarks a note of distinction (which is useful).

Unlike the header, a document's body is where the majority of your visible, natural, (default), and structural distinctions occur. Much as a toolbox has different devices to help you achieve your DIY goals, HTML offers a range of elements that provide impact to the aesthetics of a site (until overwritten). Every tag within the body can have style applied to it. If you want to override the browser defaults, use CSS.

Reference

To learn about the specific functionality of a particular HTML element, you can check out the list at `http://meiert.com/en/indices/html-elements/` or visit the handy, free reference guide (which also serves as a good tutorial) at `http://reference.sitepoint.com/html`.

How are these elements distinctive? In some cases, such as with the DIV tag, elements exist to highlight a block of content or tags. Headings increase the text size to give an impression of increased importance. Some elements use indentation and markers to promote individual parts, such as lists or tables, and some have root styles applied to them, such as B, I, A, STRONG, EM, INS, DEL, and Q to highlight their unique role and importance within the page. Table 6-1 shows how elements are interpreted visually (by default), but they have some semantic and contextual meaning as well.

Table 6-1   The Default Stylistic Differences in HTML Element

Visual Difference	Elements Affected
Default text	P, DIV, ABBR, ACRONYM, DFN, SPAN, FORM, LABEL, and LEGEND
Font change	PRE, CODE, SAMP, KBD, and TT
Text size	H1, H2, H3, H4, H5, H6, BIG, and SMALL
Bold text	Headings (H1–6), STRONG, and B
Italic text	EM, VAR, I, and CITE
Lined text	DEL, INS, and A
Indented text	DL (DD), OL (LI), UL (LI), and BLOCKQUOTE
Other effect	A, HR, BR, BDO, Q, SUB, SUP, BUTTON, FIELDSET, INPUT, SELECT, TEXTAREA, TABLE, FRAME, and IFRAME
N/A	AREA, IMG, MAP, OBJECT, and PARAM

Beyond the power of conventional text or image elements that provide a certain level of distinction within the page, form elements within HTML exert a level of distinction that visitors easily recognize. Although GUI components such as text boxes, drop-down menus, and buttons are easy to recognize, they can also retain unique styling (with restrictions) to provide users with something that is also interactive, though it may be worth retaining the recognizable design trends (as shown in Figure 6-4).

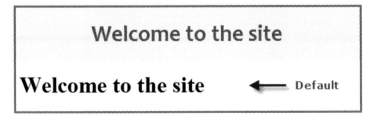

FIGURE 6-4: Many form components exist, and each has its own visual style and functionality.

Some elements naturally look and feel distinctive (such as the STRONG or EM tags). One in particular, the HR horizontal rule tag, helps form a visual separation of the content. By balancing the use of these types of elements (and being careful about how they're externally styled with CSS), you're drawing on the theory behind making text more distinctive on a page.

For a quick and easy way to see how elements are naturally styled (and how much emphasis is assigned by default), experiment and try out the code. Ultimately, you want to use CSS whenever possible to give your site the unique feeling it requires (HTML was designed to structure, not to style). Black-and-white text styled so basically that it looks primitive won't win you visitors on the basis of visual aesthetics (see Figure 6-5), but understanding how to use it is knowledge worth having.

FIGURE 6-5: Default styling isn't anything special, but it does have some undertones of distinction.

When building a site from scratch, consider either taking advantage of those tags' natural inclination toward style (such as keeping headers large or anchors underlined) or using CSS to layer enhancements. For example, when using the KBD tag to denote a keyboard shortcut, you can add a background image to make it look like a key on a keyboard. In this way, you are neutralizing or enhancing as necessary. At a more basic level, the STRONG element naturally receives distinction through the bold default style.

Because this book focuses on design, you need to know about the meaning and use of elements within HTML. You can find plenty of books and tutorials with that information. As a designer, you need to pay close attention to every element that appears on a page. Not caring is a big risk! For example, even if you add emphasis to a word (but reset the visuals), it still impacts a site's distinction. The process of coding a design is to represent your content in the best way possible. Be sure to do just that!

As you mark up your site's content, consider whether you are using the right tag for the job. Some elements are naturally more suited to producing a distinctive object than others. For example, you wouldn't replace the IMG element (holding tag for images linked to HTML) with a SPAN element (for grouping inline elements)! In addition, search engines notice how content is marked up. The benefit of being as semantically relevant as possible is that you will make your site easier to find (a site composed entirely of images will get little SEO recognition).

Important

If you want something stylistically italicized, don't just use the "I" tag (because it has been largely replaced with a better, CSS alternative). Your site's visual appearance needs to complement the substance of your site. Although using deprecated or stylistic tags will emit distinction (using "I" creates italics), it makes better sense to code properly.

Here are some other good practices (visualizing element styles):

> Using bullets or numbers in all lists (except those used for navigation)

> Giving links a different color than the body text for easier navigation

> Using a dotted underline to indicate hover effects (non-hyperlinked effects)

> Avoiding tags (deprecated or otherwise) that have low browser support

> Using tags such as SUB and SUP as appropriate (they're often forgotten)

Ultimately, HTML provides some basic styling opportunities that can be important for situations when CSS isn't likely to be as helpful or available (for example, with screen readers or text-only browsers). Therefore, give some care and attention to occasions when your site may appear "naked." Many designers focus purely on how CSS or scripts give a site visual impact, but making your HTML distinctive has a role to play in the underlying aesthetic.

Microformat magic

As designers, you spend a great deal of time applying CSS to your layouts as you produce your web interfaces, but you also need to remember that substance over style still plays a critical role in a site's distinction. The code marking up your content describes its purpose and relevance in relation to the other objects on the page, and while this may not be visual, it's still distinction. At its core, HTML serves to bring contextual meaning to your content.

HTML served through your favorite browser may showcase some basic stylistic aspects in order to allow CSS-less sites to remain usable (keeping the site's emphasis as balanced as possible), but you also have additional tools at your disposal that can enhance the value of content and give passages of text the potential to receive the recognition they deserve. If you want to enhance a site's meaning, using code structure is a great way to do so.

The layers of your structure include the following:

> Content (the textual data that makes up an interface)

> HTML (the code that defines the text's purpose)

> Microformats (the names that determine meaning)

The popular method of enhancing this semantic, contextual value is commonly referred to as *purpose-built microformats*. They provide a series of name conventions that you apply to elements in order to highlight the special meaning that (say) a particular paragraph has in context with other surrounding elements. You can use microformats and this "meta data" to reference events, locations, and identities. Browsers and social networks can actually extract this useful information and do something with it (such as create an address book entry). Figure 6-6 shows a basic microformat at work, an hCard giving a telephone number.

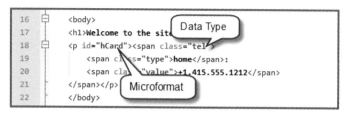

FIGURE 6-6: Microformats attach themselves to existing HTML code to express data types.

Considering subjects like information architecture and design, the need to structure your valuable assets (such as content) effectively is part of the uphill battle that designers frequently face. Although having code that barely affects the visual side of the layout may seem rather poor in terms of the design, remember that an experience is about maximizing the effectiveness of code and visuals, so microformats should be welcomed with open arms (especially because, when they are supported, they give visitors added functionality).

A great example that emphasizes how distinctive microformats can be used is hSlice, a proprietary feature build by Microsoft (for IE8+). Using just a bit of clever coding, visitors can save and dynamically rip out a section of the content (a slice, so to speak) that can then be delivered in a smaller pop-up window within the browser. It can then be activated by clicking the specially formed bookmark and the "slice" refreshes. This has distinctive value because the resulting action is that a user's focus is drawn only toward the content within the page slice (as shown in Figure 6-7). Other great distinctive microformats exist, too, some with more impact than others. Consider using them in your projects. They could be valuable assets, and may give your visitors' browsers added usefulness.

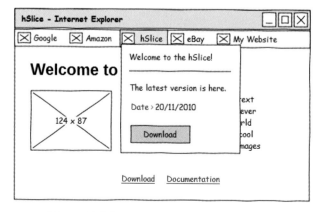

FIGURE 6-7: Microsoft's hSlice microformat makes bookmarks both distinctive and dynamic!

The benefits of these recognized code conventions go far beyond the visual distinction that CSS alone provides. Microformats can become powerful enough to aid memory (hCard), highlight licenses (rel license), boost minimalism (hSlice), and even help with tasks such as search engine optimization (rel nofollow). It's like saying that not only is a paragraph on the page, but also that the paragraph contains a specific type of content that relates to something people will find relevant and useful (and browsers can take advantage of this).

You'll find that microformats have good support. Search engines are starting to take the content on board and do something with it. Social networks and some web browsers are, too (though it's not a case of equal opportunities). In addition to these microformats, which give added meaning to your pages, there's also a case for using traditional metadata, like you find in a web document head or within a formatted RDF file (an XML document that models and describes information, expressing meaning to objects) with a defined index.

Tip

As with any type of descriptive data, it's important that you don't abuse the position you have been given. The keywords "META property" got dumped by search engines because of keyword stuffing. Don't let the same thing happen to RDF metadata or microformats!

Code plays a powerful role in design, and although they work behind the scenes, microformats shouldn't be overlooked. If they can get you a better search position, your content will be easier to find (for visitors using search tools). If you have some function-based ones in action, they can boost productivity and attain easier communication with visitors. Maximizing your HTML and semantic status boosts the effectiveness of your work and that's what you're aiming for. Distinctive designers can't afford to miss out on such a powerful infrastructural effect.

Subliminal (noninvasive) code works behind the scenes and lays down the framework for your visual endeavors. If you get the balance right between element usage and the style applied to it, you reduce waste (from surplus tags eating bandwidth) and produce an elegance and distinction with speedy results. That, in turn, can give you an advantage over competitors in the race to make sites that work and interact well at the browser level.

Reference　To learn about microformats, the best place to start is the site that holds the individual specifications: `http://microformats.org`. To learn about Microsoft's own proprietary hSlice microformat, visit `http://msdn.microsoft.com/en-us/library/cc304073(v=VS.85).aspx`.

Cascading with Distinction

HTML does have an underlying level of distinction, which shouldn't be ignored, but for most web designers, the majority of a site's aesthetics and visual layout will be provided through the application of CSS. Because the average website will have a whole range of objects positioned on a page, when producing something for the web, you need to know the selectors, properties, and values that define how content renders on a screen.

Among the many features that CSS offers designers, you'll find properties useful for giving objects a little more (or less) white space, positioning objects around a page, and highlighting the regions around objects. You can also use them for customizing lists and tables, to give parts of a page a background image, to change colors at the back and the foreground, to give the text a more distinctive appearance, and even for changing the cursor. Lots of fun to be had! Figure 6-8 shows a few of the things you can produce by using CSS (relating to text).

FIGURE 6-8: You can use CSS to change fonts, sizes, and colors of your text.

The ideal method of giving a site as much distinction as possible is through the separation of a site's structure (HTML) and the style (CSS). There are many justifications for this, though it remains a fact that if someone wants to view a site without visual extras, he or she can do so without too much trouble. Although you may want to force users to see your content things in its most elegant and creative state, as always, the user remains in control of the experience.

For designers, CSS is the equivalent of a Swiss army knife. It gives all those who enter your site an opportunity to have a tailor-made experience that (unlike HTML) doesn't give off an embarrassing feeling of blandness. Although it's not a perfect language, CSS gives you a high level of control over the layout, colors, typography, and appearance of objects held within the web browser (so consider it a must-have for creating a distinctive design).

Tip

Remember that although you can make a number of changes to your content's visual appearance, it's important to justify each tweak in respect to how it affects the other objects on the page. Using the principles and elements of design will help you, but as with most things, common sense and logic need to reign supreme!

Just as with HTML (which is constantly evolving), CSS is coming a long way. CSS3, the cool new standard that is progressively being adopted, enhances a whole bunch of extra design aspects you can control. As this standard becomes more widely implemented, you will be able to produce ever-more complex, elegant designs relying less upon images to convey a visual impact (for a certain effect). Of course, getting it to work across browsers is an issue!

What makes CSS a great design language is its progressive nature. With HTML, we see elements come and go from the specifications (this affects the contextual distinction it holds in regard to browsers, search engines, and those who understand it). Every incarnation of CSS layers additional features on top of the previous ones. So you've nothing to lose and everything to gain. Because CSS is based within presentation, each property (used appropriately) can make your site extra distinctive (so you need to know about them).

Suitable styles using CSS

So what effect on distinction do all of these properties have? Well, that's something you take a look at right now. It's important to know what tools are at your disposal to present your lovely range of content. Unless you resort to using third-party components such as Adobe Flash (which allows custom objects to be created), the level of control you have over your interfaces is quite limited (beyond stylistic flourishes provided by CSS). As older browsers have varying levels of support, implementations may not be perfect.

The first properties worthy of attention are those setting the size or scale of each on-page object. Because size is a critical factor (you want to dictate whether something dominates the landscape), the ability to adjust the *width* and *height* of elements (see Figure 6-9) can't be underestimated. Also, some useful and available properties include *min-* and *max-* extensions on width and height (for example, *max-width*) that can set boundaries for your content's visuals. The smaller the objects, the less distinctive they become, so use size and scale carefully (if you push something together too tightly, it'll overflow and your content may be cut off).

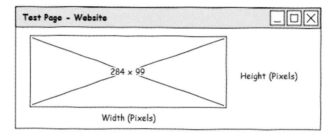

FIGURE 6-9: Width and height give an absolute scale of how much space an object requires.

If content is forced to overflow against your wishes (post setting dimensions to the object), you have the *overflow* property to either let the content be hidden or scrolled internally accounts. (CSS3 also offers *overflow-x* and *overflow-y* on the axis. Those properties are well supported, too.) If you feel adventurous, the clip property lets you cut a hole in an object so that anything behind it becomes visible!

Tip

If you want to have a box of scrolling content within the screen, it's much safer to have the content embedded within the page with overflow providing the scroll bar on the fixed dimension object than to rely on iframes (which contain serious accessibility issues). Overflowing content boosts distinction by ensuring that less relevant content appears only as the user scrolls down (past the important content, at the top of the box).

Now that you can define an object's size, you need to consider how much white space exists around the outer edges (giving your content breathing room from other brother or sister objects). Two properties responsible for giving the desired white space are *padding* and *margin.* You can assign different levels of white space to each side (top, bottom, left, or right). Padding provides space between objects and borders. Margin provides space between borders and other objects. Within browsers, this combination of width, height, borders, padding, and margins comprises the "total space" used by an object, often referred to as the *CSS box model.* Figure 6-10 shows how certain forms of spacing affect readability.

 Spaced Content Is Much Nicer To Read.

FIGURE 6-10: Spacing your content (text or otherwise) makes it look less cramped on a page and easier to read.

Although white space is useful for defining an object's relative relationship (by effectively emphasizing the edges of objects), unless you draw a line around its edges (to highlight where content should be grouped), users may assume that nothing is related. You have a few options. You can use the *border* property (see Figure 6-11) to add a line (colored with varying widths or styles), use *outline* property (which has a similar visual effect but won't let you define each side separately), or you could potentially add some funky CSS3 effects like *border-radius* (for rounded corners on borders) or *box-shadow* (for the impression of depth).

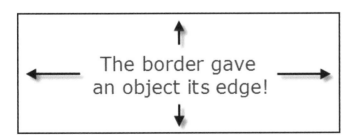

FIGURE 6-11: Borders allow you to group content visually and show the extent to which an object spans.

Now take a look at how you can position objects on the screen. Within distinctive design, position is everything! Luckily for designers, CSS has the *position* property (which lets you keep an object with its neighbors, fix it so that no amount of scrolling will change its visibility, or have it in a specific place but scroll like everything else). If any of these options excite you, making use of position along with the *top*, *bottom*, *left*, and *right* properties allows you to state where objects should appear on the screen. Otherwise, you can use the *float* property to make parts stack next to each other (the *clear* CSS property ends this floatation effect).

Tip Internet Explorer 6 does not support fixed positioning, which is a shame because it offers some distinctive benefits by remaining visible when a user scrolls. Although some hacky workarounds exist, you need to account for this issue when designing for IE6.

On occasion, you may want content to overlap or become invisible. If you're offering progressive disclosure, this will prove to be a valuable asset! Besides hiding the text using a negative top or left margin (or via their properties), you have *visibility* (with a value of *hidden*, leaving visible space for the object) and *display* (with a value of *none*, leaving no trace of its existence), which can render the effect. With overlapping content (and positioning set), you can use the *z-index* property to set a priority order for displaying content, assigning a numerical value to an object in the cascade (it's technical and cool).

Tip Overlapping content can be cool, but remember that if your content becomes illegible as a result, you could hinder your visitor's progress (and limit the content's distinctive effectiveness). As with proximity, you need to balance the effect with its usefulness.

So far, you've learned how CSS can change dimensions, priority, positions, visibility, and even how to deal with overflowing content. If you have lists on your page (organized or unorganized), you can define a custom bullet point (Figure 6-12) or image and position those images to your tastes (depending on the type of list you want to use). Although this book doesn't cover all the gory details, you can alter the appearance of tables and their borders and add some spacing between cells, too, which can help to promote a distinctive appearance.

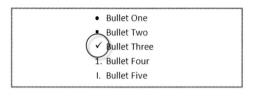

FIGURE 6-12: Use a custom bullet point (by creating an image) to give the impression of a specific type of list.

It's now time to examine the two parts of CSS that have the greatest effect on how visitors interact with your content (not taking anything away from positioning, which happens to play a significant role in organizing your visual order and hierarchy). These two property-laden concepts are *color* and *typography,* which you're already familiar with — because color and typography are so prominent within design, I've dedicated other sections in the book to those topics.

First, consider color. You already know that color plays on people's emotions and is a powerful psychological tool. CSS allows you not only to set a foreground or background color for an object, but it also enables you to set a custom background image and position it to give that object some cool flourishes or textures. CSS3 can use alpha transparency and opacity as well. You must ensure that you have good contrasts and that the final effect looks good (see Figure 6-13).

Color In Text Is Great!

FIGURE 6-13: Pick a color and be sure that it contrasts well within the page (using strong or subtle tones).

Following color, you have the typography values, which are pretty exciting if you want to give your text some distinctive ambiance. To begin, set fonts (using *font-family* to declare a web-safe font stack — see Chapter 4 for more on font stacks), using a popular typeface such as Georgia (see Figure 6-14), Trebuchet MS, Arial, or Verdana. Really turn on the visual charm by way of *font-size* (to make text larger), *font-style* (for italicized), *font-weight* (for bold), and *font-variant* (which allows you to make capital letters the same height as lowercase ones).

Do You Like Georgia?

FIGURE 6-14: Picking the right typeface for your design requires some web-safe considerations.

Next, you have the textual style rules such as *text-align* (which allows you to shift your text to the left, right, or center point of the parent, or justify it to span the whole box), *text-indent* (to indent text either inward or negatively outward), *text-decoration* (which can give distinction via underlining, overlining, strikethrough, or blinking text), and *text-transform* (which changes text case to uppercase, lowercase, or initial capital letters on every word). Examples of some of these stylistic techniques are shown in Figure 6-15.

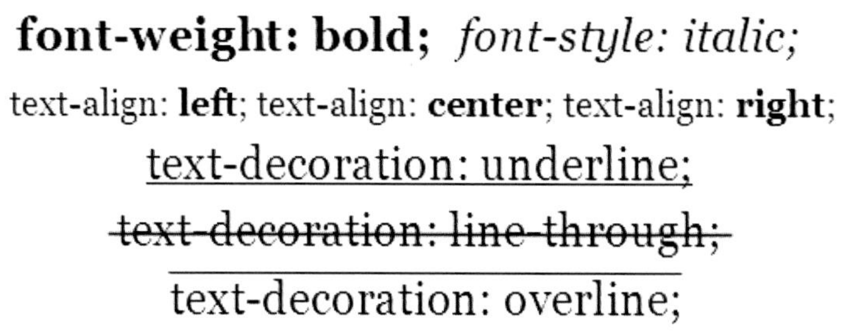

font-weight: bold; *font-style: italic;*

text-align: **left**; text-align: **center**; text-align: **right**;

<u>text-decoration: underline;</u>

~~text-decoration: line-through;~~

text-decoration: overline;

FIGURE 6-15: You style and organize text in myriad ways to give it distinction.

If all of that isn't enough, you also have properties such as *letter-spacing* (giving white space to characters), *word-spacing* (breathing space between words), *line-height* (which provides breathing space between lines), *vertical-align* (such as text-align, except for the top and baseline in preference to left and right), and *white-space* (which renders white space in line collapse events). A few others affect text visuals (and more in CSS3 if you want to use the latest cutting-edge techniques), so just experiment to see what works!

Tip White space is important, especially within your text. Although there isn't a specific formula that gives you a perfect reading experience, take the factors mentioned into account and play with the properties until you find something you (and your visitors) can be satisfied with. After all, visitors want to enjoy their time on your site.

A couple of other properties are also worthy of mention because of their uniqueness. The first is the capability of CSS to tweak the UI of the browser (perhaps to make your content more attuned to the visual style). Altering the color of the scroll bar (a proprietary bit of CSS that works only in certain browsers) or altering the *cursor* (see Figure 6-16) may initially seem like a good idea, but doing so could confuse some of your visitors.

FIGURE 6-16: Custom cursors look like fun, but users will find it hard to track their position on the page.

One property becomes the exception to this rule — custom text *selection*. If done correctly, it can improve the experience and readability for users who highlight text as they move along the content (marking their position). When the selection color is altered, you must ensure that the content marked remains visible and has sufficient contrast so that users will know that they made their selection successfully.

With a CSS property aptly called *content*, you can insert content (for stylistic purposes) into a page. I advise you not to use this CSS property for content that could be deemed critical to the content's context (in case CSS is disabled or a screen reader is used, such instances will render the text, hidden from view). Essentially, using *content* gives you an effective way to describe objects on-screen that are separate from the content.

Finally, the *font-face* at rule in CSS3 deserves a bit of attention because it allows you to use custom typography (as long as you have a license to do so). If you can find legal typefaces that reflect the sentiment within your design better than the web-safe variety does, take advantage of those typefaces. Like many aspects of CSS3, font-face has varied browser support, and a cross-browser standard is still hard to come by.

Reference If you want to learn about the specific functionality of a particular CSS property, either check out the list at `http://meiert.com/en/indices/css-properties/` or visit the handy, free online reference guide (which serves as a good starting point) at `http://reference.sitepoint.com/css`.

Mobile, print, or default design!

The many choices in CSS 1, 2, and 3 can be overwhelming for beginners. However, choice is a good thing, and it pays to consider all the options available with each object on the page to determine its optimum distinction level (or neutrality, as the case may be). If you're experienced with code but just aren't very design-oriented, consider testing a few ideas (or get feedback), and then place your ideas, tests, and doodles in something real.

Media selectors allow you to target specific types of devices (such as printers or projection devices) with styles oriented toward their needs. In the past, it was argued that for the web, the best situation would be to have a single stylesheet or visual layout for everything. But this argument was a bit over-ambitious. Designers now realize that one size cannot fit all. Use of the web, print, mobile devices, television, and other devices should differ based on the needs of the device, the user, and expectations of how style should function. (Figure 6-17 goes one step further, by showing media queries, which build upon selectors to style based on features such as window size.)

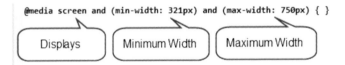

FIGURE 6-17: CSS3 media queries allow you to target specific variables of a working environment.

CSS allows you to take all your concepts and layout ideas and make them a reality. A well-thoughtout design may look great on a desktop or laptop screen, but if you view the same design on a smartphone with a small, touch-sensitive screen, the effect may not work as well. Handheld devices are popular, so you need to consider them!

Tip

Some of the designers who are hell-bent on making use of fixed width designs and using device-specific widths have adopted the same flawed technique on mobile platforms. Using a set width may work for a device such as an iPhone, but it'll all go out the window for an iPad user! As things stand, fixed width design is no longer a good idea. Fluid layouts are better.

Trying to cater to all of the available devices is a formidable task. In regard to CSS, the "handheld" media query is, to this day, still pretty lackluster in its support from device makers. As for your options, you can make mobile users utilize your existing desktop site (not the best plan), utilize CSS3 media queries and the handheld media type to help a few smarter devices get a customized mobile experience from the existing site, or you can give mobile users an independent site (making a few optimizations for the consumption method). If you have the time, go with all three types, starting from the last and working to the first. If you're on a time-sensitive project, work from the first to the last!

Important Most designers assume that resolution is the only factor affecting the space they have to work with (distinctively), but the fact that most users don't have windows maximized, along with DPI, full screen, open toolbars, and sidebars diminishes the overall viewport size.

Remember that you can provide alternative stylesheets for any situation you want. If you're really adventurous, provide several themes so that visitors can choose one that matches their personal tastes. Adding choices is time-consuming, but it can really hit the mark in respect to personalization and encouraging user interaction. With alternative stylesheets, you can put out a high-contrast edition to meet accessibility needs.

Studying Scriptable Solutions

CSS is a great language for arranging sites to be visually distinctive, but it isn't a language steeped in interactivity. It doesn't provide the experience that users expect (beyond the traditional static site that so many of us have grown accustomed to). The web provides designers with a language that far outweighs CSS in terms of overall complexity but that offers in reward an ideal platform to give visitors the interactivity they desire. That language is JavaScript, and it's a very powerful tool indeed!

First and foremost, although JavaScript isn't the only method that provides users with interaction and behavior, it's one of the few that does so on the client side (in the user's browser rather than by processing scripts before serving them). More than that, it's the type of language that lets people respond to keys being pressed, mice being clicked, and touchpads being tapped! So JavaScript is ideal for distinctive designers.

Tip Client-side scripting languages such as JavaScript allow you to interact with visitors' input devices, but don't forget that server-side languages allow you to remember and process these actions into something both productive and customized. It's a two-way street!

If you've worked with JavaScript, you know that its main downfall is that people frequently turn off scripting or selectively have it enabled (see Figure 6-18) to avoid intrusive behavior that many scripts wrongly implement (such as those highly intrusive anti-right click scripts). As a distinctive designer, your job, as usual, is not only to ensure that the site works when scripting is disabled (so use scripts, but have a fallback), but also to avoid harming a user's experience or ability to access and use your site.

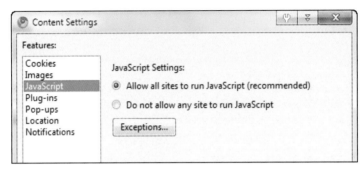

FIGURE 6-18: Scripts can be turned off in several ways, so don't assume that your site is safe.

Although style breeds distinction through visual stimulation, behavior (via scripts) solutions offer a more engaging experience by allowing the user to do more on the site than just read. This level of interaction helps people remember their experience because action fires up the brain's visual memory (rather than just the parts used for reading). This interaction also gives them a way to avoid boredom, presents them with activities to undertake, and offers exploration tools (really, the world is your oyster in this regard).

JavaScript does more than simply provide interactive elements that respond to user input or activity. The reaction of scripts can also include things such as changing CSS or HTML code or swapping out content for other content on the page. This dynamic behavior allows you to alter experiences via the choices users make and to evolve an experience into something customizable, flexible, interactive and user-oriented, as well.

How scripts became distinctive

The power of JavaScript is undeniable. Although it's had its fair share of growing pains (such as the days of poorly made copy-paste scripts), the language has enough bits and pieces built in to allow you to create almost any kind of application or functionality. Because your imagination is your only barrier, if your users require a particular aid or piece of functionality (such as a product wizard), you can implement it unobtrusively (with a bit of know-how, perhaps with the help of a framework such as jQuery).

For distinctive designers, making a choice between a dynamic or static site can be difficult. On one hand, you want your visitors to feel as though they're part of the experience. On the other hand, the added complexities of developing functionality can hamper the evolution of a site if not handled carefully. Although this book doesn't cover the range of things that can be built using scripting (this is, after all, a design book), JavaScript does offer a few tricks that provide designs with a bit more interactivity (and grab people's attention quickly).

 Interactivity actually holds more distinctive value than something that's been animated, such as a video! When action is instigated by the end user rather than flowing across the screen, the brain recognizes the reaction to an event.

Tip

The first tool JavaScript provides for improving your design work is commonly referred to as the DOM (or *document object model*). This particular feature enables you to target particular aspects of a page's structure (and, by association, style) by filtering down the hierarchy of the document and referencing objects. Each object within the page has a reference (whether it's the element name or a class or ID reference), so the object can be targeted for specifically applying behavior, too, and this is where the stylistic asset helps.

By using a mixture of functions and statements declaring "if something happens, then do a particular task," you can interact with the user by waiting for a certain event and reacting to it. Being able to target tags and events like *onclick* is great, but being able to apply CSS style changes to those objects presents you with some cooler options. Imagine being able to change fonts on demand, for example. A very crude example of DOM scripting is shown in Figure 6-19, but you can just add a class reference to an element to reduce the need for long-winded scripts that alter styles, one at a time.

```
document.getElementsByTagName("p")[1].style.display = "none";
```

And it disappears just like magic!

FIGURE 6-19: JavaScript can change CSS on demand and can produce great, interactive aesthetics.

Of course, being able to alter the appearance of objects in almost infinite ways does offer a wide range of options, not just in giving or taking emphasis away from objects as needed. Providing users with (or asking for) information as they need it (progressive disclosure) is one goal that JavaScript can accomplish. In addition to adding and removing content from a page on demand, JavaScript also can use more sophisticated mechanisms, such as AJAX, thereby setting or grabbing content without requiring page refreshes or other changes.

JavaScript used to be thought of as a language that didn't really have much going for it, but developers' dedication to improve interfaces (rather than add surplus, pointless, or bad functionality) has lead to amazing achievements. It's clear that interactivity and sites work together beautifully, and if you want to give your users something more than a basic reading experience, consider JavaScript's potential benefits in your distinctive designs.

Frameworks in visual design

JavaScript deserves plenty of credit for giving you a wealth of functionality to make your sites dynamic. However, with the changes in how scripting is being used, it's also important to mention JavaScript *frameworks*. They simplify the process of gaining interactivity and functional animations (on par in some cases with Flash) and inspire designers to do increasingly cool, unique things with their sites.

Of the many frameworks, none have caught the imaginations of designers worldwide quite like jQuery. Many arguments claim that it isn't necessary to use frameworks. Although in some respects, it's true that you do need a working knowledge of JavaScript to use them, their straightforward and tightly optimized nature (along with also degrading gracefully) makes them worthy candidates for potential site use, especially if you are in a hurry.

Note   A framework is a library of prebuilt code that can perform certain functions based on a developer's needs. It cuts out the hard work of developing such tools and lets you get down to business by embedding it in the code and calling the function, making it far easier for novices to include sophisticated JavaScript effects in their designs.

The ability to simply plug in functionality on your sites can make users' experiences easier more fulfilling. In recent years, people have come to expect interactivity within websites, and because such dynamic behavior can improve an interface, interactivity offers new levels of distinction to explore. Just don't overload users with too much content at once or use intrusive animated effects just to gain attention.

The web isn't expected to be like print. People interact with sites in a controlled manner (using precision mice and fixed-function keyboards). You can take advantage of this behavior to influence your users. Earlier, I explored the psychology of stimulus and response, and you discovered that conditioning your users with certain events (such as clicking an image may launch a lightbox, a dialog box that forces focus — see Figure 6-20) lets you reinforce expectations of what might happen in future scenarios.

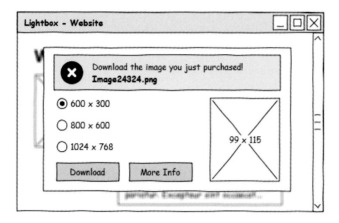

FIGURE 6-20: Lightboxes, distinctively, draw focus to on-screen objects.

All things considered, JavaScript is a worthwhile tool to explore. It lets you collect data on your users via analytics (to see how they browse and improve an experience), interact with users (and thereby psychologically influence them), and produce some wonderful effects that progressively disclose information or pages (with some neat animated effects on the side, such as changing styles to catch a user's eye). Although not as visually focused as CSS, scripts offer a number of things with which you can present, control, and engage your visitors. This is great news for distinctive designers. So explore your options!

The Past, Present, and Future

The capability to produce ever more beautiful and distinctive websites has been boosted (in part) by the evolution of languages such as HTML, CSS, and JavaScript. But as you're probably aware, things aren't as harmonious as they could or should be. With so many browsers and the power of whether style or behavior is enabled resting in the users' hands, you need to focus on making your site bug-free, compatible, and efficient for visitors.

In earlier times, web users lived through a browser war in which Microsoft and Netscape changed the landscape with proprietary evolutions in how content displayed (battles for supremacy are still ongoing). Some of these evolutions (for example, AJAX) still exist today and have been widely adopted. Others have failed, and in some cases, have left inconsistent rendering issues that web designers had to deal with. Your designs depend on the browser's capability to display your content distinctly, so you need to debug your work properly.

Important   Inconsistent rendering should become less of an issue for developers as more browser manufacturers work to ensure that their tools follow specifications. After rendering gains consistency, you'll only have to worry about the adoption of upcoming standards (hopefully)!

The current state of the web is, of course, much better for desktop browsers than in previous years. With old versions of Internet Explorer being the odd one out in terms of rendering, you have the proprietary techniques of conditional comments to aid patching. The issue to deal with now relates to the handheld market in which standard expectations no longer apply. The next frontier of design will revolve around the concepts of flexibility and usability, so be sure that your designs are distinctive and match those needs.

Despite the current issues and the old wars, the future of web design looks bright. Compatibility will remain an issue because the devices and tools people use change and evolve constantly. Plus, trying to wean users off old versions of Internet Explorer is a challenge. Going forward, making a distinctive design will be based not on what you can make from limited tools but on your ingenuity and creativity. Consider how HTML5, CSS3, and JavaScript currently alter the visual landscape, and you'll understand how powerful the web is becoming (see Figure 6-21).

With the scope for an endless range of scrolling and documents that can be as interactive as any computer game, impressing users is quite a challenge! One lesson to take from this endless array of options is that complexity may give levels of distinction, but it may not be the most beneficial experience for the end user. As you finish exploring all the tools available for code, remember that you need to carefully consider and use with restraint everything you provide in designs. The line between innovation and abuse is rather slim.

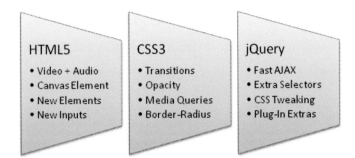

FIGURE 6-21: Here are a few things that HTML5, CSS3, and jQuery brought to the table!

Pretty progressive enhancement

Three techniques ensure that your content works when certain technologies are either disabled or unavailable for the visitor. Some work better than others, so it's important to examine the methods that impact compatibility (negatively and positively), understand which method is preferred, and debug in a hurry. Time to iron out those kinks in your design!

One method to gain a distinctive design is to follow the principle of *backward compatibility* (the basic workflow shown in Figure 6-22). Essentially, you build a site for users who can take advantage of the full experience (with modern standards), and patch your site for older devices and browsers as required. This is the most flawed technique because older or lesser-known tools may be missed, affecting potential (probably unknown) users you want to target with eye-catching experiences.

FIGURE 6-22: Backward compatibility uses a complex workflow, patching as you go.

Bug-fixing among browsers remains a common issue for compatibility, and undertaking it is a useful tool in the designer's arsenal. A flexible design that doesn't depend on specific parts looking a certain way or doing a certain task (in order to function on a basic level) leaves your visitors in a situation in which, if they don't meet your standards, they either have to exit your site or make the transition. As history shows, leaving is the easier option.

If working toward the ideal, and patching for instances where something breaks isn't considered the best solution, what is? As distinctive designers, you need to know that what you offer works for the widest audience possible. Damaged design may incorrectly render content and make the content harder to follow, which will hurt its impact and value. That said, the concept of *graceful degradation* with *progressive enhancement* has become popular.

Graceful degradation means that if you use a technology that may be unavailable, that technology must fall back to something usable (even if it isn't as pretty). Progressive enhancement, on the other hand, means that as you build a site, you layer each improvement on the otherwise working site. These concepts work in unison because layering features up (via progressive) means that if the enhancement can't be used, it degrades into something with fewer but more stable features. The testing methodology for working with layers is shown in Figure 6-23.

A basic example of graceful degradation with progressive enhancement in action is to layer your HTML structure over the content (so it has that root distinction), then place microformats on the HTML (giving it added context). Next add the CSS over the HTML (providing a distinctive visual style), then layer CSS3 over that to provide extra style flourishes, which degrade if unavailable. Finally, add some JavaScript (giving it distinctive functionality).

FIGURE 6-23: Progressively enhancing but gracefully degrading — it's distinctive stability in action.

If you have all this layering going on within your design, the design is safer for older browsers because they can fall back on an earlier layer if a fresher one doesn't work out. Layering also reduces the amount of debugging you need to undertake. You'll only need to make the odd tweak rather than outright patching entire browsers. Distinctive design requires you to know how such things will eventually work out.

Now consider how you can begin debugging or testing your site to iron out visual kinks. You don't want people to think less of your content for something that a web browser messed up. Because I expect that you understand enough about code to build the sites that will have distinction applied to them, I don't provide in-depth guides here about the debugging process. However, one method of debugging works well, so I cover it. That method of debugging, at its core, is shown within Figure 6-24.

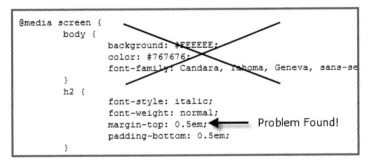

```
@media screen {
    body {
        background: #EEEEEE;
        color: #767676;
        font-family: Candara, Tahoma, Geneva, sans-se
    }
    h2 {
        font-style: italic;
        font-weight: normal;
        margin-top: 0.5em;         Problem Found!
        padding-bottom: 0.5em;
    }
```

FIGURE 6-24: Divide and conquer: Boil down source code until you find the offending material!

Debugging is a tedious task, especially if you're wading through hundreds of lines of code. If you find something that doesn't look right in a particular browser, the quickest way to resolve the issue is to go back to basics. Extract all the code that makes up the stylesheet or script and begin adding it back in groups until you reach a point where the error is replicated. At that point, you'll know what is causing the issue. Then you can research solutions, test other code, or fix silly mistakes until you resolve the error.

Getting to the stage where all the code is fixed can be a challenge, but it's worth taking the time to do so if you want a fluid experience for all users. It is highly recommended that you test your site in all the popular browsers (Internet Explorer, Firefox, Chrome, Safari, and Opera) and include all versions of browsers that a significant number of users on your site use. In the case of Internet Explorer (where this rule applies best), include versions 6, 7, 8, and 9. Luckily, you can install all of them on your computer.

Important To ensure reliability, you should test your site on the actual devices (in the default configuration format per the manufacturer). If doing so isn't an option, the next best practices are to use virtualized devices (identical) and, finally, emulators (attempted replication).

With the exception of the multiple versions of Internet Explorer, you can install the most recent versions of each browser without issue to see how your site looks. For Internet Explorer, you can download and use for free tools such as IETester and the Microsoft Virtual Machine, which enable you to see your site in the version you require. If your site looks great in all of these browsers, consider testing on some mobile platforms, if possible. The real devices are best for testing, but emulators for the iPhone, Android, Nokia, and custom browsers can be helpful, too.

The key way to see how your site looks in different browsers (distinctively and otherwise) is through use of the rendering engine (which puts content on the screen) rather than just use randomly named browsers. Accounting for all of these testing environments is tricky, but as earlier chapters point out, users will dictate the way they consume the content you provide. Your job as a designer is to make the most out of every opportunity!

Tip The mobile brand types to be emulated include Android, Apple (iDevices), Blackberry, dotMobi, LG, Mobile Firefox, Microsoft (Windows Mobile), Motorola, NetFront, Nokia, OpenWave, Opera (Mini and Mobile), Palm (Pre and others), Samsung, and SkyFire.

Distinction with future standards

The web enables your communication techniques to evolve (and market content to the public) in ever more amazing ways, but issues of compatibility will remain a problem for years to come. Because no one knows what new tools will appear in the next 50 years, you're forced to work conservatively, and think toward the future to avoid adding to the garbage of the broken web! The best you can hope for is a smooth, hassle-free transition.

As computers have evolved, and the social fabric with them, working with the Internet has become increasingly frustrating. As differences in cultural expectations collide, users must deal with diverse means of portrayal on the web. Overly complex sites and services force users to adapt their behavior to meet interface requirements. Because humans interact with computers in increasingly unique ways, human-to-machine interaction needs to be as fluid and natural as possible to avoid cognitive or behavioral barriers. The web provides essential services to mankind, and you are obliged to be professional in your approach and implementation.

Important Distinctive design is all about good communication and developing a good relationship with a visitor. Unless you can encourage your users to interact or communicate with the content you provide, you won't have a foundation upon which to build trust, empathy, and a meaningful, rewarding experience. So, be sure and make your interactions purposeful.

Consider how visuals degrade over time, not just because of the evolution of browsers, but also because of the aging process. Keeping a site up-to-date helps hold back this process, but designers also need to continually adapt interfaces to users' instinctive behavior while keeping them autonomous. While remaining aware of the varying and distinctive needs of users, designers must fashion interfaces to work in the best interests of users, keeping the user in a position of power. Figure 6-25 illustrates how time plays a signifi-cant role in the perception (and judgment) of a modern site.

Last Updated: 30/20/10

FIGURE 6-25: Humans are fascinated and affected by time. Ensure that your site doesn't appear out-of-date!

Languages such as HTML5 and CSS3, now on the horizon, and other languages continu-ally being developed will transform the way people use the web. Using the transitions and animations of CSS3, for example, you can gain attention by adding layers of animation and progression, which previously was accomplished only through the use of Adobe Flash. Graphic rendering languages such as SVG and VML also play their part by enabling you to make use of vector graphics (once supported consistently in browsers).

Summary

The web is a hotbed of new activities undertaken by people such as browser developers who want to make the web even more enriching for visitors (which is great news for your site). You can see examples of the "work in progress" philosophy in vendor prefixes in which new capabilities and languages such as CSS3 (not yet complete) allow you to test and retrofit your designs to make use of these new tools to give your site added flare. Those on the cutting edge really do push the limitations of browsers to distraction.

Distinctive design and the tools to implement wonderful, new, and intriguing features in your experiences do exist. Although you must approach code with caution, by coding with conviction and validating, testing, and enhancing your work, you can make the web a better place for your visitors. You can also give parts of a layout the best opportunity to be seen, understood, and appreciated. Code dictates visual distinction and its implementation. You have to master its power to get the results you desire, and always remember that your markup — every piece of it — is important.

Part IV

User-Centered Considerations

Promoting User Interaction

Providing distinctive interactivity within experiences

EXPERIENCES ARE MADE up of many variables, but one pivotal feature that gives life, depth, and added meaning to your web pages is interactivity. By making solid decisions and using code effectively, you can provide your visitors, in equal measure, with an enriched experience that sustains their need to explore and find the content they require.

In this chapter, I explore the root components of interactivity. I cover the types of devices that enable you to input with and output to users as well as the interactions that humans and computers encounter. I also explore the benefits and issues that are associated with user choice, along with the languages and code involved in interactivity. Later, I discuss the tools and methods used to build an interactive design. Finally, I underline the principles involved in responsive design theory that are playing an increasingly critical role in how designers build experiences.

A Click, Press, and Touch

A great deal of emphasis is placed on the distinction of a visual experience. Therefore, it seems only fair to highlight a methodology called *interaction design*, which intertwines with both structure and style to promote a more personable, useful relationship with your users. Although you could spend your days creating beautiful static sites, visitors expect more from an interface than to just read — they want to be engaged with the content. The interface must fulfill this objective.

Interactive distinctive acts differently than visual distinction. You place less emphasis on the way something appears aesthetically and spend more time creating a relationship between visitors and the services they're using. When you encourage users to interact with your service, they spend more time on a site (learning and partaking), and, thereby, are more prone to regularly make space in their lives for what you offer.

Note

Interaction engages the brain, makes people think on their feet, and encourages users to communicate and partake in activities. Although the influence won't be as strong on some as it will on others, interaction is a variable worth pursuing to evoke behavioral responses.

Interaction design is entirely user-centered and demands practical thought. It isn't just about putting content on the right page, and it isn't about wielding aesthetics to make things be more visible on the page — such as structure, style, or form. Interaction design is about making an experience more engaging and provoking a response that progressively exposes visitors to even more useful content when exploring your pages.

Designing a site to take advantage of the hardware a user may have — that's interaction! Using the full capacity of a rendering engine to make things change when a user needs more than simple text on the screen — that's interaction! Leveraging behavior to attract visitors to browse a site rather than just bounce in and out via a search engine — that's interaction! You want to design with purpose and encourage visitors to learn the cool subtleties of your site's interface. Figure 7-1 shows a simple example of how interaction can occur; using forms provides tools for text entry and submitting your input to a website.

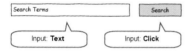

FIGURE 7-1: Entering text to be submitted is a type of interaction, as is clicking a button.

The best types of interfaces are those that are created with behavior in mind. Aesthetics improve the "ease on the eyes" feeling, but they don't take into account how users engage. Emotions and reactions are important in design. Designing sites and applications for your users is paramount to making content more useful, which boosts your distinction.

Whether you're building a search engine for content, a bookmark for a browser, or a funky little feature that allows your images to be more useful (such as sectional zooming using a lightbox mechanism), the behavior you embed undoubtedly helps make content more distinctive by giving it added contextual purpose. In addition, it also smoothes the transition between sections of a page by avoiding the need to refresh or affecting page sections. These experiences and functional aids can make or break a site. As you begin layering those wonderful scripts, consider how they will affect users.

Important

You aren't alone in trying to help users interact with a site. Most web browsers include some really cool native features, such as page zooming, text resizing, stylesheet swapping, and even extensions that can help detect functional extras such as RSS feeds within a site. If you aim to make your site distinctive, make sure it works using the native functionality. Doing so helps reinforce similar interaction as required on a web basis.

I/O hardware and interactivity

With any level of interaction, you first need to consider the range of devices that visitors may use to communicate with your sites. Various types of input and output tools allow content from devices to reach your visitors, and content from your users to reach the screen. You can't always rely on such devices to have the functionality you require. Without mechanisms such as keyboards to input data, interaction becomes limited, and missing output devices (such as monitors) increases the difficulty of readability in distinction.

With regard to hardware, input devices allow users to interact with a site. Whether it's the movement of their limbs, their voice, or even previously created documents, hardware input and output controls can help by acting as an intermediary body between humans and the web. Sites can take advantage of these types of tools (some with greater flexibility than others), and each one offers a unique method of getting tactile, visual, or positional input, or another action that relates to objects on the screen. So consider these forms of input as you build a site. Your users will rely on the functionality such hardware provides in order to use a design.

Types of input devices include the following:

> Camcorders

> Cameras

> Digital pen (stylus)

> GPS tools

> Joystick

> Keyboards

> Microphones

> Motion sensors

> Mouse

> Remote controls

> Scanners

> Tablets

> Touch screens

> Tracker pads

> USB/Firewire

> Webcams

Examples of using input methods to gain distinction include allowing keyboard shortcuts such as Ctrl+C to copy content (and save the time of going through menus), making click regions bigger for less precise devices such as touch screens, and using contact forms to encourage feedback. Also, analytics software takes advantage of input tools to track clicks and capture a bit of useful data for designers, which in turn advises you on how to design your layouts.

Tip

When dealing with input methods, consider how differently they negotiate around your screen and how they respond to requests for information. Some are better suited to certain activities, and you must be sure visitors can use the ones appropriate for their intended task. For example, although generally you wouldn't expect users to negotiate your screen by using a joystick, in some instances, joysticks may have a role in your design, similar to the way they're used in a game or flight simulator!

Contrary to input devices, output devices allow designers to relay content to a visitor. Plenty of devices accomplish this, but whether it's a physical, auditory (aural), or visual response depends on the hardware being used. In terms of interaction, you need to ensure that the balance between what you request from the user from input mediums and what they'll get is kept as profitable for users as possible. Using a "less input for more output" type of philosophy maximizes their experience. Less processing is involved, and tasks or actions can be undertaken faster.

Types of output device include the following:

> Monitors

> Projectors

> Televisions

> LED lights

> 3D glasses

> Headsets

> Speakers

> eInk

> Printers

Output mediums tend to play a more significant role than input mediums on distinctive design. That's because the result of all interaction is portrayed via the screen, speakers, printer, or other device for users to absorb and appreciate. Because all output mediums have individual specifications and limitations (size, color, or something else), to get a complete perspective, you need to recognize how such effects may be visualized or portrayed on a screen by using a range of different browsers, hardware, and tools.

Tip Output devices don't cause action, but they certainly help describe what occurs when visitors interact with your content. As with input methods, the reaction can be physical, visual, or aural, and some portray the content better in certain situations.

Although having all of these input and output devices is cool, the main problem that designers face is like that with browser functionality — you cannot really ensure that users meet your ideal set requirements. Sites requiring heavy rendering may fail to account for the visitors who lack a fast computer or good Internet speed. (This is a real problem with media on the web.) Not all users are created equal, and the issues they face degrade those users' experiences. Figure 7-2 shows that as more input and output actions are undertaken by users, the amount of stimulus and response increases through interaction.

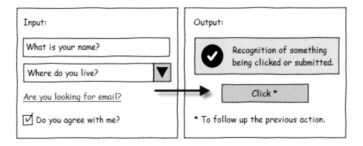

FIGURE 7-2: Input and output work hand in hand to promote great experiences through interaction.

Another example of a potential issue is the battle against discrimination that designers must face. It's called *accessibility* and is covered in the online e-book. Certain limitations that users may have, by association, affect their ability to interact with the hardware they own (such as loss of sight and the inability to see a monitor). When considering your design goals, be sure to include such critical issues. They can dramatically affect the usefulness of input or output components within the screen, which can affect a site's distinctiveness.

Distinctive design requires you to maximize your input and output methodology by providing users with an engaging interface that they navigate with their eyes and ears and that also enables them to take advantage of the input devices they use and can access to navigate around a site. Every link users click could lead them to desire or disaster, and every movement uses time and energy, so ensure that your site and its functionality do the tasks as efficiently and safely as possible.

Important

Although not distinctly an input or output medium, external forces such as a user's Internet speed, system specification, and other variables can affect the performance of interactions. So, although you hope users have a good environment, you can't count on it, which reinforces the need to be flexible in your design approach.

Human-computer interaction

Every designer should have at least a basic understanding about the way people use and interact with computers, which in the case of the web is called *HCI* (or *human-computer interaction*). The mechanics of developing an experience around your user's behavior allows you to not only maximize every interaction, but also provide something that the film industry boasts about — escapism, or drawing visitors away from the real world and immersing them in an enjoyable experience.

In computing terms, the ability to absorb a user's focus is limited because often the web is accessed on a device smaller than a television and a user may be browsing around on a tiny handheld device. So the impact of your content may be subverted by distractions from other desktop apps or from the outside world.

Space that surrounds a screen has an effect on experience, whether it's a virtualized environment (like a desktop) or a real-world one (such as devices people use or the place they are located). You can't control such variables, but consider them in your research, because users may frequently switch between your website and another one.

Common factors that affect the distinction of sites and influence the types of interaction you can provide your users include hardware issues such as screen size, computer speed, and the availability of a printer or speakers. Because the web is such a diverse medium, it really pays to stress test whatever you produce to ensure that your sites don't suffer a mechanical disability that could prevent users from accessing important features.

The aim of stress testing a site is to push every situation to its extreme and see how problems may occur if a situation goes horribly wrong. Consider what may happen if your site becomes slow to respond or if a user has a slow web connection. This situation can happen for a number of reasons, but a simple way to stress test is to use a product, such as Firefox Throttle, that allows you to slow down your browser's traffic. After you understand a problem, you can decide how to improve the situation. This could mean decreasing file sizes, increasing compression, or something else.

In Figure 7-3, the issue is a small screen. To stress test this environment, try browsing on a handheld device or using an emulator. From there, you can work out how to improve the experience, even if doing so means redesigning a layout using CSS media queries or using some clever code combination. The web is all about compromise and helping users with any situation. Doing so will aid your distinction attempts.

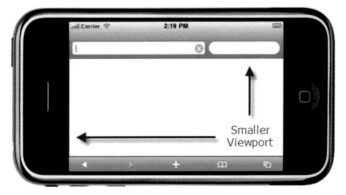

FIGURE 7-3: Smaller screens reduce the amount of distinction.

Beyond issues created by the hardware, software can intrude on your ability to provide a fluid and interactive experience. Browsers can disable effects such as "anti-right-click" scripts, marquees, blinking text, and scrolling; audio can be muted and windows resized or opened with toolbars and sidebars hogging up the available screen space — all of which distort distinction!

Important

One of the biggest design crimes is the disabling of important features for the sake of attempted protection. No scripted feature (such as anti-selection or anti–right-click) puts off pirates, so don't harm visitors by using such features in your design. Some individuals may depend on features such as the ability to select text or right-click in order to use a site!

With users being firmly in control of their experience and nothing on the screen, printer, or any other type of device or browser taken for granted, you have to be progressive with interactivity. Spend time researching what users need, when they need it, how they need it, how they consume such content, and the best method to implement such features. Distinctive interfaces don't offer unnecessary features; instead, they enhance features to maximize the visibility of what users need and want.

Ensuring that your design follows the principles of HCI by being attentive to users' needs is important. It helps avoid confusion, unexpected results, or unexpected problems. All actions within a site should be as fluid and barrier-free as possible. In fact, the less users have to think about while using your site, the better they can focus on enjoying what you provide. The only time users should be forced to think is when they must make decisions that affect them personally.

Dealing with User Choices

Functionality and interactivity introduce a bit of personality into a site by creating ways to respond to user needs and interactions. Avoid overwhelming users or providing them with stressful or complicated procedures. The aim of any site is to make the transition from page to page (or any other process) as easy as possible. Be sure to address the many potential problems that surround the idea of choice or decision-making on a page. So, if a piece of functionality can make a user's experience easier or more interesting, use it.

Designers often put so much energy into asking visitors to make decisions that they forget about providing the education behind new, exciting functionality and giving visitors the details they need to make informed choices (such as where those links take them, who gets a form's contents, and what really is required). These burdens usually fall on the visitor, who may give up and guess, give up and exit, or struggle through (hoping for more details). Figure 7-4 shows that by providing visual aids and giving supplementary functionality, you can help users decide which choices to make.

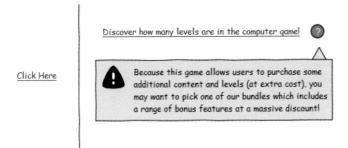

Click Here

FIGURE 7-4: There's a huge difference between unmarked and descriptive links with visual aids.

The harmony of a site's distinction requires you to acknowledge your users' requirements and to equip them with all they need to make decisions. If users don't know where to click or where to look, all the effort put into your architecture, visual design, and code falls apart, because you failed to give users what they need. To avoid this kind of breakdown in function, carefully consider the choices you offer. Too many choices cause confusion, and too few choices cause users to feel lost; therefore, strike a delicate balance to promote user comfort.

Tip

You don't want visitors to take on the burden of blame for making mistakes. Attempt to make your interfaces intuitive so that visitors can find what they're looking for as easily as possible, and set up some mechanism for undoing mistakes. Ideally, you want users to make the right choices from the offset, not spend their time running around in circles, making mistakes, and inundating your Inbox with requests for support.

One of the main ways to overcome choice-related issues is to spend time educating users about the results of their actions — for example, where clicks, keystrokes, and particular responses may lead them. Carefully considered navigation schemes, product tours, and appropriately labeled functionality can all help you achieve your goal, but whatever route you take, be sure that the interactivity doesn't make things more complicated.

If breakdowns do occur, users are more likely to ask for support, make bad or dangerous choices, or be less willing to use a site again. The power of choice shouldn't be taken for granted. Users need to be able to navigate your site without feeling frustrated or worried about using it in the future. Ultimately, you are responsible for ensuring that your functionality and interactivity lead people to make the right decisions, so never burden your site with unnecessary features. Always justify those features and make sure they're documented in a way that visitors will understand quickly.

The floods of complexity

Too much information can overwhelm people. The same is true regarding overly complex or poorly mapped-out decision points on a page. If users find themselves in a swamp of links that just say "click me," they're likely to click at random rather than with any idea about where they'll end up. Figure 7-5 shows how simplicity can reduce confusion. Consider how everything is neatly organized and that only the required details are shown on-screen.

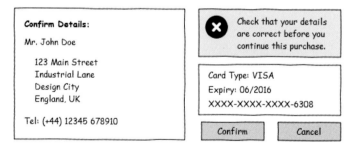

FIGURE 7-5: Avoiding confusion is important, especially when financial transactions are involved!

As people's eyes filter across a page trying to find focal points that help identify where they are or what they're looking for, they look for visuals or text to act as signposts (for example, when navigating a roadmap). With too much choice, users' brains suffer a form of mental conflict over how actions may positively or negatively influence where they will end up. Having to think among an illogical range of options results in choice paralysis!

Important

Choice paralysis initiates the fight or flight mechanism: People will do either everything in their power to understand the options (which increases the time spent working) or they'll give up and click the closest thing they can find to what they need and hope for the best. So, avoid creating such frustration whenever possible.

If you have one link on the page that says "About me," it's fairly obvious what that link represents. But having two options named similarly — for example, one named "About me" and the other "About us" — complicates things, because users may not be able to determine which page will contain the desired information. If an even wider range of choices appears with little differentiation or context (such as six "About" links), users are unable to identify the one that will take them to the page they want to visit.

Complexity in choice doesn't have to be the result of something being the same or very similar. Conflicts also can arise if two equally suitable options exist. Common issues of this kind include mystery meat navigation (MMN), where no unique label is given; associative links, where users must understand something else before they can determine the right path; and duplicate links, where users can't determine the correct route of navigation (see Figure 7-6, where users are forced to browse through a long list of links to determine which one takes them to the location they want).

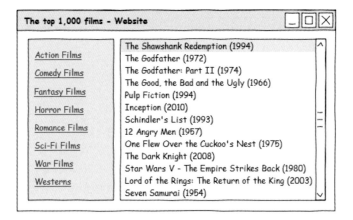

FIGURE 7-6: Hundreds of links on a page (with no real structure) mess with the visitor's mind.

Too many links on a page also dilute the distinction among the available options. Users will have a hard time trying to identify and distinguish them from one another because of the amount of "noise" on the page. This situation creates a huge barrier to entry that can cripple a user's ability to interact with a site. Clearly define important options, provide added support where needed, and don't assume that your visitors can traverse an overwhelming minefield of choices. When in doubt, the best thing to do is simplify and reduce the options. Filtering is a good idea!

The desert of simplicity

Of course, the other side of the story needs a bit of attention. Although information overload tends to be a real problem that many designers find themselves falling into, the issue of over-simplification can be equally as frustrating, and in certain cases, potentially insulting to your visitors. It's fine to dilute the number of choices if doing so helps the visitor, but when that dilution removes useful choices, it becomes a barrier.

When reducing the number of choices your visitors need to make, your primary objective is to eliminate options that offer nothing useful or to remove choices that users really don't need to make. You don't need to know their favorite color on a contact form. One classic method to simply forms and ensure that the options are retained but are easy to digest is to progressively request details as users do something requiring such details (for example, the way Twitter requires only the bare essentials at the time of registration).

Reference

Hiding unnecessary form entries is nothing new. You can find a great example of how to implement a detailed form at `http//:planner.builtbybuffalo.com`.

One classic mistake that designers commonly fall for when trying to simplify or streamline a process is removing useful choices entirely. If your users benefit from being asked for an e-mail address, then by all means leave it in, but don't ask for data that doesn't help them complete the task they want to carry out (as illustrated in Figure 7-7). Additionally, never automate decisions for which users may prefer to retain control; instead, provide opt-in functionality.

> Please enter your email address to download the free trial:
>
> Address: [name@email.com]   [Download]
>
> * Please note that the link will be sent to this address, as will some marketing messages!

FIGURE 7-7: Because users aren't declaring a purchase, you don't need personal details for a product trial.

If your visitors have to navigate through 20 pages just to find a particular part of a site, the link being used becomes a "one-way street," and the desired site will likely never to be found by anyone other than the most determined users. The same goes for orphan pages (stand-alone pages that can't be connected to other pages). Having appropriate references to pages is the right way to go. Breadcrumb navigation schemes may seem like a case of too many references, but they do provide a path to reach pages in the future (see Figure 7-8 for an illustration of breadcrumb navigation).

FIGURE 7-8: Being able to track one's progress through a site (or process) provides perspective.

The aim of distinctive design is to ensure that content of high quality has a fair chance of being noticed by offering choices on the page that help negotiate the labyrinth of options. Page functionality usually offers an increasing level of extensibility in how content can be found, used, or consumed. Consequently, a page can easily become too complicated. Good design is about reducing the barriers to entry and functionality that makes objects more accessible, but you need to take care that users retain control over their input.

Choice and decisions affect people in different ways. Some users revel in the exploration of new sites and find poking around an interface exciting and fun. Others just wanting to achieve a goal look for the simplest way possible. Interactive features within a site can help guide people to content or elements of a page that may be of interest. Be sure that options within a page are sensibly laid out and that the choices you offer encourage visitors on your sites. The goal is to end up with something easy to use, not a game of 20 questions.

Tip

Amazon's one-click purchase system has shown that reducing the barrier to entry can reap heavy rewards, as have the series of cases in which small interface changes have increased the income proportionately for big brands (in the sum of millions). In fact, with this system, users can dodge having to repeatedly enter their details, and it skips over parts of the process that are unnecessary based on the purchase choice.

Decoding Design Interactions

Behind the scenes of any website, you find a bunch of elements, properties, and functions all working in unison to render and layer functionality on that site. Although it seems like a modern miracle that such a thing could be possible, remember that every interactive feature within a site is likely to be built from a small selection of controllers. At their core, these controllers allow users to click, type, or listen for events and respond by doing something cool.

As designers, you want to ensure that your sites take advantage of the useful mediums offered to every user's hardware, and make your content more distinctive as a consequence. If you consider the power that scripting and interactivity give your sites, this kind of power literally becomes an experience-changing event. Interactivity allows users to contact you, get content on demand, explore a site, locate new content, and potentially focus in a more effective manner. They will see the object, interact with it, and await results. For a simple example, consider the anchors that guide users from one page to another (post clicking, denoted in Figure 7-9).

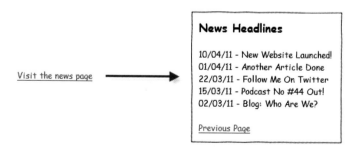

FIGURE 7-9: Users click links in the hope that new, useful content will be revealed!

This whole perception of interactivity giving distinction to a design is backed up by the way most software products are built and used. Consider how much time people spend attentively using menus, identifying clickable regions, and entering or reading text. The web isn't that much different, except that designers have the option to either maximize or minimize the functionality they provide, rather than depend on it to carry out the user's needs autonomously. Remember, though, if you're building a web app or something for a phone, you may well want to follow this effect! As for sites, it's equally as important to retain and maximize the usefulness of interactivity from input elements.

Tip   Phones follow many of the same conventions as desktop apps, except that they are optimized for a small screen. The iPhone, for example, has scrolling menus, and many apps go as far as having distinctive iconized menus at the base of the screen.

Users have different expectations of interfaces. Some show interest only in the content you provide; many more will be looking or hoping for something a bit special or unique. Static sites won't disappear anytime soon. They serve their function well and do still have some raw interactivity via clickable links. Don't ignore the power that interactivity can bring. Giving users a distinctive experience requires much more than just a bit of beauty that sits there silently catching the visitor's eye — it needs to tell a story, guide users, and help them narrow their focus on the page to content that matters. In addition, functionality doesn't always have to be abrupt. Many sites have proven this with subtle and delicate flourishes, such as auto-completes in searches.

User interface controls

With any challenge, you need to know what tools you have available. As with earlier parts of the book, this chapter examines things in the order of structure (HTML), style (CSS), and behavior (scripting). JavaScript has the most to offer in terms of interactivity, but you can get a few interactive aspects running with just HTML or CSS, which is great for designers and fans of progressive enhancement.

Tip   CSS3 offers plenty of advancements in respect to interactivity, but remember that older browsers won't have the native support for such interactivity. You may need to add some unobtrusive scripting to provide a functional fallback.

HTML interactivity

In HTML, two primary elements enable you to embed useful interactive features within a site, the first and most common of which are anchors. Most links are, by default, set to redirect users to another page or a section or fragment of an existing page. The method of cross-linking among files is a primary aspect of interactivity because the pathway to a particular page can require several clicks and directions. Redirect users only when necessary because the action breaks the natural reading flow and too many links confuse users (see Figure 7-10). To break down long lists of content, some sites have multiple pages, with a defined number of features per page.

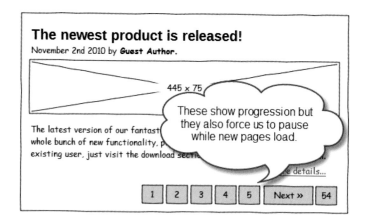

FIGURE 7-10: This lapse of concentration often occurs when content is broken into multiple pages.

In addition to links, HTML offers a second and more application-oriented set of elements based within the form tag and the numerous input elements that provide interactivity. If you've ever entered a lot of data on a form to sign up for a service, that's interactivity at work. Forms are not simply to direct users to a certain path, but to ask them to enter information that can be processed. This provides an opportunity to customize an experience for visitors based on their willingness to offer the relevant response or information (which, of course, you must store safely and not abuse). The one downside of both links and forms is that without scripting or other interactivity at work, the focus tends to be a bit one-sided in favor of the user, as shown in Figure 7-11.

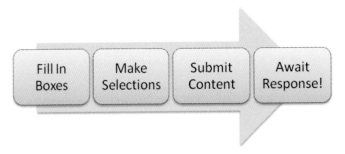

FIGURE 7-11: Forms allow users to enter text, make selections, respond to clicks, and submit information.

CSS interactivity

CSS may be a stylistic language, but you can use a few event-based behaviors within designs to help make them distinctive, too. These pseudo-classes usually work around the aspect of a user's interaction with stylistic elements on the page. They are great tools to take advantage of when support exists for them in browsers. Some of the coolest advances in terms of behavior on pages have appeared out of CSS3, such as transitions and animation, so they are worthy of experimentation and perhaps a bit of unobtrusive JavaScript to help older, less forgiving browsers along.

The most widely recognized of these pseudo-classes are those associated with link events, such as hover, focus, visited, or active. These items may not seem that powerful, but they provide the opportunity to change stylistic content when a link is clicked or rolled over, for example. A classic example of this is the drop-down menu. CSS3 lets you take this a bit further by issuing events based on explicit choices made (targeting for fragment links selected, for example).

Important Links should have a visual distinction from regular text in order to actively maintain visibility. Also, if you choose to alter the visual styles on an event such as focus, don't hide the CSS outline, which is helpful to those browsing with a keyboard.

The potential implementations for languages such as CSS3 may include progressive disclosure and lightboxes (dialog boxes focusing users on a particular area on-screen), as seen in slideshows or full-sized images on some sites, or in more content (upon clicking via progressive disclosure) as users require it. It could also include giving more information about something on a page by selecting from a list of other options that disappear once a mouse moves from the component (not good for permanent effects).

The benefits of such selector components are astounding. Beyond the benefits of providing cool drop-down mechanisms or attempting to attach special focus events to elements of a page, the CSS3 components offer you the ability to serve or refine an interface based on physical activity. By turning links into anchor fragments, for example, you can restyle the entire design or make something appear that was previously not visible on the screen, but that existed within the page. This practice is commonly implemented in non-refreshing in-page content tabs (see Figure 7-12).

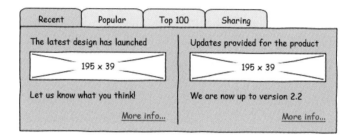

FIGURE 7-12: A simple example of CSS3 disclosure could include a tabbed navigation effect.

JavaScript interactivity

If you want to go beyond the hovers or disclosure tools or want more event-based controls, then you must leave CSS in favor of the wonderful power of JavaScript. Scripts allow you to set up a response to occur when a user does something requiring a response, leaving a required field empty, for example. The ability to have your site react to a user's machine or equipment is potentially limitless and can be set up in an unobtrusive way.

JavaScript also has allowances for events that can be triggered by setting up something in a certain way (such as adding or removing content via AJAX) and when something happens at the input level (by mouse, keyboard, gesture, interface, form, or even touch events). This is where interactivity really cranks up a notch. You can enhance your site's distinction based on how users react, and you can engineer functionality by using the DOM event handlers and listeners. If you're not that comfortable working out how to implement such features, a whole range of frameworks such as jQuery can help you.

Coding for interactivity

With all this potential for interactivity, it's worth spending a bit of time highlighting how distinction can occur as a result of such functionality. With so much power at your finger-tips, you may be tempted to go over the top and automate everything you produce to perform some quirky yet aesthetically pleasing task on the page. So, you need to be aware that potential downsides exist in distinctive interaction.

One easy-to-see disadvantage of interactive design is its distractive value. Adding the animations or visual flourishes that can improve an interface (such as progressive disclosure using the *target pseudo*) still means that hidden content will be stuffed on the page, which could dilute the semantic distinction of the code. Accessibility can also be problematic when AJAX or other script-dependent tools are added, which can really damage a user's experience. In addition to being distracting in terms of raw visibility, the distinctive value can be affected by the movement occurring, perhaps unnecessarily.

Tip   Animation in the form of content can attract attention, but animation used for stylistic flourishes within a site can draw attention away from the content. Having a bit of subtle background interactivity can breathe life into a design, but use it with caution!

Everything that you add to a design could potentially distract users from other content, and everything you remove could potentially reduce the some quality features or useful aids. Gaining a balance of quality versus noise requires weighing the pros and cons when deciding what to include. Interactivity aims to share something on the page that helps visitors on their journey through your site, so strive to make all interactivity useful!

Common interactive features include the following:

> progressive disclosure, providing more or less content

> special effects, such as animations that can be provided by CSS transitions or animation-based scripts

> enhancements, such as providing sound or video

> contextual effects, such as altering the style, structure, or behavior of the page based on the manner in which it's used or by who is using it

By using code, all of this and more is made possible! If you're curious about the potential for scripts to give functionality or interactivity, why not experiment with code? You may find that in some cases (as illustrated in Figure 7-13) small tweaks can have increasingly useful effects.

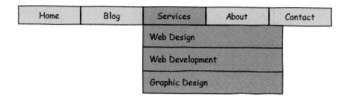

FIGURE 7-13: Increase the stability of use by setting a delay on navigation menu closure.

Producing an interactive site is one thing, but creating an experience that engages users, provides them with something useful, and has enough distinctive merit to draw attention away from other objects (only when doing so is a real necessity or of practical use) is a challenge. Adding functionality based on perceived value rather than on usefulness can cause sites to have unnecessary excess noise. If what you want to add isn't critical, your best option may be to exclude it.

Encouraging Interactivity

Interactivity can be a great thing. With it, you can encourage visitors to be more hands-on, and what you provide can run at either a cognitive level (using psychology to make visitors think and react) or a social level (encouraging people to communicate and build a community). Or interactivity can trigger page events that improve the situation and even give layouts a more polished look and feel. Explore the web for implementations from which to draw inspiration and build your own feature set as you require it.

Regarding functionality on a page, interactivity falls under two main categories: *features* or *effects*. Features enhance what exists on a page, and effects cause a reaction when several components come together. All things considered, there's plenty of justification to include interactive objects on the page.

Although effects follow the principle of responsive design (discussed the section, "Responsive design theory," later in this chapter), your page's functionality usually includes a mixture of effects that allow the feature to have its effect. After all, there's no point having a feature that doesn't actually do anything.

Most functionality falls into one of two camps — *productive* or *unproductive*. Productive features are probably the best types of tools because they help reduce the amount of time people spend browsing a site, which increases satisfaction levels. RSS feeds, for example, are features that send content to people's digital In boxes, like a virtual mail carrier. An example of this preformatted effect is shown in Figure 7-14. Other types of productive functionality include complex navigation systems, content-on-demand, and even social sharing icons, such as those icons seen on websites that identify how many retweets, likes, and stumbles a page has received (or those giving a web bookmark link).

Although productive functionality aids distinction of pages by helping people get to the content they desire, it can also help filter out some of the less useful clutter on the page. For example, you can produce a script that highlights the text where the mouse resides or focus on that part of the screen by fading the rest of the page by using opacity. Sound great? Why not consider it — you may find that these effects increase responsiveness to parts of a page!

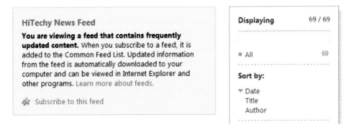

FIGURE 7-14: Syndication feeds are a productive feature because they save your visitors time.

Unproductive functionality may seem like a waste of time because it's not used to draw attention to content that users desire. Rather, it exists primarily to highlight content that a user may not be aware of but may find useful. Adding such functionality doesn't mean that you spam page links everywhere. Instead, you use it as helpful signposts or as fun exploration events to provide a secondary level of impact, after achieving goals.

Distinction in unproductive functionality works on the theory that users will stay on a page longer and perhaps find something equally useful elsewhere on a site. You can also use this functionality to give people a working knowledge of an interface. Take treasure hunts, where you lead people around a site looking for a free prize (as illustrated in Figure 7-15). Such features give sites some humor and personality and give users a sense of satisfaction.

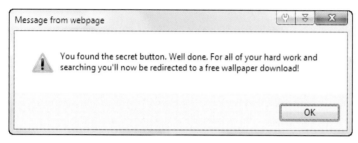

FIGURE 7-15: Easter eggs and hidden functionality have become staples of software, media, and websites!

Focus the sustainability of interactivity on providing short-term and long-term solutions for a user's needs and personal goals. If you happen to have a Black Friday sale, then why not promote it with a bit of interactivity, which could encourage people to browse your other content? For a public holiday, such as Christmas, perhaps throw a few snowy effects on the screen, if they don't interfere with content readability. Personality gives users an emotional connection to a service, and giving upgrades to site functionality may give your work a greater feeling of maturity than your peers' work.

Tip

If you are promoting a sale on your site, one common interactive method to really keep visitors hooked is to use a *countdown script*. It not only plays on people's value of time, but it also justifies their revisiting a page in order to be the first in line for rewards.

Designing for interactivity

When building sites or apps, consider the role and impact that each individual piece of functionality has on your designs. Sometimes you may want to offer instructional materials that help people accomplish a task. Other times, you may want to assist users who have specific needs of an interface. The challenge for designing interactivity focuses on every page having a purpose that must be implemented so that its benefits outweigh the costs to both you and your users — users hate wading through reels of junk content.

A whole range of tools can help you create functionality that users will appreciate. In addition, some features help promote certain objects of distinction, whereas others withdraw such focus. When you research your users and their needs, examine how they navigate around a site or what they commonly ask for in feedback. This information may give you loads of ideas to work on!

Reference   Although a number of tools are included, the following site has a fantastic table that describes each tool's category and function. You won't need them all, but consider which ones can help your visitors: `www.edtech.vt.edu/edtech/ id/interface/tools2.html`.

Seeking tools

The first tools due examination are commonly referred to as *seeking tools*. They help users find information. Examples are search engines (shown in Figure 7-16), tables of content, sitemaps, resource lists, social bookmarking sites, and anything else that either helps users pass on the word about your awesome content or helps them and others find the best pieces of information on the site. Users spend most of their time browsing a site, so it's not surprising that helping them navigate the maze of content is a basic goal of functionality.

FIGURE 7-16: Search engines allow users to "seek" pages for which they don't know the exact location.

Generators

Second on the list and worthy of a look are *generators,* those features that produce new content rather than seek answers through existing materials. Although traditional systems such as chat rooms, bulletin boards, feedback forms, and forums remain staples of this type of feature, wiki, video conferencing, commenting systems (see Figure 7-17), and upload services (such as YouTube and Flickr) have helped push consumer-driven sites into popularity. Communication is a major part of design. When visitors can contribute high-quality content, you have more distinctive material with which to work.

FIGURE 7-17: Comments on a form provide some great discussions and increase contextual value.

Scaffolding

The third item on the list is commonly referred to as *scaffolding* tools. The goal of this functionality type is to advise or inform visitors about content within a page (whether its purpose is function or something else). If you consider how much information the average page includes, you can imagine that people can find terminology or content hard to follow. The aim of scaffolding is to provide tours, on-demand help, advice, annotations, tooltips (see Figure 7-18), or on-page aids that add context to an interface and clarity to content.

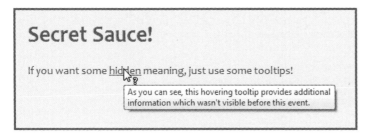

FIGURE 7-18: Tooltips can explain the meanings behind words that a visitor doesn't understand.

Enhancement

Fourth on the list are *enhancement tools*. Their primary objective is to alter the existing page or how it functions in order to better reflect consumers' needs. Sometimes, content, on its own, doesn't do the job of engaging a reader. Cognitive psychology shows that if you not only grab users' attentions, but also turn something into an experience, they're more likely to remember it! So use tools such as quizzes, visual or otherwise (see Figure 7-19);

slide shows; practical demos; and other on-page enhancements to improve the distinction of your site's content (reinforcing attention and concentration).

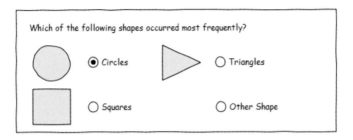

FIGURE 7-19: Providing a quiz at the end of an article reinforces memory retention and recollection.

Assistive tools

Finally, assistive tools have the straightforward goal of ensuring that what you provide functions equally well for all your users. These tools play a primary role in accessibility — for example, with browsers and sites combined, you can help users who would otherwise be left out, which isn't good for distinction or popularity! Page zooming, contrast altering, magnification, screen reading, and more help users; however, on-page tools such as custom stylesheets, mobile-friendly pages, skip links (hidden off-screen or shown on-screen as in Figure 7-20), and highlights or overview blocks can assist users, too.

| Skip to content | Skip to navigation | Skip to footer |

FIGURE 7-20: Skip links within a site can help users jump to a specific part of a page!

Although each of these tools, on its own, provides visitors with an enhanced experience, adding small subtle flourishes, such as auto-completion and theme-changing, can aid a design. Check out such implementation on other sites for inspiration; then experiment for ways to improve aspects of your site and how it functions. You never know how big of an impact your changes might have on users!

Responsive design theory

By designing with functionality in mind, the tools you provide may serve as a natural outlet for visitors' reactions, which may encourage continued use. Because visitors negotiate around a site, the notion of reacting and adjusting the page became popular in the design community. If each action has a reaction that benefits users, then it's worth aiming for. Obviously, you can't depend on users having a Terminator-style intelligence — computers aren't that smart at detection — but analyzing users' actions helps you redesign with logic and perspective.

Providing interfaces that adapt to users' needs gave birth to the theory of *responsive design*. The ideal scenario is to aim for a site that matches users' requirements, browsers, software, and hardware. Responsive design also requires distinction so that visitors are aware that their actions netted the desired result. If you have a button that does something behind the scenes but has no imprint on the page, users may assume nothing happened and keep clicking. This common effect only increases impatience.

Reference   The article at the following site focuses primarily on user-interface design, but its influence throughout interaction are profound. As you build interactivity, consider each of these principles (along with those mentioned in the following sections): www.sylvantech.com/~talin/projects/ui_design.html.

A few conventions exist within interaction design, and they can help ensure that your features match user expectations. The ideas behind them are improvement of the quality of your interfaces and how distinction can apply within the functionality produced for your site. The following principles share similarities with the principles and elements of design, so understanding their goals should be straightforward.

User profiling

The first is *user profiling,* which requires you to understand users' needs and then to calculate how to wield their strengths in a way that helps users achieve goals. For example, don't offer features to a group that will be unable or for some reason refuse to use those features effectively. Another example is the unavailability of Flash on iOS devices. Look to your audience to see exactly what's right for the task!

Metaphor

Next up is *metaphor*, which states that if you can borrow from a system that people are used to, then you'll lower the learning curve and increase the general usability of a site. (Consider the shock people got when the Ribbon replaced the menu and toolbar system in Microsoft Office 2007!) On the web, you can use traditional buttons in an MP3 player (such as Play or Stop — as illustrated in Figure 7-21). The hope is that people will recognize the mechanism and its convention and adapt accordingly.

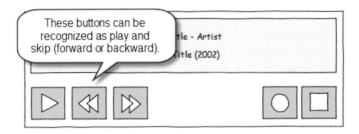

FIGURE 7-21: In an MP3 player, buttons follow the trend of actual hardware devices.

Feature exposure

Feature exposure is a principle stating that anything that may be useful to users should be visible to them at the time they require it. This principle is an extension of progressive disclosure, something you've come to know and love while exploring simplicity and distinction. Having a navigation system that's always visible may be helpful in some sites, but in others, you may want it to remain in a static position. Also, it may not be necessary to fill in some form elements at certain points, so new parts of the form can appear only as required.

Coherence

Another founding principle of interaction design is *coherence*. This concept stresses the importance of structure and asks you to do what you can to make sure that the functionality you offer behaves as expected and in an order that makes sense to users. If, for example, you have a site that asks people to order a product, don't make them sign up for an account just to add items to a basket! You need credit card details only when they check out. This example has been shown to particularly affect buying habits.

Tip

When browsing for an item to purchase, consumers like to do a bit of window shopping. By allowing them to add items to an anonymous cart, they can easily remember what they have seen and perhaps pick between two comparable products with ease.

State visualization

Another important principle in interaction is *state visualization*. State visualization focuses on actions that require a reaction or some kind of visual recognition — for example, when users need to know that a form they filled out has been properly submitted. If a user submits an incorrect or incomplete form, the error needs to be highlighted and the user immediately made aware of the issue (instead of by way of a cryptic message). Visuals draw attention, and a reactive design motivates users to make decisions based on what's recently happened.

Shortcuts

You also need to understand the importance of *shortcuts*. As visitors get used to your site or app, they will build up a mental image of how the objects and navigation are mapped out. Although you need to have concrete navigation menus leading to areas of the site, quick routes to content through on-page shortcuts are welcomed timesavers. (See Figure 7-22.)

FIGURE 7-22: Follow the shortcut principle to help people find important content quickly!

Grammar

On top of the preceding principles, you need to remember *grammar*. Consider every interface and piece of functionality as though they were the elements of a book. A few pages direct readers (in this case, users) to important parts (like chapters in a book), and some help users seek particular objects (like an index). Also, always avoid treating users like children; just tell them the rules of an interface so that they can intuitively work their way around a layout.

Every visitor to your site has a safety threshold within which he or she can withstand the occasional quirk or issue. That's lucky, because sites can suffer the misfortune of being disabled or breaking down because of unforeseen circumstances. Because your site's functionality is dependent on it doing the job right, you need these appropriate fallback mechanisms to sustain a user's level of appreciation and interest.

Important You may be surprised by how often your visitors need a safety net. Gracefully degrading code and progressively enhancing features help to weatherproof your site against most situations! Even the most compatible layouts can fail if the navigation methodology, content quality, or other variables are neglected.

Context

Another principle to consider in interaction is *context*. All actions take place within a region of the screen. Occasionally, that context is within a dialog box or model dialog. In the majority of cases, however, it takes place within a defined space in the window. For all on-screen functionality, try to keep the effect close to where the event was triggered. Users don't like surprises. Linking the association helps to smooth the flow and transition. A good example of this is tooltips, which hover under the link or object that needs explanation.

Time

Finally, you need to be aware of *time*. People spend time using your functionality and waiting for the ensuing response. Every page they navigate to takes time as well, so the time spent browsing can add up, as noted in Figure 7-23. With this in mind, ensure that you don't waste more of their time than necessary. Optimize your code to be responsive, optimize your visuals to be easy to navigate, and don't forget that the time users spend waiting is time they could use more productively (reading content, for example).

FIGURE 7-23: The less time pages take to load, the more likely users will remain on the site.

Summary

Of the many existing best practices and perspectives about interaction, the conclusion to draw from this research is that users always come first. Regarding distinctive design, note that interactive elements of a site boost the visibility and extensibility of objects within a page. If something can be given a helpful feature without abusing the privilege (or hurting the content's readability), consider making your users' experiences easier with some interactive goodness. Such features really can bring life to your interfaces.

As you layer interactivity within a design, consider the principles mentioned in this chapter. Understand your users, build upon existing conventions, expose features as required, and ensure that everything works as expected. Also, let visitors see the result of actions, provide helpful shortcuts to save time, make the content flow correctly, offer fallbacks for glitches or compatibility quirks, relate features appropriately, and don't waste users' time! These goals sound simple, but can be quite a challenge to accomplish, especially when they're all needed at once!

The Foundations of User Experience

Customizing an interface for your visitors' benefit

YOUR SITES FALL short of your goal if people don't visit and enjoy them. Even though the web in which you design is rich and immersive, your users can remain in a position in which they rarely get a fair deal. Visitors want and expect more from designs, and designers expect and demand more from users.

In this chapter, I examine the fundamental principles of the user-experience field, which lead into all sorts of directions in this book and the e-book. You explore the importance of customization and personalization, as well as subjectivity and objectivity. Then I cover some information on value-based design, along with attention grabbing and feature layering.

Customizing Creativity

Designers have put a lot of energy into creating artistic sites that people can browse dynamically. In this book, I put a great deal of emphasis on giving users an experience. The simplest way to convey *user experience* is by the sights, sounds, feelings, sensations, and responsive elements within an interface. The *experience* is the memory and reaction to those elements.

Although it can be argued that a web experience is less tactile than a real-world experience, people emote and connect to what is being served in front of them, in a sensory way. Website customization and personalization becomes paramount.

A designer must build an interface for a mass audience, but provide each user with a personal experience. The illusion of giving a mass-market appeal with "local ties" that identify with individuals is somewhat of a "holy grail" for all designers, but it is possible, especially if you consider the web's flexibility! Figure 8-1 shows some basic examples of how using clever words or images can inject personality into a site.

Allowing visitors to customize a website and the content shown on-screen is nothing new. Many sites offer user profiles that identify users by name and give them a seemingly crafted way to experience a site on their own. Communication methods such as forums enable users to identify themselves as individuals and participate. Including a shopping cart gives users a sense of being an individual customer rather than one of millions of anonymous users.

FIGURE 8-1: A distinctive use of language and personality positively affects how users relate to information.

The creativity behind giving people an element of self-expression is a powerful force in the user experience toolkit. By identifying the uniqueness of users in a way they can recognize, you customize a site and give them something memorable and a place to often return.

Personalization protocol

So how do you provide such a creative flourish in your designs? Often, you can reflect lower levels of personalization in the way you write; however, in today's sites, visual representations provide the greatest impact and interactivity. Static sites are composed only of style and substance and aren't able to participate in higher levels of distinction, which introduces your need to turn to scripting.

Although it's not entirely reliable because it can be disabled, you can use *client-side* scripting to achieve high levels of personalization. Examples include the use of AJAX (a way to send and receive data without refreshing) or allowing parts of a window to be relocated (such as moving widgets around a screen, as shown in Figure 8-2). You do this by interacting with the DOM structure (by manipulating HTML and CSS on-demand) and altering the content and visual appearance. Client-side scripting also allows interactivity with the machine to a certain extent, which could prove useful in catering to a user's device choice (if supported).

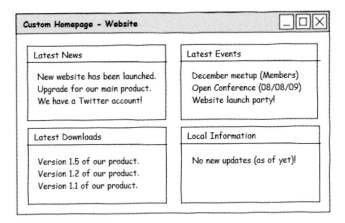

FIGURE 8-2: Client-side scripting allows the customization of widgets around a page.

Server-side scripting, on the other hand, is a real powerhouse. Although it lacks features that identify a user's computer or that give you any force within the browser, server-side scripting allows a more globalized experience so that users potentially can have a remotely-hosted account (like their Twitter stream). From any machine with web access, users can log in to take advantage of the tools allocated for their personal use. This approach helps to define an experience and allows preferences to be provided on any computer, which is how most sites implement user accounts and host cloud-based applications (see Figure 8-3).

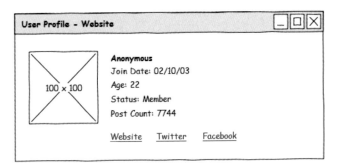

FIGURE 8-3: Want a user profile containing useful member information? Use server-side scripting.

The ability to interact with something that remembers how you left the site, what you did previously, and even gives you some measured form of control says much for an experience. Consider cookies and databases. A cookie acts as a form of short-term memory and provides some quick, stable ways to anonymously customize a layout. Databases, on the other hand, can "remember" a larger range of variables and can give users a sense of measurable progress, though privacy often becomes an issue when information is being stored or offered up.

Many examples exist for the different types of scriptable interaction that you can give to your users to provide them with a sense of experience and distinction. They recognize that their efforts remain stored and achievements framed, and have a sense of belonging and ongoing participation. Your job as a designer is to allow your users to have this sense of practical interaction so that they have an incentive to return, whether that's to purchase more goods, continue evolving their blog, or to post on a forum — it's up to you!

Tip

When coding for mobile platforms of situations in which scripting may be limited, site interaction is best placed within the confines of a server-side environment. It's the one type of scripting that always manages to deliver the goods!

Trends and implementations

Regarding the types of implementations that exist, the custom home page (such as iGoogle or its competitors provide) is one of the best examples of how a formed level of experience encourages user interaction. The service has no real content; instead it has a series of applets that visitors can customize. So, its success is based on allowing users to build an experience on pure functionality and utility, while being able to carry a useful, personalized environment around the web.

Achievements are one of the defining parts of an experience, which, as the game industry knows, adds to the powerful psychological tools that encourage users to spend more time and make more contributions to an environment. Consider providing web-orientated game mechanics, such as experience points, awards for contributions, and even prizes for contributing to a community. Offering such gifts of varying value (see Figure 8-4) promotes healthy competition along with a healthy sense of satisfaction and achievement.

FIGURE 8-4: Rewarding user interaction is a great way to ensure regular visits and content updates.

Personalization doesn't get much bigger than it does in advertising. No matter what content, product, or service you put on your site, if you want a financial benefit, you need to ensure that users know that what you offer is right for them (which requires some convincing), and you need to justify the payment. Google's advertising model shows that personalization has its place in monetization. Users won't purchase something that doesn't appeal to them. Targeting users (behavioral engineering) can therefore be very powerful.

One of the main trends in personalization is steeped in the art of communication. You've likely had the experience of calling a business for assistance, only to have an automated e-mail response or recording state impersonal stuff that you don't want to listen to. When dealing with website visitors, you need to identify user uniqueness. If you send out e-mails, never spam. Allowing users to opt into e-mails showcases the balance between user power and a potentially appealing experience for that user; it also gives users and incentive to read the message, rather than leave it in a spam folder.

Important

Bad experiences are often more memorable than good ones and the effects can linger long after the event. Offer unobtrusive, good experiences to visitors and do your best to handle problems promptly and with sensitivity.

Other examples are CMS (content management system) engines such as WordPress. These engines work provide previously set interfaces that give individuals the ability to use the product (and publish content) without needing to know how to code, and with instant results. Ultimately, you need to define and sculpt your sites into a standardized format to avoid confusion among users; providing small personal touches and a recognizable route to interaction gives users the impression of acceptance and that you care about them. Your site will have higher satisfaction ratings if you reduce barriers to entry.

The benefits of invisibility

Customization and personalization appeal to visitors because it gives them an opportunity to see a layout that matches their requirements and adapts to their own usage — by showing them how they interact, and what they want, as they want it. You also need to recognize, however, that some people won't be comfortable giving you the kind of information you request before providing them with an experience, which doesn't encourage long-lasting relationships!

Sites constantly ask users for information for gain (financially or otherwise). Unfortunately, instead of building experiences to better meet users' specific needs, many designers try to up-sell things users don't want or need. Heed this advice: Avoid such tempting pitfalls as you develop your distinctive design features and respect your users' right to anonymity, not just their rights to privacy.

Important Some aspects of distinctive design can be obtrusive or abusive. Realize that although you can do a great many things to demand your user's attention, the fallout from unbridled acts of attention-seeking can be disastrous for your reputation. Try to apply distinction when it benefits your users, not yourself!

When thinking of anonymous users, you may have the impression that they don't want to return or have ties to your site, and that is somewhat true. But in many ways, users feel more comfortable when they can't be identified. This behavior isn't so much a case of them being up to no good; rather, it's the primary human need for safety and feeling secure. Allowing anonymous browsing may feel like a missed opportunity, but it can paradoxically work in your favor if users sign up when they're ready for the commitment. Users who are given a choice to register (see Figure 8-5) will value their membership and be more receptive to handing over information in the future — and they'll be less likely to provide false data.

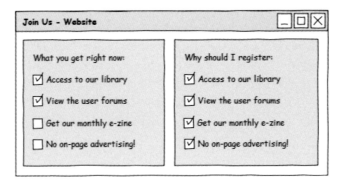

FIGURE 8-5: Give users a choice, along with an incentive to register (for a range of benefits you offer).

Consider one of the many online shopping sites. A common convention is the shopping cart. It has a level of customization and personalization, but no real need for data. Sites like Amazon cleverly allow users to window-shop and fill their carts as they browse. Then if users like what's in the basket, they simply sign up or log in and make the purchase, which follows the principles of progressive disclosure and privacy enablement.

One of the key reasons it's important to allow anonymity until identification is either offered by the user (to further personalize an experience) or required (say, to make a purchase) is that those being asked for more than they want to disclose may give falsified information in order to meet the criteria. Because fake accounts aren't useful to you, it's better to progressively customize at a level visitors will naturally accept and to increase demands for information as your site needs to.

Important Although you may want to stamp out false registrations, a number of sites like "Bug Me Not" exist, which aim to allow the public to use previously created fake IDs. If you ask too much of users, they'll just get defensive. So don't ask unless you really need to know!

Positives and Negatives

Design is a subject that receives more attention in terms of overwhelming popularity or utter negativity than most other aspects of the web. Site design usually reflects the ideas of a site's publishers, who want to promote their thoughts and goals with the hope that those viewing the offerings will relate and continue browsing. Despite being such an expressive medium that throws opinion to the edge, you need to explore the pros and cons.

Your visitors will hope to gain an experience from the services, tools, and products you offer on your website. To make these as distinctive as possible, recognize that every user has his or her own expectations of an interface. Likely, nothing you produce will please everyone. Design is an art, and ultimately, the experiences you provide can be interpreted in various ways.

Consider implementing user-defined preferences and customization so that your users find what they want and so that it displays in a way that's meaningful to them. How visitors interpret your work and see your content is determined based on their own perception. If your design appeals to their sense of aesthetics and works well, the experience will be positive. This is one reason for preferences, because users determine an aesthetic layout they prefer. You can provide a menu with some previously defined layouts, as in Figure 8-6, or allow a handcrafted theme.

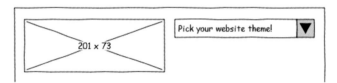

FIGURE 8-6: Personalization can be as simple as a drop-down menu with alternative stylesheets!

Determining what is good and bad within an interface requires a great deal of skill. As a designer, take into account the recommendations and needs of your visitors by removing things that the masses complain about or by resolving problems that have specific merit, even if those cases affect a small number of users.

Opinion is the ruler of the web. Put your time and energy into cultivating and crafting your interfaces into a format that your visitors will enjoy. Determining what does and doesn't work is a tricky business, but in the field of user experience, it's a balance of meeting the needs of the many and addressing the genuine concerns of the few that absorbs the majority of your time. Understand this methodology. It's critical to distinctive design!

Tip

Some critiques are paradoxical. Consider the classifieds site, Craigslist. It isn't that aesthetically pleasing and doesn't have much in the way of experience beyond pure functionality. Yet to this day, it remains a very popular site on the web.

Website saints and sinners

The boundaries between good and bad sites are proportionately measured by the very users who experience the environment. Consider how many times you have seen a film and then thought, "What is all the fuss about? I didn't like it." This is pretty much the same for all mediums, so you need to appeal to your chosen audience in the best way possible. Users should enjoy your sites, not suffer in silence.

The concept of the perfect website is a little far-fetched, especially because everyone's idea of perfect is relatively unique. There is a good point worth making on the benefit of imperfections, though. Although ironing out critical bugs and issues is important to the site's capability to give users what they need, imperfections do draw attention, discussion, and even become memorable; therefore, in some cases, purposeful quirks in a design might actually benefit the distinctive value. In fact, the dominant accidental quirks often hold more distinction than some deliberate visuals. Broken typography is shown in Figure 8-7.

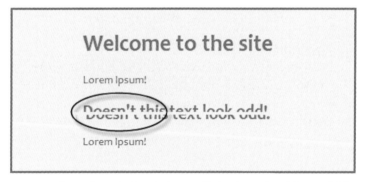

FIGURE 8-7: Inconsistencies in a design are distinctive and could be useful for giving a site "character"!

One fundamental issue relating to design and the concept of good and bad technique is the issue of necessity. Many sites add features that aren't required, such as "print this page" links that go to a printer-friendly page when a print stylesheet will do or links that attempt to replicate a Bookmark or Back button. Training users to use features that are unnecessary not only instills bad habits, but also causes problems when they leave the site and find others that don't follow suit. (This negative trend is known as an *anti-pattern*). If something is unnecessary, don't put it there or, if there, remove it!

The result of the debate over what makes a quality site can be confusing for all involved. Distinctive designers want users to have the cleanest and smoothest experience possible, and sites must evolve to modern standards. As you design sites or build layouts, consider the positive and negative impact for objects on the page and the page itself. Make every feature beneficial.

Websites are usually considered "bad" by the masses if they fail to contemplate or meet their needs. (Often this happens when designers design for themselves rather than for those who use the sites.) Interfaces need to appeal to your audience, which is possible only if you make the decision to implement, refine, repurpose, publish, and continue to evolve your work to your users' needs. Visitors come and go (as do regulars), so needs may change over time, which is why redesigning from time to time is useful.

Reference

If you're looking for some inspiration for whether a design may be considered good or bad by people with an eye for creativity, this "hot-or-not" gallery (and other inspiration galleries) is great for getting a few general design ideas: `http://commandshift3.com`.

Subjectivity within distinction

The key principle to consider when aiming for a distinctive and useful experience depends on the users of the site, what they want from the experience, and how they interpret what you offer through content, visuals, and interactivity. The main idea at work here is *subjectivity,* which reinforces the idea that users see things only from their, perhaps restricted, perspective.

Because subjectivity is hard to measure, when designing a site, use the opposing force, objectivity, to offer what you hope will appeal to the masses and then make refinements based on group behavior and feedback. If you provide visitors with a medium to personalize their experience, subjectivity becomes the strongest force and lets people see things as they want.

Tip

Being objective seems straightforward. You just consider the facts and variables at work, without your own opinions or thoughts. Of course, this is easier said than done because people's biases dictate much of what they perceive to be good design!

Every user's taste differs. Be sure that the base layer of your user interface promotes clear and objective thinking in order to appeal to as many site users as possible. It should provide the slice of interactivity, choice, and distinctive customization that will match users' subjective needs and also present the content in a way they can enjoy and put to the best use (see Figure 8-8).

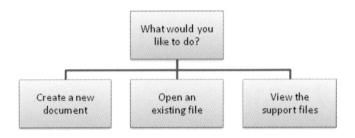

FIGURE 8-8: Offering choice is one of many distinctive routes to objectivity in experience design.

Overcoming the problems of subjectivity can be tricky if you try to account for all possible variables a user may want to control. Many sites to this day have gone through a whole series of reinventions and redesigns to strike a good balance between what most users expect and what individual users want. The most distinctive site you can produce needs to account for this balance, so don't forget the value that a user's identity brings.

Tip

Reinvention and renewal are important in maintaining a distinctive design. People get used to interfaces over time; if redesigns occur progressively while keeping the central elements in place for usability, the change catches users' eyes and draws their focus.

When designing your site, never forget that your visitors are individuals. If you believe tweaking a customization or experience to their personal tastes is practical to implement and useful, then consider the tool of personalization. It's one method to ensure that the content requiring attention from a specific type of user gains that person's interest and will be easy to locate in the future.

Value-Based Web Design

Within design, the construct of the page and how users can relate or personalize content to match their tastes is important. You need to ensure that less useful materials aren't presented to users who won't find a use for them. Without the site having some form of inherent value, however, there's little to no point going to all the trouble of having the site. After all, content is king!

The concept behind *value-based design* is simple. In the case of user experience, don't design your sites primarily to provide an experience, especially because what is considered an experience is subjective. Aim to provide the user with the occasion and environment to experience something. If you design your site well and make your content distinctive, visitors will naturally rate their experience based on the whole system.

Tip

Think of your site as a house. When you enter the house, the objects within it don't give you an experience; instead, it's your exposure to those objects and the memories you form that become part of the experience (as you attach other experiences occurring within it). Design is about gaining exposure, not tangible ownership!

Although you can design a site, designing an experience or a particular type of value is much more difficult. What users get out of visiting a site will be unique to them. Every one of your users will experience something different. In fact, if your site is deep in content and feature-rich (not "mock-up" text, as in Figure 8-9), users may gain new experiences every time they visit. If value exists and users are ready to explore, they get more from a design.

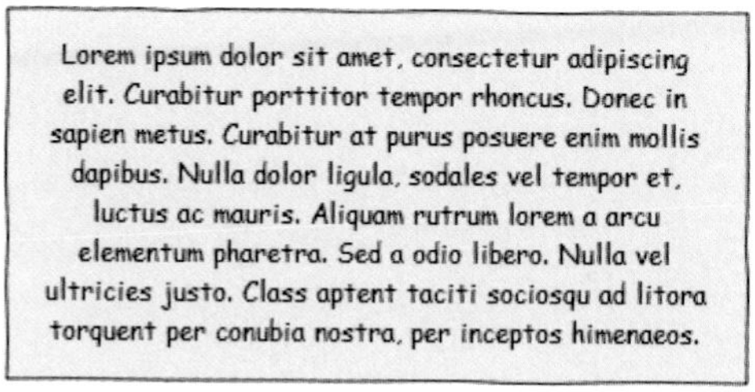

Lorem ipsum dolor sit amet, consectetur adipiscing elit. Curabitur porttitor tempor rhoncus. Donec in sapien metus. Curabitur at purus posuere enim mollis dapibus. Nulla dolor ligula, sodales vel tempor et, luctus ac mauris. Aliquam rutrum lorem a arcu elementum pharetra. Sed a odio libero. Nulla vel ultricies justo. Class aptent taciti sociosqu ad litora torquent per conubia nostra, per inceptos himenaeos.

FIGURE 8-9: A site with nothing but Lipsum (placeholder) text has no chance of survival because it has no real value.

The need for value is underpinned by the notion of the *content gap,* which states that if quality and value are missing from a site (or the design doesn't appropriately allow that content to be used, or doesn't synchronize well), then the power and meaning behind the content will be lost. Templates are a classic case of how such a gap can occur. Generic layouts don't add to the emotion and reflection that a site's content needs to impart. Wireframes alone are equally void of personality, as shown in Figure 8-10. The point is to always design sites around content; don't write copy to fill in a design. This is yet another case for substance over style.

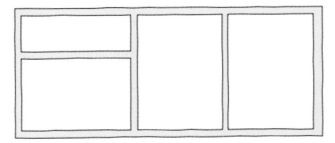

FIGURE 8-10: A wireframe has no emotional attachment; enrich it with digital furnishings.

Distinctive design isn't only about the aesthetics or the functionality or even the content. You need to consider the wider perspective and acknowledge that everything you produce must be user-focused and user-centered. Having something of value is a primary goal, but it must be valuable to the end user rather than just exist for its own sake. Having a layout that removes barriers to access and helps readers digest content is second on the ladder. Customization and interactivity mixed with value-based design emphasizes this point.

Attention within the substance

You've spent plenty of time looking over the methodology for giving your site's interface the boost and distinction needed to draw attention to the right places. You must also consider what actually matters within the interface. Sometimes designers attempt to draw distinction with good intentions but accidentally highlight content that perhaps doesn't deserve the attention that something more profound and less understated would require.

As you design your site, think of your content as being built from various artifacts, and each of those items must relate to the environment it sits within. Your visitors ultimately will expect to find what they're looking for, so every flourish you produce needs a functional purpose. What really matters on a site are your visitors' perceptions and, by extension, the amount of attention they devote to your visuals in order to make use of the content.

The idea of *affective design* was born from the design field of HCI (human-computer interaction) and focuses design skills on bonding with users' needs, because experiences are emotional, and you want to create a lasting relationship with your visitors to increase the likelihood they will return to your site. Layering features or content that trigger emotions, thereby provoking reactions that build upon behavior, enables users to engage, respond, and find something distinctive within your interfaces.

These types of features trigger emotion:

> Comical or humorous material on the page (like satire)

> Trolling in comment blogs (causes anger and frustration)

> A clean, balanced aesthetic layout (professionalism)

Consider the value that features give your interfaces. Although they aren't directly part of the site's content, often it's the elements that create an experience that makes lasting impressions and builds brand reputations. If your site has a useless search feature or some poorly conceived navigation system, users may justify not returning because the site isn't user-friendly, rather than on the quality of the content.

Services also play an understated role in distinctive design. Content, although the main focus of many sites, isn't always the center of attention. Many brands place their focus and distinctive aims on selling goods or services. Although descriptions and content help users make choices in regard to services, the functionality and quality of experience are based primarily on how things work and how visitors locate the result they seek. Therefore, aesthetics and functionality give things life.

Important

Although you don't need to include services or features in a design for a site to work, the site will seem more lifeless than more interactive layouts. But it's also worth remembering that in addition to providing services and functionality, visuals give a sense of freshness that can breathe life into a site.

Layering features for emphasis

Value comes in all shapes and sizes. What your users may appreciate may end up being a quirky feature you see as helpful or just plain fun! Layering a site's functionality and features with the hope of gaining emphasis and users' adoption involves the appropriate disclosure of materials and ensuring that the main priority of your site is scaled correctly. Some items have more inherent value on a site than others, so it's always worth considering how "in your face" components appear to be.

So what is the order of priority and how do you determine what parts of the page get the most attention? The simplest answer is the following: Content and the context it holds are the most critical parts of the page. Services come after that (content entices use), then come aesthetics (visuals complement usage), then interaction (the way sites react to use of the visuals), and finally features (tools that await interaction until needed). See Figure 8-11.

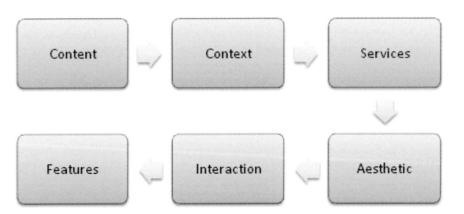

FIGURE 8-11: The order of priority for layering functionality according to its importance is central to the design.

Drawing a balance between gaining the focus of users and distracting them with action on a page is always a risk. In design, you must consider the variables that can pose problems for users. Distinctive design relies on a delicate and often carefully considered balance on many levels, so it should be of no surprise that you need to balance value against medium (tools to help you navigate the space).

Tip

The mechanics of a website are like the mechanics of a computer. The components that appear on the inside dictate the way it operates and how people will interact with it. Use your best judgment about which objects will produce the best performance.

Interface customization requires progressive disclosure to avoid throwing too much at users and making them suffer information overload. The way visitors scan a site, identify key pieces of information, and then follow the clues to get the answers they're looking for is remarkable! Content takes time to read, and functionality requires an adaptive mind. Do all you can to streamline the process.

A site's interface primarily will be composed of content, and that's how it should remain if you are offering knowledge rather than services. However, plenty of scope remains for giving sites interactivity and features that allow visitors a new and exciting range of methods to communicate with your layouts. Being clever with interaction gives your visitors something a bit more memorable, and its distinction will likely become ingrained in them, more so if the interface is built around their needs.

Expansive Experiences

As you build experiences that scale from page to page, think of the bigger picture. Although the objective of a site is to help the business or individual hosting it receive something in return (such as money or recognition, which are, of course, important), the user should always hold priority; remember, "the customer is always right."

Central to your goal as a designer is giving users something to remember and something that progressively provides new and exciting value. Although offering your users a well-structured and organized site is fine, consider giving the site more depth, beyond just changing the page by progressively including more content.

Important

Depth in a page doesn't have to be just value-orientated. You can enhance the level of functionality within the pages by having interaction with third-party sites (such as how the AddThis script provides a mechanism to market links that users find interesting).

Awareness of your interfaces and how users react is important to providing an experience. The choices you make dictate how the design will evolve. Giving your site a bit of depth or the sense that there's more to the interface than meets the eye will engage users' minds and may motivate people to explore (see Figure 8-12). Many single-page sites follow this principle and see a great level of success as inspirational web sculptures.

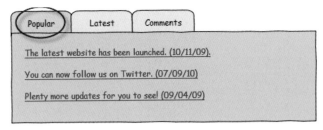

FIGURE 8-12: Providing multiple layers of content promotes a feeling of hidden depth.

Making an impact is also vital if you want users to have an experience and remember it for all the right reasons. Make statements in design. Aim for something that is useful but noninvasive that encourages users to let their thoughts and actions guide them toward something of value. Make your content appear in front of their eyes with the distinction drawn as required and throw in some responsive design, if possible.

As Chapter 5 asserts in its discussion on psychology, an experience requires meaning and purpose. Memory defines people's experiences and the distinction designers assign them. (Memorable content will be easier to recollect on pages.) Recognize that memory is fragile, it degrades, and you can't expect users to absorb everything. Also, don't expect users to transfer their skills without becoming acclimated to the environment. So, you need to help users find the key points and relate them to something that can be converted into long-term memories. By doing so, they can associate distinction with recognizable objects.

User-centered considerations

Memories are built and stored based on people's experiences. Because no two users are alike, several factors determine the importance or dominance users give objects. By avoiding stereotypes and targeting users only if you're sure that a pattern matches a group's behavior, you can promote a sense of interaction. Users do conform over time — trained behavior based on instinct.

The ideas put forward in regard to user-centered design are based largely on psychology and the way users interact (as well as sociology and group dynamics). Although distinctive design requires you to understand enough about behavior to determine how your users are likely to make use of the mediums you provide, predicting problems before they occur is a good thing. Being empathic, responsive, and observant are worthwhile skills, and not just when hosting a site!

Important Tolerance is another trait many humans could use. You may become impatient with visitors who struggle to find what appears to be obvious to you. If a visitor misses something you think is obvious on your site, find out how and why the problem occurred. Maybe a better method exists!

So what practical conclusions can you draw from the whole concept of making your users the center of attention? For one, trying to please everyone by being generic or not acknowledging dominant regions that use the site will lead to trouble. If you don't research and try to understand your audience, you run the risk of losing their attention and alienating users who otherwise may become regulars. It's all about following trends as they appear.

Consider the fact that many users may have special needs, whether for a disability (as the companion e-book explores in more detail) or another issue (perhaps a user may require the content in another language). The features you provide, and the content or services you offer are only good if visitors can make sense of them. You can offer more help than is needed, such as order tracking, shown in Figure 8-13. But make sure that the help you provide isn't invasive or obtrusive to any of the site's users.

With features that you provide in your sites, the main objective is to think outside the box. If you want a search engine, improve it with auto-complete or some other useful enhancement. If your users want another navigation route around the site, experiment with new features to achieve that goal. Ideally, you want to expose content to as many users as possible, so don't settle for a second-rate, generic design.

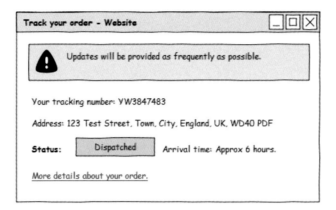

FIGURE 8-13: Examples of distinctive help include tracking the delivery of an order on a website.

A storybook with plenty of twists

Every site aims to take its visitors on a journey and guide users through roads and sights until they find what they're looking for. Unfortunately, they can easily get lost in the jungle of features and pathways. Their vision can become distorted, and the path can fork in so many directions that users end up in a labyrinth or maze that doesn't seem negotiable. To prevent such an experience and avoid dead ends or wrong turns, you need to create a smooth, straightforward, friction-free path!

A simple way of catering to the philosophy of turning a site into a journey is to treat it like a storybook. Visitors who enter the site should find themselves on a page with many roads and signposts to guide them. As users delve deeper into such an interface and pages, they learn more about the site (which is useful for future visits) and will likely reach their destination, gaining something of value from the experience.

As you've explored, providing informative signposts and useful aids to negotiate a site can be useful (such as breadcrumb links showcasing a hierarchy, as shown in Figure 8-14), but more importantly, providing such details can actually be a form of on-page narration in which users can find distinctive content quicker than otherwise possible. Design is as much about being descriptive and using a mixture of visual and tactile tools to gain meaningful responses as it is about putting content on the screen.

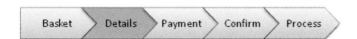

FIGURE 8-14: Breadcrumb navigation menus explain the primary path to the page as a story.

Summary

Providing an expansive experience requires adapting your sites to an increasing range of devices and potential routes of consumption. Sometimes, the ideal solution is to break away from convention and consistency (such as how the iPhone alters its keyboard layout between the browser address bar and normal text entry). Other times, you need to stick to expectations to avoid complexity. Being adaptive is central to being distinctive, so always consider subtle flourishes that can provide extra contextual value.

All things considered, what makes a good or bad experience really gets down to a wide variety of variables that you can either choose to ignore or you can adapt to. Consistency is fine, but not at the expense of your users' needs for a particular page. In addition, you need to assist and reassure users, rather than limit the use of content you provide them, and educate them as the need arises.

Users appreciate simple tools such as an "escape hatch" on the site. If they enter a page that they didn't expect (but know they are on the right site), they may attempt to click the logo to return to the home page before clicking the Back button or closing the tab.

The future of design is going to be primarily user-focused. Although some designers tend to hold onto forcing users to adapt to interfaces and layouts that they produce, the web is becoming increasingly social and users have a lot more control and power than in the past. Regarding distinction — don't reinvent every page as though it were unique because that might be confusing. Instead, adapt pages as unique content requires.

An ever-increasing array of devices and products appear, which removes the safety bar of an already "hard to design for" market. Because you want important content on the screen noticed first, transcend the idea that one size can fit all and that users can be grouped based on general statistics. Designs must become more flexible and customizable so that users gain ideal experiences, and redundancy needs to be minimized.

Perhaps in the future, the technologies and languages that designers use will leap forward in a way that allows distinction to occur faster than before. For now, the web is still a static society littered with interactive aspects that fish for a user's attention. As customization becomes less invasive and personalization gains a bit of decentralization so you remain in control of your details, content will become smarter and more distinctive. With new levels of intellect, you want to do all in your power to improve the situation for your users.

Part V

Designing for Ubiquitous Users

The Construct of Usability

The importance of recognizable, easy-to-use sites

THE IMPORTANCE OF designing a site around the needs of its users goes without question. As the complexity of your layouts increases, so will the demands of your users. The aim of usability is simply to promote an evenhanded interface that users can negotiate without incurring complications.

In this chapter, I expand on the ideologies of user experience, accessibility, and design theory by exploring the world of usability. I discuss how to make an adaptive, flexible design as well as the ways to make your work unique. You examine the objectives of usable design, the basis of trends and conventions, heuristic design, anti-patterns, plus some content on inspiration. Then I share some insight into the design and arrangement of the common layout elements that matter most, including information about eye-tracking and usability testing.

Universal Usability

Throughout this book, I emphasize providing a user-centered design in which your visitors' needs remain a priority. This chapter reinforces this point with a subject that plays a big role in the usefulness of websites, applications, and products. The case for usability directly follows the idea of user-experience design and that everything you produce needs to be free of all barriers to entry, if possible.

The companion e-book has an independent chapter examining the case for accessibility and reinforces that visibility is what primarily allows your distinctive content to be seen (and thereby gain the user's focus and attention). Usability builds on accessibility in such a way that after the user sees the content on a page, the page's design reduces friction (*friction* refers to items that detract from a smooth flow on the page), offering good functionality and ease of navigation. Figure 9-1 shows how a mixture of good accessibility and usability improve visibility — which aids distinction.

FIGURE 9-1: Accessibility is your first priority; usability is always second in importance.

When you build sites, you do so with the intention that every page will have content or some level of functionality that offers something useful to visitors. (If nothing useful is on a page, why create it?) So ensuring that users can negotiate around your layout is paramount. If sites aren't usable or accessible, no amount of high-quality content can overcome the struggle your users face. They're likely to find another site for the information they seek.

As much as you may wish otherwise, users may not share your train of thought. Your challenge is to make your site durable enough to adapt to their natural ways of thinking and how they were trained to use computers. For example, many users don't know what a browser is, yet they're competent enough to use the tool when it's active on their screen. Most users can identify things such as the Back button.

The justification for taking usability into account is that you know very little information about your users. You don't know which browser they use, if they have a disability, or how familiar they are with an interface. Ensuring that they aren't overwhelmed allows you to reach out to visitors to give them what they need in order to use your offerings.

In terms of distinction, usability plays its part in ensuring that your content maintains the "Can you see me?" context, which highlights the importance of visibility in a design that pushes the relevant content ahead of the essential noise — the bits that explain things in greater detail. Usability forces you to acknowledge that although distinction can increase obviousness by drawing focus to active elements, it shouldn't undermine a user's natural thinking process.

Essential noise refers to the objects on a page that require a user's attention, either over a short-term period or for the entire duration of a visit.

Note

Dynamic, adaptive design

So how do you account for usability within your designs and avoid losing focus on what matters? You begin by making decisions about how distinctive content should be. Getting your priorities in order and deciding what is necessary within a page plays a critical role in the usability of your layouts. Designers need to develop their designs based on the needs of content and functionality. As you give or take away distinction, you need to build around your visitors' browsing habits.

Being user-centered can be deemed central to usability, but it's probably better to say that usable sites tend to work in spite of users rather than because of them. This perspective may seem harsh, but the undeniable way that visitors can end up in the right place via routes other than the ones you provide is a testament to your site's adaptive and flexible nature.

You cannot hope to win over users with a single method of navigation. Users may find your site from points of entry such as a social network or a search engine. You have no way of knowing what obscure setup users may have at their fingertips (in terms of device, browser, or hardware). Therefore, in addition to being recognizable in terms of form and function, your site's implementations must be dynamic and flexible.

Tip

You cannot hope to catch every single user requirement, so don't fret if your site doesn't look "pixel perfect." The idea of having such a design goes against the dynamic nature of the web. Just do what you can with the resources you have available.

Users can turn off technology, so Flash and scripting can evaporate from an experience. Alternative content, both in context of accessibility and usability, has become a must-have feature. The mechanics of a site need to bend to demands; although you can predict occasions when some visual truths will occur, usability now requires you to think outside the box as you package your beautiful content.

With this in mind, in distinctive design, one highly regarded issue of usability is how designers handle errors. For example, you can design your site so that when a user submits an inaccurate or incomplete form, you offer "live" help, rather just than an automatic response telling the user something is incorrect or missing (see, for example, the form validation in Figure 9-2, which can be cleanly implemented and may increase a user's tolerance for errors). Even offering a funny or enhanced 404 error with some useful links can reinforce your users' confidence and reduce their frustration. When errors do occur, the recovery process is often more critical than the error itself.

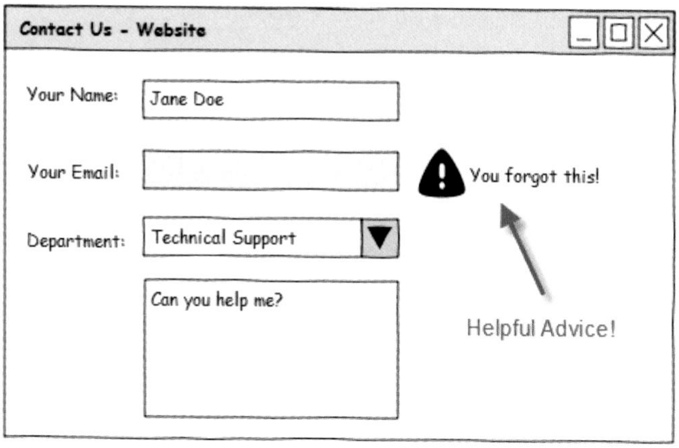

FIGURE 9-2: Form validation can be helpful. Why refresh when it isn't necessary?

In addition to the issues people encounter on a page, the tools they use to navigate need recognition. Remember that users may access your site and services by using any number of strange devices or input (or output) elements, or they may have limitations requiring special tools (or a more thoughtful design). Testing your sites with Zoom (shown in Figure 9-3) or resized text, screen readers, and other accessibility aids can help to reduce potential usability friction.

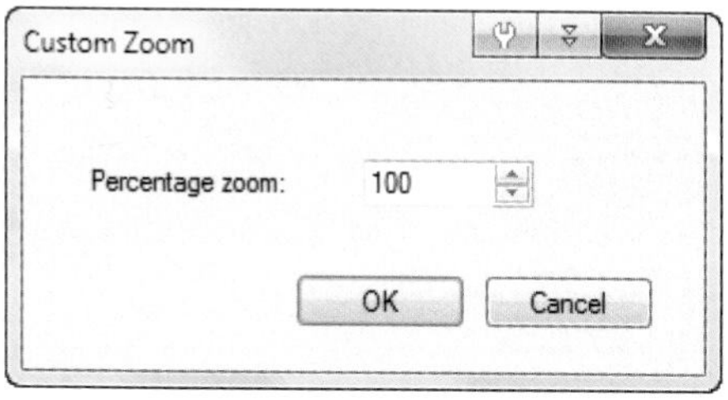

FIGURE 9-3: Each web browser comes with a range of tools; consider testing them on your sites.

Ultimately, usability has as much to do with discoverability and how much work users must expend as it does with anything else. Browsing the web can be time-consuming and can weigh heavily on the minds of some users. Distinctive design hopes to improve this situation by increasing visibility, but you need to include usability and other user-centered design approaches in the mix to ensure that your sites are as efficient and agile as possible. Splash screens (those little images that appear when something is loading) are an example in which redundancy quickly lowers usability.

Tip

Although you want to reduce the amount of time your users waste trying to navigate an interface (or accomplish tasks), don't be afraid to help your users spend their time on the content that matters (such as purchasing goods or using your services).

Identity crisis challenges

One issue relating to usability is striking a balance between ensuring that your interface meets user expectations and ensuring that the results don't look like a generic template. Playing it safe with commonly recognized parts of a page may be good for some visitors — less cognitive action is required. They will see the same positioning and objects, relative to other sites. (You don't need to follow everyone else's design to make a site usable, so copying others' work isn't appropriate here; just ensure that conventions you do alter get the visibility they require.)

Important

On your interface, base familiarity decisions on the people who access your site regularly. If they are experienced, feel free to experiment more than if they are less competent with web navigation.

However, because you want to remain in your visitors' minds, giving your site a unique look and feel plays a significant part in how content is consumed and memorized. Remember that you want users to be able to recognize objects on a page, and at the same time, you want to create a unique site that visitors will want to keep exploring. One successful method is working with a grid. Most designs are composed of rectangular content boxes that affix a stereotypical boxy shape. Using graphics and positioning to work around this grid to give a page a unique display can help you establish quirky identity. Figure 9-4 shows a wireframe — note that certain points of the layout are easy to identify.

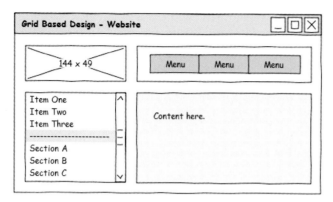

FIGURE 9-4: The grid on a site can look boring, so consider breaking out with style!

Another method for working around stereotypes is to experiment with the latest technologies and features that the web offers. Following the idea of progressive enhancement, you can ensure that the site degrades gracefully, yet offers practical enhancements for browsers that support them. The e-society is moving toward a web that evolves beyond "versions," so why not follow suit with a bit of innovation (who knows, others might adopt your cutting-edge technique)!

Tip

Remember that visitors may not understand the meaning of betas. If you decide to make a test version of a site public, be ready to receive criticism for bugs that you're perhaps aware of but haven't yet fixed. Be sure to inform and acknowledge users!

Some of the most usable sites are as rudimentary as you can get, but accomplish their purpose elegantly. Others make a name for themselves by improving traditional techniques to make them more useful or by deviating from or setting new trends. Whatever route you take, remember that users are the ones who will be using your design, so you need to weigh the cost of implementation (or exclusion) against the benefit to users. It's all about showcasing your talents in building elegant designs.

Terrific Usability Trends

Although maintaining a unique yet usable interface is one of the primary goals of design, consider adapting your skills to lessons taught over the years. As is often the case in usability, research offers significant insight on how people use products and services and, perhaps more importantly, gives designers direction on reinforcing distinction. The three core objectives involved (as shown in Figure 9-5) are *efficiency*, *ease-of-use*, and *satisfaction*.

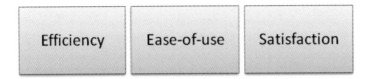

FIGURE 9-5: The three objectives of usability are easy to remember but can be hard to attain.

With usability, the first objective is *efficiency*. A great interface requires little more than a glance from visitors in order for them to know where to go. Although you hope they recognize and appreciate the visuals you produce, visitors should be able to achieve tasks without having to understand the mechanics involved in the functionality or a quirky interface.

The second objective to usability is *ease-of-use*. This objective ties directly into efficiency. Reducing the complexity of an experience reduces the learning curve and training users need in order to adapt to an interface. Unlike efficiency, however, people's primary focus is less on how quickly they can achieve a task and more on the ease of the process. For example, if a long form needs to be filled in, intuitiveness becomes critical. Many users are willing to sacrifice speed for a better experience.

Another principle of usability is how *satisfying* an interface is to use. Perhaps this objective is less appreciated than those previously mentioned, but ironically it may be more important. If an experience is satisfying, people are more likely to want to encounter it again. Ultimately, the amount of time, effort, and energy visitors put into an activity will increase if they enjoy it. Sometimes, the satisfaction of an interface can result from its efficiency or ease-of-use, but those two variables may not always satisfy users.

Tip

Measuring your site against efficiency, ease of use, and satisfaction is worth the effort, but remember that your visitors' interpretations of these objectives are what matter. You may think that your site is awesome on all three levels, but the crowd may disagree!

The consequences of not meeting these objectives aren't worth thinking about! Doing so will probably result in your site having a few begrudging regulars and a majority of one-off users who will change sites as soon as something better comes along. Consider the social networking scene. Facebook pushed mySpace into obscurity. Facebook won because it's a more usable site and presents itself to a willing audience.

Quick, useful conventions

So what common best practice can you rely on to ensure that your sites are as distinctive and recognizable as possible? Enter the documented and successfully implemented practices called *conventions, trends,* and *patterns.*

You can find numerous best practices, tips, and tricks for your design work on the web and in books oriented around usability. This book focuses on distinctive design and examines just a few primary best practices to showcase aspects that can affect a site's distinction.

Reference

If you're looking for some great best practices, consider examining the list by Jakob Nielsen at www.useit.com/papers/heuristic/heuristic_list.html, or check out some of the lists of patterns, conventions, and trends published in articles, books, and other websites. You'll really be amazed at the sheer number of them!

The first common convention relates to light versus dark designs. Audiences have been divided for years about whether to use a light-colored background or a dark background. Some people like sites that use dark gothic colors or vibrant deep shades; others prefer clean and bright visuals. Each option creates very different visual styles, and some sites are more suited to one style more than the other, as shown in Figure 9-6. When deciding which is more appropriate for your site, consider your content, weigh your options, and match the color scheme to the subject.

FIGURE 9-6: The decision to use light or dark depends on the type of site.

Layouts that promote something industrial or minimalistic may benefit from light designs (white emphasizes visual breathing room more than black does). A benefit to using dark designs can be seen in specific communities (such as the video-game industry, where rich textures are often presented), or in individual subjects in which the environment effectively reflects darkness (for example, a rock band's site or a horror movie). You want to match a visual with the environment it naturally occurs in, because visuals reinforce the senses.

Another common convention is the minimalist versus complex layout debate (see Figure 9-7). Specific types of content may perhaps lend themselves to a more clean and simplistic layout. This is the case for personal portfolios, corporate sites that aim to emit a polished infrastructure or mobile layout. For example, Amazon showcases millions of products and needs to compare objects on the screen.

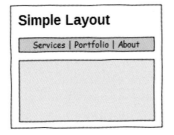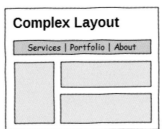

FIGURE 9-7: You could use something clean and minimalist . . . or something packed with action.

With any aspect of usability, the context of the environment matters. If you want to portray yourself as a rapid, fast-moving business that is constantly releasing new things for people to purchase, you need to be less generous with white space in order to showcase your wares. Using less white space makes the task of building a distinctive UI tougher because you need to spend more time applying emphasis to critical elements.

One other example is the ever-popular single-page design. Back in the 1990s, the idea of stuffing everything onto one page seemed crazy. With advancements in how designers code and progressively disclose content gaining traction, being concise is no longer something for those with little to say. Today, people produce portfolio sites with numerous layers of content that users can access as they browse and interact, which for some sites, resolves the issue of the time it takes for subsequent pages to load.

Important Use one-page sites with caution. If users have a slow connection or are in a low bandwidth environment, every byte counts — one-page sites tend to be size-heavy. This issue can be especially notable with novices, who "stuff" content instead of logically breaking it down into individual pages that provide separate, unique purposes.

Common examples of trends following this progressive disclosure pattern include tab panels, drop-down menus, and even the accordion technique (which collapses content that has been read and shows fresh material on the screen as users click). This technique isn't ideal for every site, but for controlled portfolios or other sites that want to avoid the dreaded refresh, it can be a useful convention, and is worthy of consideration.

Of course, conventions and trends don't need to be something as sweeping as deciding between light and dark or one page and many. Placing your logo in the upper-left corner and linking it to the homepage is a convention. Using breadcrumbs or drop-down navigations (see Figure 9-8), profile pages, blog comments, avatars, social sharing links, and tag clouds are also conventions or trends. At their peak, you could find yourself following one of many trends to gain distinction.

As for best practices, who knows how many common-sense approaches you can follow? Following trends and conventions automatically increases user awareness because of the level of recognition, so be sure to explore using them in your designs. Whether you're using a widely accepted trend, following a best practice, or trying to alter perceptions with something new, consider the consequences for every action and ensure that what you produce is in your users' best interests. After all, not all conventions are good ones.

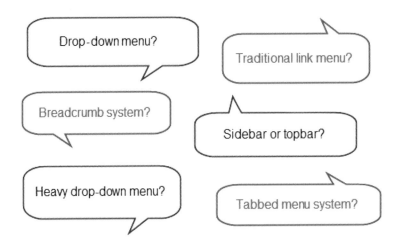

FIGURE 9-8: Many conventions exist in design, and choosing suitable solutions is tricky.

Tip Don't be afraid to break with tradition and convention if you can provide something usable for visitors: Single-page sites may not require a navigation menu, and enabling commenting on blog posts may be a bad idea if you receive a great deal of spam.

The danger of anti-patterns

Plenty of great thoughts about what will work best for a particular site or situation exist, but following trends and patterns blindly is a bad idea. Not only do sites' audiences differ depending on the content provided, but also research shows that user habits and trends frequently change.

Ultimately, opinion and subjectivity have their place in providing meaningful, usable designs for a particular audience. Still, you need to base your conventions and site habits on sound research, rather than just on what's being implemented on the web.

Tip Consider a logo. Most trends and conventions show that a site's logo typically appears in the upper-left corner of a page, but perhaps your design has a unique enough interface that you can place your logo in the vertical middle section instead.

A great example of why following the flock can be a bad idea is illustrated by *anti-patterns* — which highlight trends that negatively affect a user's experience. One of the classic cases of a design trend failing to have a specific purpose was the Web 2.0 phase many designers went through. In this case, rather than talking about the next evolution of the web, many assumed that Web 2.0 indicated that sites should use glossy buttons, zany badges, beveled corners, and give off the sense of an artificial, almost plastic or reflective surface. Figure 9-9 shows this kind of spectacular design — although it grabs users' attention, the purpose behind its use is lost.

FIGURE 9-9: Web 2.0 took advantage of eye-popping badges that often had little to no purpose.

Ultimately, people chose to follow the Web 2.0 convention purely on its aesthetic appeal. At its core, what it offered was a popular set of effects that used bold colors and shiny effects to give off a distinctive feel. Because of the scale at which the Web 2.0 was implemented, it lost the underlying value that designs should provide. People used the design for all sorts of sites, thus the look and feel didn't really match up to the content it housed. The convention became a generic blueprint. Design allows you to impart emotion and cultivate a sense of atmosphere; wasting it on pretty but useless visuals sacrifices its distinctive value. If use of a design isn't satisfying, usability suffers.

Other primary examples of anti-patterns in trends or patterns include mystery meat navigation such as the Click Here button, Lipsum (placeholder text) in live sites, validation buttons, and counters showing the number of visitors to a page (see Figure 9-10 for an "unpopular" account).

FIGURE 9-10: Web counters can showcase unpopularity as a side effect.

With so many good practices and so many bad ones, you cannot simply rely on copying your competitors or following a whole bunch of outlines laid down by one group. Only you understand your audience. The knowledge you gain by reaching out to a community for feedback and testing ideas determines whether a particular method is right for you. Design with purpose and maintain good intentions and you should be fine.

Inspiration from the muses

When it comes to trends, patterns, and conventions, nothing beats real-world implementation and knowing that substantial user support exists to verify that a particular design method is easy to use. You can now begin looking at competitors and their established designs for information. Although stealing someone else's design is unethical, drawing inspiration from them and adapting existing solutions to your needs makes sense.

One reason for seeking inspiration from other designs is that as the web evolves, you need to test your ideas to come up with workable solutions. If people just used templates and rarely got involved in the actual building of sites, the web wouldn't be as rich and dynamic. You don't need to reinvent the wheel unless you have a good reason to do so. If it weren't for other sites, you wouldn't have trends or conventions to follow.

How you make use of inspiration is clear-cut. If you have a particular piece of functionality that can benefit your users, it pays to examine how others have successfully used the technique in their sites. This approach obviously will be more effective for large-scale solutions such as forum products or search scripts; nevertheless, the focus is on customizing and improving techniques to match an audience's requirements.

Tip

You can build a shopping cart (such as Zen Cart), forum package (such as vBulletin), or CMS engine (such as Drupal) if you aim to gain some experience in coding or perhaps to build something more agile than what already exists. If, instead, you require something basic, consider the range of awesome tools provided by the likes of Joomla! and WordPress.

After you find a website that uses the trend you want, consider whether you can improve it rather than simply embed it. You may be able to come up with some site-specific tools that give users a more engaging experience. If you find that after a period of time, a particular feature will do better elsewhere on a page or if something you've added isn't being used as you expected, either refine the object or remove it.

Being inspired isn't just about taking a cool toolkit or technique and reenacting it. You want to learn from others' mistakes and tests, improve on existing models, and give your visitors a better experience. There's no shame in being inspired by others, and thousands of CSS galleries and showcases highlight beautiful sites for you to explore. You may find some bug or feature you'd never considered, though remember that every idea isn't a good one.

Reference If you want to explore some inspirational sites, consider visiting `http://bestwebgallery.com`, `http://commandshift3.com`, `www.drawar.com/gallery`, or `http://onepagelove.com`. Each has a unique way of picking sites (other good galleries exist, too, so don't be afraid to shop around).

Logical Layout Methods

Many trends and conventions exist, but none have as much visual emphasis on a page and its usability as the layout. One aim of usability is to ensure that sites are logically structured and that everything flows correctly. By following trends and conventions, you can ensure that regular users and those requiring screen readers alike get a fantastic and stable experience without inhibitions. (after all, you must structure your content to increase readability.)

Within CSS, a range of unit values dictate the relative or absolute width and height of objects that helps us to assign distinction. Certain elements such as images may require fixed dimensions to avoid distortion, which decreases readability. Other elements may require something a bit more flexible and fluid to ensure that users on devices with restrictions such as screen size aren't punished for using a less capable or durable device.

The basic layout measurements are as follows:

> **Absolute (PT, CM, MM, IN, etc.):** Use this measurement for traditional print design, but it's a poor choice for web designs. Everything remains static and affixed to a set canvas.

> **Fixed (PX):** Use this measurement for inflexible elements in a site design, but not for site widths, because of Internet Explorer's lack of PX-based text resizing.

> **Elastic (EM):** This measurement is better than fixed-width designs, but still imperfect on small screens. Because this measurement bases itself on the relative font size, the width can stretch a bit.

> **Liquid (%):** Use this measurement for single-column sites and flexible durability.

> **Hybrid (mixture of the previous items):** The best solution for most sites. You make use of several different unit measurements for a stable layout.

Tip   Other measurements include relative (100% height or width), scaled (CSS3 orientation into portrait or landscape mode), equated (via CSS3 calc), fluid (min or max width or height), and conditional (CSS3 media queries). Choose a mechanism carefully and always test for compatibility because the CSS3-powered ones may not work in older browsers.

The way you lay out your sites and provide your content in the hierarchy and cascade of your designs affects the end user. Five principles have great visual impact — *object nesting, object separation, column usage, content positioning,* and *scrolling.* As you can imagine, the visual distinction provided by each of these is unique.

Nesting is the first key principle of design theory related to the layout mechanism. With nesting, you group related content together. Nesting can occur in the hierarchical sense of objects gaining priority over each other, or it can result directly from the visual impression of an object being held within another. Regarding usability, a great technique to give objects distinction and a sense of relating to each other is to use nesting and group objects within the same columns or content blocks.

Another principle relating to layout mechanisms is *separation,* which can use white space around sections of a page (or object) that shows either global representation among pages (such as navigation) or sections that need to be identified as independent or unique. Lightboxes are a classic example of both nesting and separation. Some forms of separation in layout are as simple as highlighting the differences among groups of objects (such as columns); others are all about dominating the landscape. As you go about building that visual architecture, consider how you define independent objects.

The third convention is the subject of *columns.* In practice, good liquid layouts expand or contract columns as the user requires. The best layouts reduce the number of columns based on the space available on a screen (for example, collapsing to a single column on small displays). If your layout redraws the content to match the screen, great. Otherwise, the convention is to have one to three columns. As mentioned previously, columns provide a good method for both nesting and separation. As your eyes scan for relevant content, breaking a layout into parts makes sense.

The fourth convention is the practice of putting content before the navigation in the site's structure. You can use *positioning* to place content toward the top of the visual hierarchy as convention dictates. The justification for this practice is based in accessibility, in that visitors using screen readers get to hear the content and pick where they want to go from the navigation menu. A good practice is to match this technique with skip links so that users can skip to the navigation menu.

Scrolling is a big layout issue because it affects every design you produce. Because people are used to vertical (up and down) motions when browsing, one recommendation is to avoid alternative scrolling actions. Scrolling in both directions may be problematic because of the sharp increase of control needed to reach a specific bit of content (see Figure 9-11). In rare cases and if implemented in a safe, usable manner, horizontal scrolling can be distinctive. The difference gives it distinction but can increase a user's learning curve.

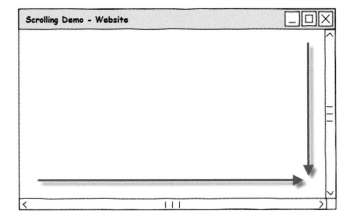

FIGURE 9-11: Most people are used to scrolling down or across, but never involve both!

Organic arrangements

Users expect a range of sections to appear on every page. Although some sections need to be visible all the time (a navigation menu, for example), others may need to appear only after useful content has been examined (for example, the header and the footer — probably the most recognizable objects because they're built to look different than the content).

Some pages include all of the sections users expect and others may not, but the content within each section needs to follow trends and convention. You can design these sections independently and then pull them together in a fluid manner to ensure that the page is identifiable. Try using a variety of distinctive principles to maximize the use of the space — trends exist for each of them.

Header

The first section usually found within a site is the header, as shown in Figure 9-12. Here are some items commonly found in the header:

> A logo or branding, usually located in the upper-left corner, that identifies the place hosting the content

> A navigation bar with links to pages or categories, such as products, services, and the about us and contact us links

> A search box to aid navigation based on keyword searches

> Skip links to aid in traversing the site

> Breadcrumb navigation for deeply linked sites to show progression and help users identify categories of content

> An abstract or page overview of content

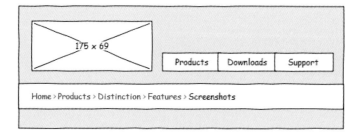

FIGURE 9-12: The site header may include a wide range of items that users seek.

Footer

Next, examine the footer, the last visual displayed on a page. Though last, the footer often includes useful tools or places of interest that build on the content found in the header. Many page footers contain links to policies, copyright details, contact information, and social sharing links for the site. Some footers even have other pieces of information such as awards and honors, memberships, site archives, links to sitemaps, subscription links, and occasionally a bit of text quickly explaining the site's purpose. Footers can be as big or as small as you need them to be, as shown in Figure 9-13.

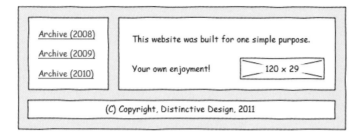

FIGURE 9-13: The footer has gained a lot of attention recently; don't ignore it!

Sidebars

Now, look at the next most dynamic element of a site, the sidebar. Some sidebars contain navigation links; others may contain features or functionality for a page so diverse that there's too much to mention! One interesting yet cool aspect of sidebars is that you can include more than one of them in a page. They usually hold content and separate features or links. As individual blocks, sidebars are usually grouped together under one roof, perhaps down the side of a window.

Note

Sidebars aren't necessary components, and they won't be found in single-column sites. There's no sense in adding unnecessary features, and sidebars absorb a great deal of screen space. So, if you want to ensure that your content maximizes its focus, sidebars may not always be the best idea. Keep in mind that you can make them appear on demand by using a script.

Choices for what headers, footers, and sidebars contain depends on your site (you may not even use one, two, or any). One thing they have in common, however, is that in most cases (for sites), they remain static on every page (the content rarely changes). With your site's main content (the body of text for each page), of course, the opposite is true: every page and its content needs to be unique.

Conventions within a page's content box will differ depending on the type of content being displayed. Content boxes are more dynamic if, rather than content alone, they feature some core service functionality, such as comparisons to other products, a portfolio gallery, site-related images, or web apps. The possibilities for a content infusion are limitless!

Eye-tracking for efficiency

One reason to follow trends and conventions is based a user's natural flow through a site. How you identify natural flow isn't just a result of aesthetics or the way your visuals dictate direction. Eye-tracking and the way eyes naturally orient toward certain areas of a page for unique tasks and how you can then manipulate this movement have gained the attention of designers over the past decade.

Important
Tracking the user's eyes alone gets you only so much data. Consider tracking how often forms are used, which keywords are searched, where a user clicks and other actions, as well as how long a user spends on a particular page or section.

In terms of readability, most users start their journey at the upper-left corner of a page, move across horizontally (say for navigation), and then scan downward.

Beyond reading gravity, users tend to get used to seeing parts of a page reserved for certain conventions — such as a logo in the upper-left corner or similar location (as shown in Figure 9-14), which usually links to the home page; the navigation menu clearly visible either at the top or left side of a screen; and a footer at the base.

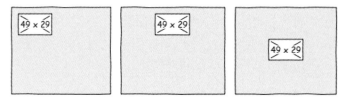

FIGURE 9-14: Logos typically appear in one of three positions (or atypically at the upper-right).

Whether you put certain expected items in their conventional place on a site is entirely up to you. You must decide to follow or forge trends. Although following trends reduces cognitive friction, sometimes a little cognitive friction can actually improve a site's interface by forcing users out of a "zombie browsing" state, in which little or no thinking is required.

Eye-tracking offers insightful observations about how people use the web. Plenty of variations on the technique can be applied, such as heatmaps, which you can find in certain analytics packages (for example, what Google offers). As you build, launch, and monitor a site, consider studying how users click and negotiate around pages to see if you can make improvements, and how following their eyes can lead you to optimizations.

Testing to Benefit Usability

In terms of usability and distinctive deign, you spend a lot of time analyzing the best way to implement a certain piece of functionality or region of a site. Following the trends and conventions of existing implementations and models of design is good, but you need to base the majority of your decisions on empirical evidence that applies to your own audience's needs and expectations. Be sure to undertake usability testing!

Usability testing differs from traditional research because rather than referring to statistics or other people's findings, you place more effort on asking an audience how you can improve your services (without bias). In doing so, you attempt to make the design more usable or accessible. Figure 9-15 shows browser usage testing.

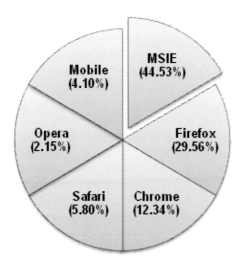

FIGURE 9-15: This chart shows statistics on browser usage by NetApplications.com for December 2010.

Ultimately, usability testing is about discovering what works and what doesn't. Every site and project is different because every audience is composed of a wide range of users with varying skill levels and backgrounds. Distinctive design showcases that you can do certain things to catch your audience's attention (and make good content visible). How you portray your content and its visibility largely dictates your site's overall usefulness.

Tip   Taking usability testing on board can improve your site's distinctiveness. Allowing user customization or preferences ensures that a user can consume the content in his or her way. And physical testing may help to improve layouts.

Traditional research is usually right there in black and white awaiting your interpretation of how to incorporate a trend or best practice into your design; usability testing requires more than just a quick question-and-answer session. Design it in a way that gains meaningful data. After you collect the results, analyze the information to ensure that the majority of those involved in testing agreed with the test results.

To cultivate your site in ways that your audience will appreciate, testing must occur. You risk alienating many users if you base all of your decisions on your own experiences. If you base a design solely on existing research (such as the needs met by another site), the layout will work but may not have the effect you're looking for. Usability testing breaks this barrier and gives your users a voice in the design challenge.

The heuristic evaluation

Before you distinctively test sites to ensure that they appeal to your product's audience (rather than rely on advice based on research for other sites), review conventions and parallels drawn from the best practices others have uncovered. Yes, it is important that you independently test rather than just rely on research, but heuristic evaluation and research give a good starting point.

The general concept behind heuristic evaluation is to look at previous experiences and works to see how you might use the knowledge and techniques gained to benefit your own sites. Your visitors' needs may differ from the conventions that exist for a specific type of site, but it's amazing how often crossovers occur between one site and another in terms of usability conventions.

Reference Many people are wary of using citations from Wikipedia as proof of anything, but the data gathered in this article shows a well-researched group of globalized and independent statistics: `http://en.wikipedia.org/wiki/Usage_share_of_web_browsers`.

A plethora of sites rely on the same grid layout of fixed-width dimensions or follow conventions for specific types of pages in terms of the content such as portfolios, About pages, and blogs. If you want to know whether what you're thinking about implementing may be harmful to a user's experience, look to the work of other designers. (It's proven, for example, that iframes are bad for accessibility.) Many places have researched best practices and consulted books and tutorials on the subject. How subjective or objective they are depends on who undertakes such a study. If you don't have the time or energy to set up your own user-testing methodology or if you just want to verify your results, all you need to do is use a search engine to find some interesting statistics. You may, for example, find that a mobile site (see Figure 9-16) is necessary.

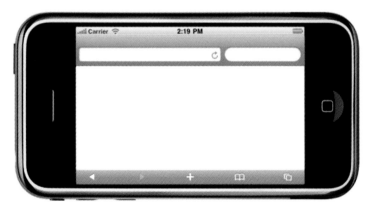

FIGURE 9-16: Research has shown that mobile browsing is on the rise, so a mobile site may be useful.

If looking through piles of research sounds like no fun and you just want some direct, easy-to-follow advice, the other part of heuristic evaluation is to simply seek advice from experts in a particular field (whether it's about usability, accessibility, or something else). You can gain insight from their years of practice about how to best implement what you want or how to maximize distinction. Expert advice can become expensive, but it is full of value, cultivated from years of experience. Heuristic evaluation comes into its own, though, with the idea of refinement. If you see someone else's research claiming something isn't a good idea, and on another site you see something contradictory, you can use existing research from both camps to experiment and carry out your own trials. Your findings ultimately add weight to one theory or the other. Accept others' results, but never be afraid to test their validity so that you are confident about how your audience will respond, and don't forget to publish your findings!

Roots of usability testing

So now it's time to move on to the most important, yet often overlooked, aspect of ensuring a usable and successful site — the humble usability test. The most successful sites put more experience and study into their interfaces than less successful ones and thereby gain the greatest level of reward. Even if their layout isn't the most beautiful, the planning behind it will be recognized.

Usability testing can be simple or technical, depending on how much you invest in gathering user metrics that guide your design decision-making process. Sometimes, you may want to grab some quantitative numbers by using a form in which visitors enter feedback. Other times, you may want to monitor users using your site to study behavior.

Tip

If you don't want to organize your own testing environment and want a quick solution, consider using professional organizations that can organize and help you gain the feedback you need from real users. Focus groups can also provide meaningful results.

Many tools, apps, and sites on the web contain usability principles, cool check lists, patterns, and conventions that seem to be developing a trend over a set period of time. Regularly upgrade your knowledge about what new languages, specifications, and research may help you improve a site's experience. Staying informed about the latest conventions is essential for maintaining a distinctive design. What works for your site right now may not always be so distinctive in five to ten years time!

So what are the components and process of undertaking a usability test? To simplify, after you assemble users, assign them a task or a series of tasks. Figure 9-17 shows an example of such a process. The task can be as simple as answering questions, or you can send users on a treasure hunt around the site to look for that all-important content or to purchase a particular item. Observe how they interact with the site and where they stop or get stuck, record all the results, note any common areas where you can make improvements, and finally make any necessary changes.

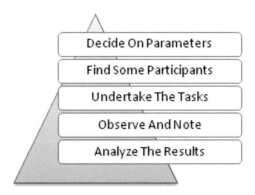

FIGURE 9-17: The process of a usability study is straightforward, but it requires plenty of organization.

Obviously, I've simplified the steps up to avoid complexity. If you want to maximize your usability testing potential, you can consult many books and guides on the subject. Again, for the sake of simplicity, the following list serves as a starting point.

Testing methods include using the following:

> **Polls:** Polls are easy and quick, as shown in Figure 9-18.

> **Quizzes:** This method takes longer but reveals more information.

> **Questionnaires:** Use questionnaires to get ideas from your regular audience.

> **Surveys:** You can ask users about particular features.

> **Interviews:** Interview by using instant-messaging services, phone calls, or in person.

> **Focus groups:** This method is a good way of getting users to bounce ideas off of each other.

> **Alpha and Beta tests:** These tests help uncover bugs and missing features.

> **Observations:** Use observations to see where special considerations need to be made.

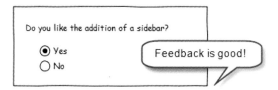

FIGURE 9-18: A poll on your site qualifies as meaningful feedback, even if its scope is limited.

When you carry out a testing method, read the questions and check the setup first to ensure that users aren't just going to tell you what you want to hear. In that same step, if you have an existing site, the criticism may prove to be the best thing you can find. If a genuine issue surfaces, use it as motivation to improve your site.

Summary

Whichever way you go about understanding your audience and its needs, you must take action to improve your site at every opportunity. Distinctive designers consistently and progressively aim for improvement, taking on critiques both positive and negative in order to improve their sites. The many issues of usability, accessibility, and other user-need-based elements will always need to be resolved. The best way to create a great experience for your visitors is by regularly innovating and improving a site.

Focusing Facets of Findability

Outside influences affecting distinctive design

CREATING AN IDEAL, distinctive design encompasses more than deciding what to place on pages and fit into code. The way you increase visibility affects the likelihood of users finding your site, understanding your interfaces, and becoming site regulars.

In this chapter, I examine the external influences that dominate the digital landscape. I explain how users sit firmly in control of the web as well as how search engines affect design. I round off the chapter, and book, with some helpful hints that you can follow to justify using the design rules in this book, should such an occasion ever arise.

A Game of Give and Take

Producing a distinctive design requires you to examine how your site and service operate and how you present your content to the public. The visibility (and the quirky variable called *findability*) of your pages and the on-page assets you provide have dominance over how distinctive a site becomes, but it's become more important than ever to also recognize the influence that outside forces have on distinction.

From within your sites, you have the power to control the visibility of certain objects. You can also use conventions to customize an experience for your audience's needs by considering factors such as *accessibility* and *findability*. Being able to create or design a site gives you some level of control and responsibility as you build an experience in the hope that visitors will discover your site and return to it.

Important

In the introduction, I write that "users sit firmly in control of the web." The idea of resigning control may seem crazy, but it's important to realize that the pressure of having to evolve a community by yourself can be even more demanding than does having loyal visitors who can offer kind words and free promotion for your site.

You can have the most distinctive and elegant site in the world, but if people don't enter it, then all your hard work is for nothing. Visibility plays a big role in this area. Figure 10-1 shows just a few of the routes individuals can take to locate your website's content.

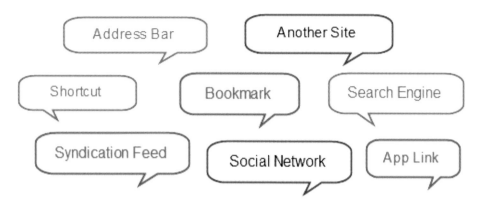

FIGURE 10-1: Many routes lead to a site, but some are vastly more popular than others.

Outside influences are not limited to the tools and services — search engines and social networks — that help users locate your site. You could consider your own audience within the design process and how they communicate about your site (both internally within the feedback systems you provide and externally by linking and reviewing). You can benefit from your site's visibility by distinguishing the findability of your services from others.

The justification for building a distinctive site is undeniable, but you need to consider how your work appears to first-time users. Communication has a big role to play in cultivating an audience. If you haven't considered how your site is seen by others, now is the time to ensure that it's perceived as distinct from your competitors' sites.

External sites that either promote or advocate frequent visitors play a central role in the development of a community. Even something as straightforward as e-mail newsletters show some external influence on your site.

Important

Out of site and out of mind

One of the most critical points regarding the success of your site occurs when users first visit the site. In order to convince them to return, the site must portray the professionalism they expect, and it must be appealing and work well. Their first experience on your site may well be their final destination in seeking something important to them.

Every experience can have a different point of entry — for example, users may decide to look for something, go through the process of looking for it, decide that your site matches what they're looking for (this is where distinction comes in), and then decide to click and check out your distinctive and well-crafted layout (see Figure 10-2). (If you haven't used the tips and tricks in this book to improve your interface, now is a good time to revamp your site.)

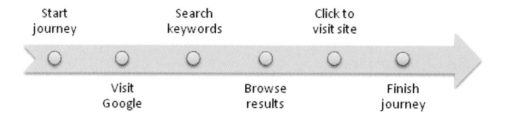

FIGURE 10-2: This figure illustrates an average journey for users looking for a specific website.

The sites you produce can project either positive or negative reactions. Although you can, to a certain extent, influence or control perceptions or opinion in moderated environments, the web is increasingly socially motivated. Sites can gain high visibility through viral marketing — sometimes referred to as the *Slashdot effect* — and the content that is promoted can significantly boost the number of visits to a site.

Note

The Slashdot effect can be viral marketing at its best, or it can be dangerous. This effect generally occurs when a popular website (such as Twitter, Mashable, and StumbleUpon) links to a smaller site, greatly increasing traffic to the smaller site, and possibly a flood and crash scenario!

You need to consider the outside influences on your work's visibility because every site centers on a brand or an item that users should commit to memory. Promoting sites enables a larger audience to find and enjoy your carefully crafted experiences. As users begin to trust and enjoy your content, community spirit increases, which helps to create a bond that can produce regular visitors. Even the social networks you choose to use affect your site (profiles become extensions of your site's content).

Distinctive design requires you to focus on user-centered experiences. You need to ensure that what you provide is visible to and usable by all visitors. The process you set up to help users find and discover your site plays a central role in gaining a continuous audience.

Rolling with digital punches

The two central facets of findability are *search engine optimization,* or SEO in the context of search visibility, and *social networking.* Both features have come a long way in a relatively short period of time and have produced many useful services for gaining attention.

Important   I'm not strictly against SEO practices, but the web includes a lot of misinformation. If you're going to follow the route of optimization (rather than just an organic, natural search rank), be careful about whose advice you choose to follow.

Making a site distinctive was at one time relatively straightforward, because designs tended to be static and lacked human interaction. Although interactivity has played its role in the revolution of the web, the ways in which people connect, share, and talk about sites and content have changed, too. Society is no longer bound by print media — you can reach a diverse audience on a modest budget and with accounts on popular sites, along with some well-written online content, of course.

Using interactive features plays a critical role in your site and your ability to retain an audience, and these features can encourage visitors to bond and be involved in the site's success. As a designer, you need to identify the external tools that can help you succeed and then take advantage of those tools to benefit your audience. Promotional methods range from using social bookmarking sites right up to developing micro-communities of fans (interacting through sites such as Facebook). Figure 10-3 shows some popular social networking features.

When dealing with off-page visibility, one difficulty you encounter is the level and amount of existing noise. Trying to gain a good search position is hard because billions of other sites are trying to do the same. Moving with the tides of social networking can also be tricky. Using outdated or less popular services (such as mySpace) may weaken your ability to get users involved in the community part of your project.

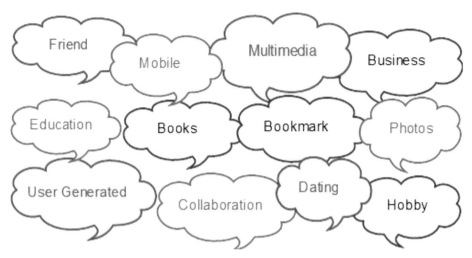

FIGURE 10-3: Many types of social networking exist, and some of them could prove to be useful.

Damage control is another problem you face while dealing with external forces. If a user bad-mouths your site within your own forums, the comment may be easy to resolve or remove. When negative perceptions are projected on your site from an external location, you can do little to nothing about them (without violating free speech or trying to pressure a site into removing the content). You must remember to make your choices carefully or risk doing irreversible damage to your site and brand.

Be proactive in handling negative situations — do not try to hide them!

Important

Designing Search Data

So how do you ensure your site's findability? The best known method is through search engines. In the past, people had to deal with a whole range of competing search engines vying for attention. In your favor, Google and Bing have reduced the amount of work you need to do to ensure that indexing occurs because these two search companies control the lion's share of the market.

When users first visit your site, chances are they found you by using certain keywords (for example, see Figure 10-4), and your site appeared in the results. So, to be sure your site is indexed properly, search for it and then upload a sitemap to ensure that everything is indexed correctly. Google offers a set of free webmaster tools and has plenty of useful tutorials to help you do so.

Search: | Distinctive Design | | Search |

FIGURE 10-4: Search engines can be helpful if you don't know have a specific site in mind!

If your site is visible to search engines, you've completed an important step, but simply existing isn't enough! Make sure your appearance in search engines achieves the visibility and recognition required to ensure that users continue entering your site. Although optimizing your site for searching can be tricky, because search engines, or spiders, tend to give you less control over how your content appears, it's entirely possible to achieve.

The first step to designing your search data is choosing the right keywords and ensuring that the site's title and description match what users expect to find. Simply hoping that Google picks the right content to display is pointless. Also, consider the benefits that paid advertising can bring. In SEO, every little bit really does help!

 Well-written content should naturally gain a good position in search engines. Remember that other factors, such as hosting location (for regional sites) and document formats, can have a critical effect on your site's search engine position.

Tip

Always keep in mind that trying to manipulate search engines with false data is a sure-fire way to get your site banned. Be transparent and honest rather than tricky, especially because the end user is often the one getting hurt, in the same way honest users are hurt by anti–right-click scripts and auto-playing music.

You can find many book and articles on SEO. However, you can also gain visibility through word of mouth and through techniques used in print design and other non-digital methods (for example, in business cards, as illustrated in Figure 10-5). Print may have become less popular, but it certainly isn't dead. So, use it to increase visibility to your targeted audience, in a way your competitors may not have even considered.

FIGURE 10-5: Well-designed business cards are great for promoting a site's visibility.

Another way to promote your site is through *link building* (having others link to it), which promotes and adds credibility to your site by association. A possible side effect to this technique is spam, which people frown upon. Not every site will have "followable" external links, and sites that too readily pass out free or paid links often do more harm than good. Always focus on relevant, high-quality links that potential visitors will notice.

Maximizing on-page visibility

Making your content search engine friendly is primarily about ensuring that your content can be seen outside the pages on your site. Remember that decisions you make on a page affect how visible and distinctive your content appears to users. How your content is written determines which keywords are indexed. Metadata you provide can affect the way your site is listed in a search engine, and design decisions can affect the usefulness of what you provide.

Important

The language in which a site's content is written dramatically affects its visibility in search engines. If you predominantly write your content in something other than English, prepare for the search engines to rank you lower for English-searching users.

Preserve the quality of your writing. In SEO, sometimes in an attempt to gain a high Google or Bing placement, people sacrifice the quality of their content by entering extra keywords. Doing so can affect the readability and usability of your information. Always build content for human consumption, not for machines!

Beyond the problems caused by abusing keywords, certain technologies have the power to affect the ability to find information. Sites written entirely by using Flash illustrate how problematic indexing can become. Although Flash can be indexed in a limited capacity, the output has little context in comparison to HTML within the scope of the page, which diminishes the distinction to what search engines recognize as most credible. This problem is reason enough for having a fall-back mechanism for ensuring that your work degrades gracefully in Flash-free situations.

Tip

Anything of importance on a page must have a text-based alternative. With images, this comes in the shape of alt attributes; video requires transcripts; for plug-in tools, such as Flash, you want an HTML-alternative site layout.

One prominent way to help search engines and social networks recognize and select content of specific relevance is through the use of metadata. Providing a good description and title is important, but also using tools such as RDF (Resource Description Framework), microformats, and other semantically useful specifications such as the DCMI (Dublin Core Metadata Initiative) can quickly improve a page's visibility or a site's subject matter, as well as help certain browser plug-ins.

Because of the way search engines work, try imagining that the search engines and social networks that visit your site are accessibility-dependent users. Making your site accessible and using structural conventions means that your site is far more likely to be SEO-friendly. See Figure 10-6.

FIGURE 10-6: Search engines notice certain structural conventions to aid a user's navigation.

The final point to make in ensuring that your content works well off-site is to consider your method of navigation. If you have a one-page site, the speed to find the right page increases (obviously), but the speed to find a particular detail decreases (users need to browse within the internal structure to find it). With multipage sites, be sure that your navigation system flows well and can cope with user demands, which helps search engines index and link pages.

Maintaining the off-site rule

Within distinctive design, making your site visible is critically important. Standing out from your competitors lets those who have an interest in your goods see the design you've encased it in, as well as gain a meaningful experience from content you provide. Promoting your identity on the web requires planning and an understanding of what works for a particular system. You can do plenty to help and guide search engines and users who link to your content, but it's important to also understand the impact that external sites can have on whether a visitor decides to click the link to your site. Users are manually typing URL addresses into the address bar less frequently. Note that users prefer to rely on referrals they find in websites, social networks, search engines or bookmarks, where they copy URLs and then paste them into their address bars (as shown in Figure 10-7), so do all you can to convince potential visitors to return to your site.

FIGURE 10-7: Users tend to copy and paste URLs rather than manually type them in the address bar.

Beyond visibility and standing out in an audience's mind, be sure to focus your attention where it matters most. Joining a service simply to post links is pointless if no one is watching. In SEO and social networking alike, you primarily want to build up your audience and then progress to publicizing your site (without going too over the top). Designing with external sites can be tricky, but doing so becomes easier as you get used to the concept.

Ultimately, with any method of promotion, you need to be careful about sustainability. If you are the type of person who hopes for instant results, distinctive design probably is going to be a challenge. Finding out what users want, how they want it, and how to deliver it can be time-consuming. Sometimes you optimize your content for a particular feature or service (such as a social network), and then the service disappears or falls into disuse over time. The solution is to use what your users use, and gradually introduce them to your site.

Note A couple of examples of social networks and search engines that have fallen into disuse are mySpace (which failed to compete against Facebook in the social sphere) and Ask Jeeves (a small UK-based search engine that, despite an aggressive marketing campaign, has never managed to compete with Google or Bing).

Another principle for dealing with off-site promotion is to be active and progressive. Don't be consumed by a successful campaign or attention-grabbing stunt and think that all your hard work is done. Competitors won't sit still and let you gain all the credit. They're trying for the same top spots. Maintaining visibility is critical to showcasing your distinctive design and continuing to plug away is vital.

One way to define search distinction is to be what the user needs — nothing more and nothing less. You want to tell them about every loving detail your services offer, but you also need to realize that with restricted space for promotion, you may need to leave the exciting extras for users to discover when they're on your site. Distinction is about making what needs the attention visible, so with limited space, give priority to the necessary elements and let the others naturally fade into the background.

Important Finding the balance between providing too little functionality or experience and providing too much of either is difficult, but if you find that users either won't adopt a new feature or complain of complexity, something may be wrong.

Sexy Social Engineering

Although search engines have their uses, social networks have become a force (both good and bad) in getting better communication and market solutions to users. You can do anything from rallying supporters and followers to having an environment for resolving bugs to producing a socially orientated microsite.

Twitter and Facebook promote not only more instantaneous responses to support requests, but they also add personality in contacting sites. Social networks even promote the production of more content-like images (in the case of Flickr) and video (for YouTube) to help monitor visitor numbers and highlight the freshest material.

Tip

Sites like Get Satisfaction center on gaining feedback or critique for bugs, questions, and requests. They certainly don't replace traditional methods such as e-mail or Skype, but they can give you a fast and flexible solution if you're constrained for time.

Toolbars, extensions, apps, and widgets that can be downloaded or built into devices or browsers have enhanced people's instant access to services. Such tools give your visitors new levels of customization and functionality (as Figure 10-8 shows). Distinctive design is fantastic when you can control it within the browser, but it really steps up a level when you can apply theme and enhance and develop your profiles by using third-party service providers.

FIGURE 10-8: Browser-based enhancements can affect rendering and enrich distinctive content.

Users of social networking tools tend to be open to the possibility of revisiting a site. In Chapter 5, I discuss the psychological implications of attachment (bonding with your sites). If users connect to your brands, they'll revisit your site. Gaining customer credibility and commitment boosts distinction.

Phones and the next wave of technology indicate the increasing importance of socialization on the web. The ability to share details and make purchases while in the middle of nowhere (as long as you have a 3G connection) has changed occasionally sitting at a computer into something that touches people's everyday lives. The web is becoming an extension of the real world. Although levels of contribution may vary, you need to evolve past one-way communication.

Studying for social success

When you make use of social networking — whether it's something simple like Twitter, which has one basic purpose, or the multifaceted Facebook — the ideal situation is that you portray the same message you display on your site. The cool thing about sites such as Facebook is that they allow you to tweak an environment to almost the same level as a complete site, so you really can push design boundaries.

Developing bonds with users on social networks is important, and a common way to increase visibility through these mediums is to make your users the first to know about the latest news, offers, and activities within a site. You can use social networking to keep your visitors informed as well as to help them gain the best possible experience, such as through the medium of regular tweets within Twitter, as shown in Figure 10-9. Using these tools to boost the effectiveness of your site can help reinforce your brand's awareness.

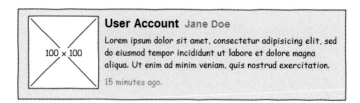

FIGURE 10-9: Sending out tweets can ensure that your regular visitors find out what's going on.

Every service has different applications, and you need to ensure that your published content is appropriately organized and contains the right kind of social connectivity. Many people click Like buttons or retweet content that they believe others will find beneficial. Try to focus your social integration on quality and on enhancing or supplementing sites, not replacing them or providing unnecessary functionality. Focus on users' needs and smoothly integrating solutions.

Crowdsourcing (asking for visitors' experiences, motivations, and assistance to increase the usefulness, value, and notoriety of a site) best exemplifies the power of social networking. Not only can you monitor how people use a page and get feedback, but also you can actually instigate some high-quality usability testing. Consider how many people follow the progress of your site (or just you). Adding a message that asks for willing testers to come forward may yield enthusiastic results and help ease the issue of finding participants. Some famous examples of crowdsourcing in action include Wikipedia, the Linux OS, and software products such as the OpenOffice suite (Microsoft Office alternative).

Some social networks provide APIs (application programming interfaces) to help you hook your own site into the service; others just allow you to embed pre-hosted content. Studying the details of each social network can help you calculate how much work you need to put in versus the value of what your users can get out of it. Any social network can help increase a site's success rate (in brand loyalty, recognition, and usefulness), so you need to brainstorm how yours can benefit.

Social networks are here to stay, so be sure to consider how each type of social feature can help you. A photo-sharing site can help showcase events you've attended, or perhaps a messaging platform can help you track user-support requests. You may even invent some new uses for them.

Ripples and ego reflections

People have fine-tuned their social profiles to meet their own distinctive sites' layouts and themes. Matching the colors and textures are classic examples. Designing a social experience isn't just about marketing; it's equally important to treat those profiles as though they're sections of your own home page with a unique appearance that your visitors can enjoy.

Social networks provide a critical level of functionality by giving prebuilt (and hopefully) stable environments to which visitors can attach. The wider effect of these great tools is that they can add dimension to your service. Social networks give groups that have already joined a service a quick and painless route to interact with you.

Social networks aren't a perfect means of delivery, but you can promote yourself to the outside world through these prebuilt, useful channels. RSS and Atom do their best in helping on-site syndication (see Figure 10-10). These days, social networking is expected, so put using it effectively high on your list.

FIGURE 10-10: Syndication may be losing support because of social networks, but many users still like feeds.

Be sure to use social networks as you do all bonus functionality. Ensure that it gracefully degrades. Whereas scripting or Flash can be turned off, people may refuse to sign up for or use a social networking feature. You need to ensure that your content is available on your main page, and never try to force users to contribute. A theory called Zipf's law, or the 90:9:1 rule, states that 90 percent of a site's visitors will simply observe and decline becoming involved in parts of sites that require contribution. In addition, 9 percent will contribute, but only if they have to or occasionally want to. The remaining 1 percent will be your regular posters and make up the majority of all user-submitted contributions (see Figure 10-11).

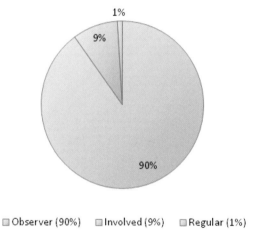

FIGURE 10-11: A graphical representation of Zipf's law and how often web interactivity occurs.

Making the most of the few contributors you're likely to have is critical. The majority of a site's users simply browse and nothing more. Don't force users into a situation where they need to interact unnecessarily; you don't want visitors to click the Back button! With interactivity comes responsibility, and you need to give users the flexibility to be as involved or uninvolved (or privacy-conscious) as they prefer.

Designing with Distinction

Throughout this book, I've covered just a few of the issues to consider when building a distinctive design that looks, works, and functions in increasingly beautiful and useful ways. Distinction isn't just about giving quality content the most attention, and it isn't even entirely about the natural aesthetic. Distinction is about using the tools at your disposal, such as design, code, science, inspiration, and even users, to help get that important content noticed. Design contains artistic, scientific, and philosophical elements (see Figure 10-12).

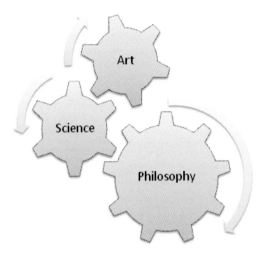

FIGURE 10-12: Every site design involves these three components.

Designers and developers have a responsibility to know their trade. Although you can potentially become proficient in many things, every site, no matter the size, revolves around the content — whether that is text, images, media, or a service. Ensuring that each user to your site is encouraged, guided, and provided with a fantastic experience is critical. If your content causes complications, you need to rethink how you publish.

Every decision you make has some level of impact on the page. Taking the time to understand how users interact with your site, what they want to get out of it, and ensuring that such content is available to them seems to most like plain common sense. Distinctive design helps you enhance visibility, prioritize ideas, and think more about how to construct a successful site, which users will appreciate.

Tip

The impact of a page depends not only on variables such as the size of an object, but also on other objects in the environment. Design equals the sum of all of its parts.

As you build or redesign your layouts, challenge yourself, question decisions you simply accepted as fact, keep learning, take the time to understand your audience, and design with purpose. Having such a design shows you're attentive enough to consider each object or line of content and code. The results of such effort and hard work can appear as unique to an audience, visible to all, and can flow in usability with the greatest of ease (this is a great goal to aim for). Distinctive design doesn't have to be pretty — it just has to work optimally!

Don't panic: Justifying the job

Sometimes you don't have the freedom to make design decisions, or you may encounter barriers imposed by management or client choices (based on wrong information or a lack of understanding). As a professional designer, your job is to maintain standards, educate clients, and build sites; so justifying a distinctive design application is critical. Figure 10-13 shows a rudimentary process in which such justifications can occur.

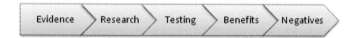

FIGURE 10-13: The general process of justifying the distinctive design ideology for your work.

If you have to deal with a boss or client who's perhaps making decisions that lower the quality of the end site, first justify your aim to produce a distinctive site through the benefits that individual aspects of the design will give users, along with evidence supporting your claim. The wealth of available *evidence* should convince any business valuing customer loyalty that it needs to incorporate practices such as accessibility and usability. Showing those businesses hard facts is a good place for you, as the site's designer, to start. If not, then you need to move from the core evidence to some extended *research* studies.

Accessibility has clearly defined benefits, such as the increase in a user group by opening up the site to a previously blocked audience. More importantly, distinctive design determines how a user will interpret a page. In cases where the evidence isn't so easily definable (and you're unsure about the right move forward), it may be worth doing some usability *testing*. Case studies that look at a group's collective opinion rather than one individual's viewpoint can justify change (for the better).

> The quality of distinctive design should never override specific needs of an audience. You could have the most empathic or distinctive layout in the world, yet it could lose some of its contextual value if you go overboard with style but offer little substance.

Important

For example, if you've shown your client or business owner evidence and research to explain your distinctive design approach, and he or she isn't convinced, then your next move is to test some actual users in order to back up your viewpoint. By going beyond general facts and showing real benefits, you can convert the person to your way of thinking. Show clients statistics so that they can see the potential for increased income. Also, show how smarter code can save bandwidth costs.

If none of this works, you have one other route, focusing on the *negatives* of keeping everything as it is (the potential for lawsuits because of poor accessibility, for example). Highlight the design flaws and critique areas that could prove to be serious mistakes. Take this route last because using positives for change has a greater effect than negative feedback. People tend to become defensive when you critique their style. If all else fails, take the approach of just doing what is feasible, implementing, to the extent possible, principles that will make a site distinctive.

> Consider those stubborn clients or coworkers (or bosses) as a challenge. Be adaptable and present a polished presentation. There's no sense in just giving up!

Tip

Summary

Distinctive design encompasses a range of tricks and tools, and that's really part of its appeal. Making the most of a site isn't just based on one core subject. Your content and your code and everything else have their place in what eventually comprises a site's user interface. How you implement the various components determines exactly how distinctive your website becomes. Although you can produce an amazing site by approaching each of the subjects in turn, any changes you implement will likely help to improve the site.

You can use all the tools mentioned in this book to improve your site's distinction. By applying them to your design, you can boost a visitor's productivity and experience. Web design is composed of so many individual subjects that keeping up can be tough. By using every object on your page carefully, you can ensure that your visitors see what you want them to see, as they should see it, and when you want them to engage with it. New devices, standards, practices, and trends are on the horizon. Determine what's right for your users and continue striving for interfaces that showcase the possibilities of the web.

Index